MAN
IN THE MIDDLE

D1714622

Books by John Illig

Trail Ways, Path Wise
Pacific Dream
Man In The Middle

MAN
IN THE
MIDDLE

JOHN ILLIG

ELDERBERRY PRESS, INC.
OAKLAND

ELDERBERRY PRESS, INC.
1393 Old Homestead Drive, Second floor
Oakland, Oregon 97462—9506.
E MAIL: editor@elderberrypress. com
TEL/FAX: 541. 459. 6043
www. elderberrypress. com

Elderberry Press books are available from your favorite bookstore, amazon. com, or from our 24 hour order line: 1. 800. 431. 1579

Library of Congress Control Number: 2008941091
Publisher's Catalog—in—Publication Data
Man In The Middle/John Illig
ISBN 13: 978-1-934956-10-6
ISBN 10: 1-934956-10-4
1. Hiking.
2. Nature.
3. Through-Hiking.
4. Thru-Hiking.
5. Continental Divide Trail
6. Adventure.
I. Title

This book was written, printed and bound in the United States of America.

To my nieces and nephew,
Emma, Melissa, and Andy,
and with great love
for my dearest little peanut,
Francis.

Also
To TEAM LOCUST

The Continental Divide Trail

CONTENTS

1
Reaching Mexico

Be bold, and mighty forces will come to your aid.

—Goethe

Crazy Cousin.

If you measure success on a hike as walking every inch of ground from beginning to end, then my two previous hikes were successful. If you measure it by how well you stay true to yourself and treat nature and those around you as best you can, then I think both my previous two hikes were successful, too. Certainly, there'd been trying times. And I've been through a divorce. On my first hike, I was young; on my second hike, I was troubled. But I think I'm okay now. At least, I'm self-aware. It's important, because this time it won't be easy. Nobody takes the Continental Divide Trail lightly. Still, it had to be done. Reason being simply that that's just what you do when there are three trails and you've already hiked two of them. It wasn't any more complicated than that.

America has three celebrated hiking trails and they follow longitudinal mountain ranges. They're the Appalachian Trail, Pacific Crest Trail, and Continental Divide Trail. A reverential subculture of long-distance hikers calls them the AT-PCT-CDT. They roll off the tongue easier when abbreviated that way. Holding varying degrees of difficulty, the AT is comparatively easy, the PCT is trickier, and the CDT is quite impossible. Proportionally, they're what addition is to multiplication is to calculus; what junior high is to high school is to a doctoral program in optical engineering; what a wagon is to a tricycle is to a flaming stunt-trick unicycle. You get the idea: the CDT is rough. To through-hike you must walk the entire length of a trail in one calendar year. Complete all three and you earn the hiker's coveted triple crown. The CDT was what all I had left—all thirty-one hundred miles of it. You save the hardest for last. Keep in mind, however, that this was just walking after all.

The Continental Divide Trail follows the Rocky Mountains up New Mexico, Colorado, Wyoming, and Montana. The tricky thing was that in 2005, the CDT wasn't yet continuously connected, so in some spots you just had to improvise and hike along from town to town as best you were able. Also lacking were lean-tos, maps, and a through-hiker handbook. There'll never be lean-tos on this one, and that's okay, but the other things mattered. Trail headquarters was the newly formed Continental Divide Trail Alliance. They claimed that their goal was to finish the actual path of the CDT by 2010, but they'd misjudged it by dozens of years, since it'll take them many decades to turn this into a continuous trail. That boded ill for me, since navigation isn't my strength. And few people'd be out there to help out. The trail wasn't finished, nor was it popular like the others. It was more like the crazy cousin. Each year only a mere twenty-five people embarked to through-hike the Continental Divide Trail. I was just hoping to meet a few of the other twenty-four.

Four Stacked Boxes.

Necessity demands that the Continental Divide trail isn't the same as the Continental Divide. The trail only loosely traces its namesake, occasionally following the actual Divide, and other times just crossing back and forth over it. The Divide is the spine that splits our continent's watersheds in half. No water crosses from one side over to the other. Theoretically, all water west of the Divide eventually reaches the Pacific Ocean, while all water to its east reaches the Atlantic. Although it hydraulically splits the country, the Divide is left of center and not truly in America's geographic middle. The designers of the trail have been fixated on keeping its route as close as possible to the actual Divide at all times, often at the expense of hiker safety, convenience, and sanity. If they'd give the trail license to occasionally take the most scenic, direct, and convenient route, then perhaps there'd be more than twenty-five people attempting it each year. Somebody should maybe tell them that.

Forming a mental image of the Continental Divide Trail is tricky but here's help: four stacked boxes, each large and left of center as they climb, are the Divide states of New Mexico, Colorado, Wyoming, and Montana. The bottom box has a funny boot-heel in its southwest, while the top box has an irregular western edge that hangs down over Wyoming as if to cling on and keep the stack from toppling. In order, south to north, these are the fifth, eighth, ninth and fourth largest states in America. The mountains run west of center up all four boxes, and the Continental Divide Trail hangs like a rope that's being hit with a stick. Upon reaching Montana, the trail briefly follows the Montana-Idaho jagged border. Idaho thus technically holds a smidgeon of the CDT, but I just sort of discount that and instead only picture the CDT as being in the four box states, for the trail soon leaves that border and climbs northward through Montana's interior. The major cities in those states lie east of the mountains. One thing was certain: the trail zigged, zagged, and was the furthest thing from a straight line that you could imagine.

Sequential.

Transient as tackling these hikes makes me seem, some alter ego inside me has somehow managed to secure roots, in that I've held the same occupation for sixteen years. I'm a coach. It's a job that I cling to and love with every ounce of my soul. I coach the obscure sport of squash and have done so at two different colleges in Maine: first were five years at Colby College, and then came eleven years at Bates College. Coaching gave me summer freedom, which let me dabble with very long walks.

My first motorcycle came after my divorce, when in 2002 I bought a used Honda Shadow. It was my sole transportation preceding this hike. I'd never owned a motorcycle in my youth, or else I'd probably be dead by now. Finally well past my wild years, I was careful and mellow on the motorcycle. It made for interesting times, driving to grocery stores through the Maine winters. It gave me practice in dressing warmly. It kept me outdoors, which I loved. I slowly got my bearings back postdivorce, until I realized one day that I'd go hiking again. It comes to you just like that—a few years pass and then you get the itch. You just know when it's time to head back out.

A psychologist once told me that I was the most sequential person she'd ever met. It's true that I operate sequentially, tackling just one thing at a time and finishing it before going on to something else. It gets in the way of my functioning, as multitasking is impossible for me. It's like how this twelve-year project of hiking three trails had kept me prisoner all the while—had perhaps kept me from fulfilling other goals. But if that was the case, then at least it'd soon be over. It wasn't too late for me. This was my last summer to through-hike. Afterward, I'd be ready for a home, remarriage, some land, and some kids. A couple of dogs, I hoped, like one black Lab and one white German shepherd. I wanted those things, wished to build my own home with a mountain view, deck, wood-burning stove, claw-toothed bathtub, windows, bookcases. I'll pour myself into that. Make sculptures outdoors. Devote myself to my family. We'll create our own holidays. Celebrate solstices. Have fun. Laugh a lot.

That was my dream. My paternal instincts were welling up in a major way.

11

I was almost through with this project. But I couldn't say that I wished it was over. Couldn't say that because I was looking forward to this hike. I couldn't wait to begin, to get back on the trail and test the waters and see what this infamous CDT was all about. See whether I could handle the tough one.

"I'll be back by September first," I told my boss, the athletic director.

"That's what you said the last time," she said.

(Ouch!).

"This time I mean it."

I'd exceeded my deadline the last time. After my Pacific Crest Trail hike of six years earlier, I'd returned to my job sixteen days late. I couldn't let that happen again. If I could begin the CDT by May 4, that'd leave me four months to finish and return for the start of the new school year on September 1. That wasn't much time, though. I'd need wings on my feet. I'd need to average one month apiece for each of the four states. I'd need everything to go according to plan. But things don't go according to plan.

Divorce was hard to go through. It took time, but I survived in one piece, and now I look back and it seems like another lifetime ago. It's possibly made me a better coach, for it's increased my tolerance for others. I have greater empathy and am less judgmental. Everyone experiences wrenching moments in life, and you wouldn't wish those on anyone.

Another thing which helps me coach was that I was such a nightmare as a college player. I'd broken rules, transferred schools, joined a fraternity, gotten in fights. The law of unintended consequences has it that now there's nothing my players can do that'll fool or surprise me. They can't pull tricks that I'm not on to. But coaching tires me. I immerse myself in the job. I'm married to my job. I love my players so dearly that they've become like a family to me. An extended family. They partially satiate my paternal instincts, because I care so much about them. But I'm still a kid, still laugh at their jokes, listen to their music. I'm no military figure who requires their fitting into a mold, acting as one, and marching in lockstep. Instead, I finesse every situation and treat them as individuals. I want them to question life, but I get tired when they question me. It's the only way I know how to do it, still I find it exhausting. Each season's conclusion finds me collapsing at the finish line, ready for a break, ready to spend my summers recovering before fall hits and the students return and the cycle begins anew.

Dreams.

With a backward twist of my wrist, I rode my red motorcycle away from Bates College on April 21, leaving my squash teams and the squash building behind. Our squash building was off-campus. The college had planned to build a new facility in the gym, but that'd fallen through, so instead we went a different route and rented a medium-sized warehouse four miles away. We'd gutted the inside and erected five squash courts. I'd call it a cold and distant outpost, except that it was spacious and warm inside with carpet, sofas, and stereo. It was a perfect situation.

Cold icy rain drenched me, testing my resolve from the onset. I bailed, having only reached Portsmouth, New Hampshire, on my first night. Next day was better. Sunshine. I bypassed Boston and motorcycled to Lowell, Massachusetts, where I parked at the library, the first building I'd come to. Inside, I inquired if they'd direct me to Jack Kerouac's grave. It was one of only two things that I wanted to do on my way to Mexico.

Inconceivable that Kerouac was here, and I lived so close without having ever before paid homage. People from all over the world thrill to come and see his grave, and I was only now finally doing it. I felt as if I'd a list of wishes and was checking them off, fulfilling my dreams while I could. It's never too late. He'd actually once worked in this very library, they volunteered. They'd a room devoted to his books. They gave me a flyer with directions to the cemetery, and back outside I went, riding to the end of town. The cemetery was average-sized and nondescript, off an average-sized and nondescript road—like any cemetery off any semi-quiet road. No fanfare. I rode my motorcycle inside, down along the little streets where dead people lay inside coffins beneath the grass in their quite peaceful final neighborhoods. I found the grave. Walked over and looked down upon it.

Strange to think of bones lying underground (and, what: clothes around the bones?). I want to be cremated when I go, burned outside on a sandy beach on a Native American funeral pyre. There were a few coins placed on the tombstone and a couple of notes. There was a small flag from Sweden— random—and flowers. But that was all. Kerouac had died at age forty-nine while living in Florida with his third wife. But Lowell was where he'd been born and raised and had been a football star. So here was where they'd placed his grave. He was troubled, depressed, alcoholic. But wide open. Unafraid. My spirit was nothing like his. I'm tight and closed, I know that. It's my brain chemistry. He was a man without borders. It amazed me because I'm a person of so very many borders. From the very first sentence, I'd cherished his novel, The Dharma Bums. That book was why I'd come here—to be near the person who'd written it. I rode away, two towns over to Concord and Walden Pond. It was my second and last pit stop.

You can actually go to Walden Pond. You can actually go there and see the water. I'd lived in New England for fifteen years, in which time I'd driven every inch of its roads to all its colleges and universities with my squash teams—but I'd never before been to Walden Pond. I couldn't think of anyplace better to visit, as Thoreau remained current for me. The image of a home just slightly removed was appealing to me. It helped me envision my future. Thoreau was a visionary poet, and he was certainly talented, but he was uptight like me. This land was owned by his friend Emerson, who'd suggested he build a cabin and live here awhile to collect his thoughts and follow his dream of writing a book—do it as a way of getting over his despondency over his older brother's death. Sensitive man, he was. That plan worked out well.

I loved being here midday, midweek, in the spring while it was deserted. In the parking lot was an exact replica of the cabin he'd built for twenty-eight dollars, with replicas of his bed, desk, stove. Now, a sidewalk circumnavigated the lake. I walked halfway around to the spot where Thoreau's cabin had stood, at the cove beside Wyman Meadow. Only the foundation remains, but you can stand and see the same view he'd enjoyed. You can see from where, exactly, he'd gotten his water. I picked up a pebble to take with me to Mexico. I found a secluded spot and undressed and slipped into the lake, submerging completely. I imagined that the same molecules that'd once touched Thoreau's skin were now touching mine. But I knew it didn't work that way.

It felt wonderful to dress again and put on warm clothes and ride off on my motorcycle. It was invigorating to balance on two wheels, draw back the wrist and lift and lower the toe and bend into turns and feel wind rush against my face as the scenery changed. Two dreams were checked off the list, and only two remained for the rest of the summer. Of course, the last two were big ones: riding across the country by motorcycle and hiking the CDT from Mexico to Canada.

Fossils.

My September 1 deadline dictated my starting the hike as quickly as possible. For that reason, I'd take only major highways to Mexico. I told you, I was no Kerouac. I dropped south to the Mass Turnpike and rode westward, picking up the New York State Thruway. The dismal stretch past Albany, of Schenectady-Utica-Herkimer almost did me in as it always does. If someone had told me to follow my heart right at that moment, then I'd simply have turned northward and ridden up to the Adirondacks to live in a mountain home there for the rest of my life. But I wasn't on that course just yet. I'd embarked on a different mission.

Upon reaching Rochester at midnight, I slipped inside my older brother's house and slept on a sofa—he and his wife and their kids, upstairs. The cash register was ringing for them in a major way, as my brother had taken over direction of his surgical practice. They were about to upscale dramatically by moving into a castle the size of an aircraft carrier, but they were still a few months shy yet of flipping that switch. I spent two days in Rochester, playing with my nephew and niece. Those kids had become the perfect age. I'm not excellent with the very small, but once they get big enough to kick and catch and throw and take practical jokes and play Monopoly and appreciate sarcasm, then I morph into Crazy Uncle Johnny and am much more fun. The lone exception for how I am with the very young is with my ex-wife's son

14

Francis. I adore that little guy. All these kids tug at my heart. Inside leaps the thought: I want this. When it finally becomes my turn, I'll be an older father, but a wise one.

I practically froze motorcycling westward past Buffalo. I was on the move again. Rain fell and pummeled me so chillingly that when I reached Erie, Pennsylvania, I aborted my plan of continuing to Chicago, and instead dropped immediately southward to escape the blustery Great Lakes. Trucks flew by and I feared for my life. I couldn't recommend this to anyone. About the only good thing was that I could lean back against my backpack, which I had bungee-corded to the backrest. I spent the night in Pittsburgh. Not in Pittsburgh but in a hotel outside Pittsburgh, in a spot possessing zero Pittsburgh-ness about it. That's how it is around all our cities. Everything looks the same now and anything can pass for anywhere. Two five-hundred-mile days took me next into St. Louis past the arch (Gateway to the West), and into Tulsa, Oklahoma. I was tiring now, losing steam. Two subsequent three-hundred-mile days took me to Amarillo, then into New Mexico. The ride had offered amazing sights—like dozens of firework stores and the largest cross in america.

New Mexico's otherworldly landscape was a vision that I'd previously seen only in photographs. I rode to the western side of the Rio Grande and turned off at a few scenic overlooks, so stunned was I by this world that was chopped up, eroded, and red—the earth all rusty and orange and red, red, red. All cratered, with strange formations, striations, lines, cuts, swales, swaths, and deep trenches. There was little greenery. It was unlike anything we had in the east. My heart beat quickly. My deepest feeling went: *You mean I get to walk through this?*

Two rest days in Albuquerque found me enjoying the only American city that possesses three Us and two Qs. The lips touch only once when you say it, early on; then it's the base of the tongue against the throat, twice, in and out. I briefly visited Old Spanish Town. A block from there was the New Mexico Museum of Natural History and Science, which I entered to spend the day looking at dinosaurs. Those fabulous animals had once lived here, running around in the places that I'd be walking through. They'd certainly been warm-blooded egg-layers. Ancestors of modern-day birds. They'd been here when there once was a great inland sea, with its western shore at the eastern Rockies. New Mexico is fossil-rich. Huge numbers of dinosaur fossils lay buried underground here, the same as they did in Montana. I stared at the skeletons and imagined them flesh-covered, birdlike, and very much alive, with quick twitches and wiry legs, chasing me through New Mexico's dry, red, crumbling landscape. I wouldn't last long in that mismatched skirmish. I'd need to make like a mammal and find a cave or climb a tree. Or use my big brain and build some fantastical weapon.

My motorcycle died three hours south of Albuquerque on Monday, May 2, ten days after I'd left Maine. Heading southbound on Highway 20, my gear shift broke and fluid spilled out. I pulled into Truth or Consequences, on the western shore of the Rio Grande. There were natural hot springs in this town that'd actually been named after the television show. I sat in a diner next to the highway and waited for a tow truck to come and collect me. Impressively, my motorcycle had made it across the country to within a mere sixty miles of my destination. Now I hitched a lift.

My tow truck driver smoked cigarettes and his girlfriend sat between us, so I kept my passenger-side window rolled halfway down for air and was just incredibly grateful for the ride, this ride sponsored and cost-free thanks to my prescient membership in AAA automotive emergency help. Modern life has conveniences. They let me out at Pacachio Storage in the city of Las Cruces. I locked my bike inside container number sixty—so I was on foot now. Pacachio Storage unit key in my pocket, and pack on my back, I walked into town and checked into a hotel.

There're people who love to help, and I'd already identified one. A week earlier, I'd called the CDTA headquarters in Colorado. They'd explained to me that no official CDT starting point existed, but that soon a permanent route would be established. They gave me the name Marc Hackola. Said that he lived in Las Cruces, worked for the Bureau of Land Management, and was charged with creating a new starting route. The CDTA sold four books with information about the trail, one for each state. I'd bought them over the phone with a credit card and had asked them to mail the books to Hackola for me. From my Las Cruces hotel room, I called the BLM and got connected to Hackola's line. I left a message on his office telephone answering machine with my name and location. I was awakened that next morning by Marc Hackola knocking on my hotel room door. He handed me my four CDTA books.

Blimps.

No exact place started the CDT in the south due to the trail's being in-complete in 2005. If any place should've been marked and well-organized it was the start, so its lack signified the kind of experience I could expect. I avoid clichés when I coach, but one thing I've always told my squash players is that Chinese characters contain words inside words, and the word opportunity is contained within the word for crisis, meaning that inside every crisis there's an opportunity. My opportunity here was to be creative, find a good route, and gain confidence. I just had to figure out the first common denominator of all possible starting points and decide how to reach that spot from the border.

The town of Silver City was the first common denominator in the south. Hikers chose different ways to get there. The original route had been to start down in the bottom of New Mexico's boot heel, at the Antelope Wells passport station. From there, a forty-five-mile, shadeless, hot, highway walk led directly northward to Hachita, and then a few more days of road-walking led to Silver

City. Antelope Wells wasn't a town but just a border station with gates, guns, lights, barbed wire. Police. I studied my New Mexico road atlas and planned my own route to Hachita. Route 9 ran parallel to lateral Interstate 10 to its south and was within a few miles of the Mexican border, so I decided to choose a random spot off Route 9—as close to the boot-heel drop as possible—and from there I'd walk southward until I reached the border, and then walk north-westward to Hachita. Make my own way. Cross country. From Hachita, the route to Silver City was clear. That was how I'd start.

I rode a Greyhound bus one hour westward to the small town of Deming with its long country blocks, Wal-Mart, decaying hotels, and visitor center. I ate in a café and made final trip preparations. I spent one final night in a hotel, and that next morning, May 4, prepared to leave. I rode a taxi westward out into the desert.

"The state flower of New Mexico is the Wal-Mart shopping bag."

My AW-Taxi driver Roy said that while pointing at brown plastic Wal-Mart bags that were stuck and flapping in the breeze on the barbed wire fence that lined both sides of Route 9. He was African American, a Vietnam War veteran, was retired from computer work, had a couple grown kids, and had moved to Deming less than a year ago. He was running the taxi just to help the town. He said I was crazy for asking to be let out at the side of the road here. No cars, buildings, homes, or people in sight. Just a few small mountains on the distant horizons, and otherwise nothing but endless barbed wire fence. Low little prickly chaparral bushes covered the desert floor. A roadrunner ran by and my taxi driver didn't bat an eyelash.

"Make sure you watch out for government blimps," he told me.

"What?"

"Government blimps."

"Yeah?"

"They're in the sky. They watch the border. They can see everything that you're doing."

He sounded paranoid and I stood hoping that this part of our conversation would quickly pass, but then he pointed up into the sky to the north.

"There."

I couldn't see anything, but he kept on pointing…and I still couldn't see, but he still kept on pointing…and then I saw it! It'd taken several seconds for my eyes to adjust to the vast openness of a sky devoid of clouds, but then there it was: I could make out a blimp in the sky far away. I'd never have seen it. Why I should care if it saw me was a different matter. It's a crazy world of secrets. A crazy world of guns and blimps and border stations.

"I wouldn't go out there because I don't like snakes," he said.

With a slow U-turn taxi driver Roy drove off. It was a lonely sound, hearing the car pulled away. I hadn't the luxury of starting out with a hiking partner. My friends all worked. I crossed the road and climbed over a chest-high

17

barbed wire fence. It was the first of hundreds that I'd climb over that summer. Ubiquitous is what they were on the CDT. The entire Rocky Mountain byway should be renamed: land of the barbed wire fence. The red sand at my feet gave way and was poor footing. Chaparral bushes were everywhere. They were just wide enough that you couldn't step comfortably over them, so I constantly had to choose to walk either left or right around each one. It kept me from enjoying a rhythmic gait on a sure course, and made the going slow.

When I finally came to a fence after two nervous southwestward hours of sandy, overheated, off-trail anticipation, it wasn't a big metal affair like they had at the Mexico-California border on the PCT, but instead it was just another barbed wire fence. A dirt jeep road led east-west parallel to it here on the American side. There were some quasi-official-looking signs on both sides of the fence, some in English, some in Spanish. I reached my hand over into Mexico, and so I'd begun. I had one international border down, one to go. It was only the second time in my life that my skin had been inside Mexico. The first was six years earlier on the PCT. Neither visit had lasted longer than a few seconds. Mere seconds with a hand stretched over a fence isn't the most thorough way to experience a country, its culture, its people. I walked westward along the border.

Dusk fell, catching me still on the dirt road at the border. I wasn't carrying a tent. I set down my blue nylon ground cover and lay on it in my unzipped sleeping bag looking up at the stars. I'd been nervous about bivying, not knowing how it would go. I'd slept in lean-tos on the Appalachian Trail and had slept in my tent on the Pacific Crest Trail, so bivying was new to me. Now, I found it was easy. I just lay down and slept. That's the meaning of bivying—you just lie down on the ground.

I was alone, and yet with me were friendly old hiking ghosts. The memories of all my old Appalachian Trail and Pacific Crest Trail friends were here with me. Thoughts of all those crazy hikers rose to the fore—Hydro, Mozyin', Ponder Yonder, Chinook, Kilgore Trout, Blazer, Easy Stryder, Hunter S. Thompson-Ron, Dana, Zoomsteen, and the Junkyard Dog. I could see them all shuffling across the deserts, skipping through the woods, sliding down the snow, jumping over boulders, climbing up mountains. Smiling and laughing as they went. I thought of all the miles and all the times we'd shared together.

Even my ex-wife Cristina was here with me, too. I can't talk much about her, for that's not what this story's about. I'll mention her once or twice, to be sure, because she's still a part of my life, but she's no longer my spouse, so it's not fair to anyone if I discuss her too much. I will say that she's a friend of mine to this day. Shall be my friend until I die. I think the world of her and I always will. I love her to an extraordinary degree. It wasn't the kind of love that made me wish I was back together and remarried to her. No, events had transpired as they'd needed to happen. It was more just a love of extraordinarily deep admiration of her kindness, patience, and selflessness. She's the best person I know. It makes me feel good about myself, knowing that I care so much about another person.

18

I'd do anything for her. So yes, with me was everything that I'd learned on my two previous hikes. My experience would come into play. My summer had begun. Little fanfare existed out here.

2
Under Way

Off Prozac.

One crazy initial feeling, postdivorce, when out on trips with my squash teams, was turning in and lying down in hotel rooms in strange cities, knowing there was no one that I had to call to check in with. I felt the same sensation here, felt it all over again. There was good and bad in it. Out here, the greatest thrill for me would come in reaching Montana and grizzly bears. Ursus horribilis is the great bear. Every moment until then would leave me no escape from the thought of it. I won't carry a gun. I'll be the intruder and will enter the northern Rockies gingerly. I won't bear grizzlies any ill will, even if one should decide to eat me. My plan was to carry an umbrella and somehow find the nerve to unfold it during a grizzly encounter, do so as a bluff to make myself appear larger, to make nearsighted grizzly bears decide not to risk a fight with strange, upright, stick-legged umbrella man.

The CDT's listed at thirty-one hundred miles, but I feel that's overestimated. When one day a complete route finally gets established, it'll surely be measured at less than that. Each state on the trail had a unique personality: New Mexico held hot exposed road walks; Colorado was snow and lightning at high elevation; Wyoming was grizzly bears calmly waiting with their mouths open at Toegwotee Pass (south edge of Yellowstone National Park), ready to chomp down on hikers much like Kodiaks behave when they stand in Alaskan streams effortlessly waiting for unsuspecting spawning salmon to fly inside their gaping jaws; and, finally, Montana was where any hiker still left standing gets eaten by grizzlies at some point before reaching Canada. It's important to know what you're getting into.

I was off Prozac. My last pill taken on the day I'd left Maine two weeks earlier. Already I felt different. It takes awhile to work into the system, and it takes awhile to work out. My glow had worn off and my sparkle was gone. But there was no one out here for whom to sparkle and glow. I didn't feel great. For the past two years I'd experimented with existing on small, medium, and large doses, the largest of which made me actually sing while walking to my office in the morning. With the middle dose I could manage, but it made me drowsy during the day, and I'd grit my teeth and feel a bit drugged. The lowest dosage allowed me to cope. With zero of it, I feel flat. It gives me a little bit of erratic behavior every time I go off it. Erratic behavior, like awakening at the Mexican border and walking through the desert. There was no great reason for me to have suddenly stopped taking the Prozac. Some people take it only seasonally in the winter, to compensate for the decrease in sunshine. Perhaps through wishful thinking I was trying to be like them. I'd gotten off it that previous summer of 2004, when I'd stayed in Maine and had played tennis tournaments every weekend. I'd started dragging, though, growing progressively worse, until by early June I couldn't take the sadness any longer and I went back on it.

Part of why I'd gone off it then and now is that having a dependency sucks. After a while you just don't want to have to be taking anything anymore. You want to believe that you don't need anything. When you're taking it you feel okay and so you forget how it feels to be without it, so you lose your fear of going off. You forget the sadness. So you go off it. Back during that previous tennis-filled summer I'd told myself that I'd get by without it because my squash season had ended and I didn't have to run practice and deal with my players' emotions. It was spring and summer, and the long days were filled with ample sunshine. And besides, if I ever felt bad, I could easily retreat and remove myself from whatever I was doing, and go home to take a nap. This time, I was repeating all those same arguments. I'd fooled myself into believing them once again. Like here I was enjoying the utmost freedom imaginable—so how could I really get sad? I felt sad, though. I felt down. All this crazy discontented restlessness never seems to leave me. I'll never be done with it. The most I can do is survive. I look and see expressions of it everywhere. It lies in the poetry of Robert Frost:

I have been one acquainted with the night.
I have walked out in rain—and back in rain.
I have outwalked the furthest city light.

Frost masked his restlessness and depression, but it's clear to those who understand. My father was a hardworking and modest attorney who always helped others. He was fine with my choices. If anything, my life in sports was partly his fault for having always played games with me and my brothers outside when we were kids. He was always throwing a ball for us. Always taking us to climb trees and dirt bluffs. The thing with me was that I'd just never grown tired of the bouncing ball. My mother, on the other hand, had grown up poor in the Deep South, and her father had died when she was fourteen. My mother had struggled with mental disease and she carried a chip on her shoulder. She'd done her best with us and had raised us to become something.

That was where Cristina'd come in and had changed my life in teaching me that I didn't have to be or become anything. That it was okay that I just was. It wasn't that I'd never heard it before or didn't know it on a rational level, but Cristina was the first one to help me truly internalize it. She'd saved my life. It's why I'd married her. It's also why I'll love her forever and will always be on her side. But it wasn't enough for us. I doubt that my place is to impart wisdom or pass down life knowledge to my squash players, but if there's one lesson I wish I could give them then it was just that—they don't need to be or become anything. If they can be decent and kind, then I already love them for who they are. Creepy for a coach to talk about loving his players, but there it is. It'll be what I want for my own children, too.

After my Appalachian Trail through-hike of twelve years earlier, my then-girlfriend the "Y" moved out west. She'd ultimately returned to New England, got married, had two children, but we'd never really found ourselves able to restart our friendship. Just a few things had happened that'd soured me. It was different after my split with Cristina. Our continuing friendship means the world to me. She'd gotten me on Prozac and that was of great help. The two previous times that I'd tried going off it have sucked. I shouldn't go off it again. I don't need a large dosage, just a small dosage has worked miracles. My going off it entirely wasn't the way for me to go. Yet here I was off it. I wondered how it'd affect my hike.

Hachita.

The mesa I walked upon stretched so widely that it offered no sensation whatsoever of standing tall. The surrounding landscape was flat in every direction, contrary to the image of a dramatic ridge-walk that a Divide connotes. Only an altimeter revealed the truth, that the ground here was six-thousand feet elevation, higher even than the summit of Maine's tallest peak, Mt. Katahdin at 5,267 feet.

Hot, dull and flat, this was nothing like the start of the Appalachian Trail in the severe, cold, craggy, densely forested irritable mountains of Georgia which are freezing in springtime, so through-hikers get rained on, snowed on, iced on while battling straight up and down, into and out of chilly, slippery, drizzly gaps. This was nothing even like the start of the Pacific Crest Trail in the high rolling desert hills of southern California, where boulders and hillsides with trees add personality to the land.

Strewn about lay discarded empty plastic gallon water jugs, evidence of whatever mysterious people who were out walking around. If the state flower of New Mexico was the Wal-Mart bag, then the state debris was the Empty Plastic Gallon Jug of water. It reminded me of the warnings I'd gotten from all the miscellaneous people I'd met over the past few days while in transit making my way here: be careful of snakes which'll bite you; be careful of Mexican border crossers who'll take your stuff; be careful of American drug runners who'll kill you; be careful of Native Americans who'll bother you if they find you on their land; be careful of ranchers who'll shoot you if they see you on their property; be careful of government agents who'll catch and detain you and give you a cavity search. It's always that way when hiking a trail—everyone helpfully, patiently telling you about all the scary, impossible obstacles that you'll have no chance combating. But I saw no one. Not even a snake.

I knelt and pushed into the sand, planting like a peanut the pebble I'd carried with me from Walden Pond; then I trudged northwestward, trailless, cross-country, on May 5, back to Route 9, feeling for all the world as if I were alone in the universe. My feet hurt and my backpack weighed too much. I'd a heavy sleeping bag and more food, books and trinkets than I needed. I'd lots of water, but I needed that. Water is heavy, but you can never have too much of it in the desert.

I reached Mad Max, Road Warrior, deserted Route 9 and walked four hours along its burning asphalt into Hachita. My feet hurt so badly they reduced me to the pace of a very, very, very, very fast snail. Hachita was the size of a football field with a café, gas station store, post office, and a few homes. With a population of fifty, it was no booming metropolitan hub. It was smaller than New York City, Jakarta, Tokyo or Mexico City. You could lasso it with a rope. Cars pass through to Mexico and back. Standing there, I couldn't help but think, What would my life be like if I lived here? I had no answer for that. William Least Heat Moon had driven through here three decades ago and described seeing "dust devil" plumes of sand spinning in the wind around town, lifted by thermal pressure. He said: "That's something else about the desert: deception. It can make the heat look like water, living plants seem dead; mountains miles away appear close." He compared his feeling of discovering a bar in Hachita to that of an ichthyologist finding the first millions-year-old fossil fish coelancanth still alive and swimming in the sea.

At Hachita's post office, I collected a long thin package that looked certain to contain a pool cue or fishing rod, but it was really an umbrella that I'd bought weeks earlier and had mailed to myself here to fool nearsighted grizzlies. It wasn't that I expected to see grizzlies at the post office or anywhere near the Mexican border, but just that I wanted to experiment with hiking with an umbrella to see if it could be a viable grizzly solution later, up north. Down here, I'd use it for shade. I took the CDTA books which cover Colorado, Wyoming, and Montana, and mailed them ahead to Chama, New Mexico, up near the Colorado border. I'd deal with them later.

"No charge," the postal worker said.

"Wait. What?"

"Yeah, there's no charge for that."

I was confused. "What do you mean? I totally have money. I can pay for it."

"No," she smiled.

First, she'd let me into the store just as she was closing, and then she'd taken an interest and asked me about hiking the CDT. Now she wasn't accepting any money. She was really coming through for me.

"Okay, but here's the thing," I said: "One day, for real, there'll be hundreds of hikers coming in here every single spring, and you can't possibly pay for all of them." But she wouldn't let me pay. I wondered where the money would come from; whether it'd come from her pocket or if she had some way for the government to pick up the tab somehow, as if it was free.

Hachita's café had capacity for twenty if you squeezed in to try to set a world record, but I was the only patron. The café was nothing more than the front room of the owner's ranch home, and she sat in back watching television. A guy pulled into the parking lot outside to sell snakes and lizards which he'd caught in the desert. Another car pulled in when he did, to look at the wares, suggesting that it'd been an arranged meeting. The reptiles were in hundreds of glass containers in the back of the station wagon. It was awful. I doubt that the guy would enjoy the experience if some technologically advanced being swooped down and scooped him up and stuck him in a glass jar the size of his body and traded him off, or cut him into little pieces for one reason or another. It made me sad. Kurt Vonnegut would agree.

Putting my feet up in the Hachita café was rude, but necessary because they hurt so much. A hiker sometimes takes liberties—moral shortcuts or allowances. Nobody with manners was here to talk me out of it (I was alone). My feet were overheated and swollen from a mere one day's desert walking, and elevation slowed my blood from rushing into them. Ice would help them even more, but I hadn't yet reached a level of desperation great enough to force me to go through the steps of procuring ice and a pan. Instead, I just sat and ordered food and drinks. I couldn't wait to eat. Hunger's the best sauce, as the saying goes. I studied my ripped-out page from my New Mexico road atlas to see what lay ahead. The answer was more road walking—sixty-three more miles of northward road walking would take me into Silver City. The roads were the "official" route, according to the CDTA's New Mexico book.

The trouble with that CDT book and those for the other three states was that the total set weighed more than a vanload of giant medicine balls. Each book had random, non-through-hiker information comprising 95 percent of its content. The books contained such seemingly endless information on side trails, flora, fauna, alternate routes, history, and hiking tips that it was hard to sift through and find the exact information you needed. Searching through the books was possible while sitting in a café eating, but I couldn't do it while out on the move in the sand beneath the unforgiving sun. Worse was that the maps in the books didn't help. They were large-scale close-ups devoid of perspective as to what lay nearby. All the pages were high gloss and heavy, and pack-weight spells trouble for through-hikers.

If the CDTA cares about attracting through-hikers, they'll need to change it. They'll need to create a true through-hiker's handbook by condensing the four books into one volume, printing it on cheap lightweight paper, excluding the photographs and all other non-through-hiker extraneous information, and doing a better job with the maps. For now, at this early stage of the trail's development, that was too much to ask. Look no further to understand why only twenty-five people set out to through-hike this trail every year. The AT and the PCT both have helpful through-hiker handbooks, and that's what makes those trails manageable and the number of hikers on them large. It was a bit like whether the chicken or the egg came first. The CDTA won't make a through-hiker's handbook because they don't think there's a market for it, but all they have to do is examine the traffic on the other two trails to know that there could be if only they'd make the book.

I walked over to the gas station store next door and bought candy bars and chatted with the owners about the CDT. In walked a terrifically charismatic dark-haired young man in blue jeans and T-shirt with penetrating blue eyes and a movie-star smile. Laughing and reeking of pot, he proceeded to roll and twist on the floor, showing us some yoga moves as well as two balancing tricks that he told us he'd learned from an amateur boxer in Chicago the other day.

"Twenty-two years old," one of the store owners told me once the young man had left.

"Just bought a large spread nearby," the other owner said.

Spread?

"He has money?" I asked.

"He won fifty-thousand dollars in eight seconds last month."

"How'd he do that?"

"Pro rodeo rider."

"He's one of the ten best steer riders in the world."

I left the café at dusk, in order to night-hike and make a few miles up the road while the temperature was cool.

Smoke Balls.

Squash is growing. People still don't know of it because it doesn't televise well. It's funny to me, and purely coincidental, that I've been a vegetarian for twenty years and that I coach the only sport that shares its name with a vegetable. There're sixty men's and thirty-two women's college squash teams in the country, and we're rapidly adding more. Most have varsity status, but a few are only club teams without full funding. Most are in the northeast, in New England and beyond, stretching to New York, New Jersey, and Pennsylvania. However, teams have cropped up in other regions of the country in recent years, too, with Stanford, Cal Berkeley, USC, Utah, Washington, Notre Dame, Northwestern, Tulane, Vanderbilt, Virginia, Georgetown, George Washington, Denison, Penn State, Drexel, and the United States Naval Academy all having traveled to play in Team Nationals this past year. Nationals was at Yale, which has a stadium court made of four glass walls and has 360-degree viewing all the way around it. Glass-backed courts have changed the game, because now it's quite spectator-friendly as it's visually and audibly interactive.

In men's squash, the national intercollegiate team champions for the past ten consecutive years has been Trinity College, in Hartford, Connecticut. They've beaten the standard bearers Harvard, Princeton, and Yale, plus all other takers for ten years without losing a match. Their win streak is 194 matches and with no end in sight. It's the longest winning streak in history for any college team in America, for any sport in any division. There's only one division in squash, and every team is able and willing to play every other team in the country. Except Harvard. Harvard plays very few matches. They ignore everyone else and focus obsessively on trying to beat Trinity.

Squash is scarcely known in America, but it's popular in the rest of the world. It's played in 147 countries. That's because the rest of the world has always played a more enjoyable, more athletic version of the game than we have, so they've had more fun with it. Up until a dozen years ago, American squash was played on a narrow court with a hard ball. Until then, it was mostly a county club and prep school sport in this country. That all changed in the early-1990s, however, when American squash converted to the international standard of the sport by playing on the wider court and switching to play with the softer version of rubber ball. Now we play the same game of squash that's played in the rest of the world. That's started an influx of international players, because here young men and women can study while playing for their college squash team. Trinity College has taken advantage of it.

Trinity's been able to recruit players from all over the world. Their current top-eight players are from Pakistan, Zimbabwe, Sweden, Brazil, and four from India. Nine players comprise a varsity intercollegiate starting line up, and the only American who started for Trinity last year was their number nine player, Tom Wolffe Jr., from New York City, who's the son of author Tom Wolffe. At

Team Nationals you can see papa Wolffe in his white suit and bow tie walking around signing autographs. Other top teams have international players, too: Princeton's current top-five men are from Mexico, Egypt, Malaysia, Hong Kong, and El Salvador; Harvard's top-five men are from Switzerland, Israel, India, and two from Canada; and currently my Bates College men's team has players from El Salvador, Zimbabwe, Hong Kong, and Kenya. I've also recently had players from Jamaica, India, and Thailand. Diversity keeps things interesting. I've hung up a quote which says, Only when all those around you are different will you truly belong.

Seventeen of the top-twenty ranked players in intercollegiate men's squash are international students. They dominate. It's because they've been playing the softball version of the game longer. And because some of the best athletes in other countries are on the squash court. The incoming talent has revolutionized squash in this country. It's a wonderful thing. Squash is less snooty now. There's diversity now. Inner city squash programs have sprung up in Chicago, Boston, New York, New Haven, Providence, Poughkeepsie, Philadelphia, and San Diego. The level of play keeps rising. There's trickle-down effect, as excellent American players who once fed exclusively onto Ivy League teams are now having to look for other teams on which to play. Duke, Emery, Boston College, Vermont, Colgate, Purdue, UNC, and NC State all have club squash teams. Stanford has built an eight-court facility and has just hired the leading American coach. Stanford's women have varsity status, and soon they'll be giving out scholarships. Look for future Malaysians on the Stanford women's team. At some point it's going to explode.

During the second half of the season each year I'm always so tired by running practices and traveling every weekend that I stop playing and I get out of shape. This year had been no different. The result was that I found myself on the CDT out of shape. It was part of the reason why my feet hurt so terribly now. The solitary miles gave me time to think of my squash teams, and of all the players I'd left behind. When each year's season ends, they catch up on their homework and there're no more practices for me to run, which sucks the energy out of me like a vacuum. The season ends so abruptly that it hurts. I discuss the phenomenon with other squash coaches and they tell me that they feel the same way.

From Hachita to Silver City, the route was nineteen miles northward up dirt road 147; then four miles westward along an unnamed dirt road parallel to busy mega-highway I-10; then through a bridge under the interstate; then twenty-nine miles up seemingly endless dirt Separ Road; and, finally, fifteen miles up paved Highway 196 into town. The way was dry, hot and exposed to the sun. And I was utterly alone. My feet hurt so much that I spent two of the next four days off the trail resting in a dirt-cheap hotel room in a defunct dying town called Lordsburg off Interstate 10. In and out of Lordsburg was a hitchhike, so I hadn't missed any ground.

Each of those first few nights, I lay by the road under the stars. Everyone'd told me to be wary of Havelinas, which apparently were little hairy pigs. I saw a group of one dozen and they skittered away. My first night from Hachita, I took colored smoke balls out of my pack and lit a few, like a kid, fascinated. It was bright enough at night to see their red and green smoke colors rise up and drift away. Fire and smoke—the world's oldest television set. Or maybe it was ocean waves. Or passing clouds. Or tree branches blowing in the wind. I'd gotten the smoke balls at a firework store on my way to the trail. I'd entered one to see if they had something which I could use to scare a grizzly, and they'd sold me a very loud banging explosive that was shaped like a crayon and self-ignited upon striking it like a match. It made a deafening noise. The saleswoman had thrown in the colored smoke balls for free.

I was starting out okay, but there were lots of things that I could've done better. I could've started the trail in better shape. I could've started with a hiking stick. I always like carrying a hiking stick, but I didn't have one now. I hadn't managed to bring one on the motorcycle and hadn't been able to find one in the stores in Albuquerque, Las Cruces, or Deming. I could've started with one metal ski pole that twists in the middle and slides down into half its own size for easy transport. I also could've begun with a lighter backpack. I could've brought just a tiny summer sleeping bag instead of my current heavy, warm monstrosity. Easy to think of these things later. Harder to figure out in the moment when you're on foot, unfamiliar with your surroundings, and unsure of what the places ahead will be like.

The north end of Separ Road led me through a narrow canyon under high cliff walls. The perfect place for an ambush. Here stood the first trees of the trail. May 11, on the seventh day of my hike, I staggered the final leg, up Highway 196. Just five miles shy of Silver City, I did a strange thing in the mini-village of Tyrone and the Tyrone post office. My feet hurt so much that I could barely stand. Perhaps brilliant, perhaps deranged, I emptied the contents of my backpack into a box at the Tyrone post office and I mailed them to myself ahead five miles up the hill to Silver City—then I walked the final bit carrying zero weight on my back.

Silver City occupies the southern border of the Mongollan Mountains, and to its north rise hillsides of increasing heights. This was welcome. Major changes were afoot. So far I'd connected the Mexican border to Silver City, with my feet. It'd been a long and painful eighty-three-mile stretch, all totaled, on a route of connected roads. The reason was clear as to why only twenty-five people set out to through-hike this trail every year. The CDTA book for New Mexico described the start this way:

The CDT at its onset is less a single marked trail than a
network of alternative routes. Vegetation here is sparse but

28

whether following cairns, walking roads, or hiking cross-country, you should be well-equipped with map, compass and a Global Positioning System unit, if you have one, as the topography can be complex and confusing. A strong imagination, a fondness for history and a taste for desert vistas reveal subtleties along this segment that will make the long miles of exposed road go more easily.

3
Silver City

It is like a finger pointing the way to the moon.
Don't concentrate on the finger or you will miss
all the heavenly glory.

— *Bruce Lee, Enter the Dragon*

The Palace Hotel.

Great fortune greeted me in Silver City. An intuitive left turn on West Broadway placed me in the miniature historic district of town proper at the doorway of The Palace Hotel. They had vacancies. I took a room. I'd made it. Built in 1882, the brick hotel had twenty-two rooms above a high-ceilinged museum-like front lobby of old mirrors, faded rug, and mismatched antique furniture, like chairs with velvet cushions that you wouldn't want to sit on for fear of their breaking. Steep stairs led to the rooms. I climbed up to find lacy white bed linen and window curtains, as well as a claw-footed bathtub. I took a bath. I slept like a baby and in the morning ate fruit, pastries, jam, and coffee for breakfast on the second-floor terrace, old murals painted on the walls. It was all quite fantastic. For the first time since leaving Maine, I closed my eyes and relaxed deeply.

A billboard welcoming tourists said: Silver City, 11,000 Years of Culture! Silver City had ten-thousand people living up at six-thousand feet elevation. It was the same elevation as all the rest of the land I'd walked over, except here

30

were pine trees and the beginning of undulating mountains and hills. Like a rare jewel, Silver was tucked away and had limited access, for the 3.3-million-acre Gila Wilderness hovers over the north side of town and cuts off travel, save from the south. A car-sized W made of hundreds of individual small, white rocks was visible on a hillside and signified the town's small Western New Mexico University.

Silver City had a hippie feel with two Olde Towne streets that were home to cyber cafés, art studios, health food stores, small restaurants, tattoo parlors, a motorcycle shop, and six bars that hosted live music and poetry readings. That funky place had a warm climate with sunshine year-round. In town were Mexicans, Mexican-Americans, Native Americans, cowboys, artists, retirees, hippies, drunks, and Vietnam War Veterans. I was overjoyed to know that I could eat well in cafés, take warm baths, clean my clothes, and lie in a comfortable hotel bed. A framed article from out of the wildly popular Modern Maturity magazine hung in the Palace Hotel lobby and had Silver City ranked as the third-best small town in America. Silver City brochures on the lobby coffee tables had glowing propaganda detailing the accolades of this crazy place:

> *Best mining town.*
> *Best American cities you've never heard of.*
> *Hundred best small art towns in America.*
> *#8 town for art & music lovers.*
> *Top-11 retirements spots.*
> *Top one percent of nation's healthiest places to*
> *   live and retire.*
> *Dozen distinctive destinations.*
> *Fifty most alive places to live.*

Billy the Kid had lived here. Next to The Palace was a replica of the original house in the original location where he and his mother had lived. Movie director Ron Howard'd had the replica cabin built while filming, The Missing, with Tommy Lee Jones. That movie had nothing to do with Billy the Kid. After filming, Howard'd donated the cabin to Silver City. That story didn't make logical sense to me, despite my affection for little Opie Taylor and "Richie The C" Cunningham—but it was written on a placard before the log house, so it must've been true.

Silver City was proud of Billy the Kid. He was born in New York City and had come west with his mother in 1873, when Billy was thirteen. They'd settled in Silver City, but his mother had then died of tuberculosis a year later when Billy was just fourteen years old. His father was gone by then. A year after that, Billy robbed a Laundromat and the sheriff put him in jail with the intention of scaring him straight. It didn't work, because Billy was extremely skinny and he escaped the jail by climbing up its chimney. He fled town for

31

good. He was seventeen when, in Arizona, he killed his first man. When he died at age twenty-one, he was linked to the deaths of twelve men. It's what Silver City was most famous for. Another was that Geronimo had been born north of town, and not only he but also Cochese had lived in the Gila Wilderness. Both were legendary for eluding capture. But nobody in that wilderness could be caught, who didn't want to be caught. My next task was to enter and find that out for myself.

It was a relaxing time. I thought back and theorized about the ideal way to begin this hike. My motorcycle ride had been fine, but also great would be to fly into El Paso, in western Texas' strange sideways shark fin. Take the airport shuttle westward to Deming and then taxi southwestward to Route 9 and the middle of nowhere, as I'd done. Or even better yet would be for a friend to fly with you; then you rent a car, and your friend drives you to the trail southwest of Deming. Your friend then spends a few days driving the dirt roads, keeping you hydrated and carrying your pack as you walk alongside the car for company, slackpacking all the way into Silver City. Hang out together in Silver City for a couple days, then say good-bye. That'd be a terrific way to start.

Unless you're independently wealthy, though, it's nearly impossible to begin a through-hike on just the right foot. You have to figure out a way to pay for the hike, and for the typical person that invariably involves working your tail off right up until your time of departure.

Jack and Mike.

Success out here seemed contingent upon chance encounters. May 12, I strolled the town's sidewalks passing art galleries and tables at outdoor cafés — and then I happened upon Jack and Mike's Hike and Bike Shop, which had hiking gear inside. I mentioned that I was through-hiking the CDT, and they claimed to be hikers, too. They gave me information which saved me. Quite fortuitous for me, but scary and sad that such random moments prove integral on the CDT. Until now, I'd been focused mainly on the beginning, getting to and from the border to start my hike in one piece. Now I needed to turn my attention to the trail north of here, which was wilderness. My only map was a ripped-out page from the state road atlas. It helped me to see the Big Picture — like how my next town, Reserve, was situated northwest of the Gila Wilderness and I'd have to walk through the wilderness to get there. The road atlas page was nicely color-coated: brown for low desert, light green for higher elevation, forest green for even higher pine tree forest, and shades of gray and white for the tallest mountain ridges and chains. I could see the Gila River, and I could broadly see my route ahead, but not the fine points. Such a large-scale view alone wouldn't suffice. The heavy CDTA book for New Mexico, however, was a disaster. Its maps didn't help because its route was insane.

The CDTA's "official" route north of Silver City followed the Divide on a

32

180-mile easterly loop around the gorgeous Gila Wilderness. According to the CDTA book, the wide loop contained precious little water and no trail towns. That, and it wasn't scenic. So why take it? Jack and Mike were intimately familiar with the area and they sold me a contour map of the Gila Wilderness, drawing for me the best route from Silver City through to the town of Reserve. Their route included a forty-mile-long walk up the Gila River. They said that people go birding there and that 265 species of birds have been found in the river canyon. It was something not to miss. After five days of near dehydration, the river-walk sounded heavenly to me. Their route even offered a place for resupply halfway up the river, at Gila Hot Springs Village, which contained the Gila Cliff Dwelling Home National Monument. Amazing! CDT through-hikers often call their Gila River walk the highlight of their summer, but the CDTA would've had me avoid it entirely, opting instead for a longer, blander, aidless, waterless route at the expense of all common sense. Instead of simply altering its route, the CDTA very strangely bad-mouthed its own route. Of its own official route—its 180-mile loop eastward around the Gila Wilderness— the CDTA book for New Mexico warned:

> Sorry, but no town could even remotely be considered near this segment. There are no supplies, services or accommodations anywhere near this route. Many CDT thru-hikers bypass the "official" eastern route and go through to Reserve, primarily because it is direct and goes through perhaps the most scenic section of the Gila Wilderness, past the Gila Cliff Dwelling National Monument, along the Gila River.

The Twisted Vine.

More fortuitous, still, I entered Morning Star Sporting Goods to buy a pair of running shoes, and there met Jessie Gibbins (not her real name). Something occurred at that moment which hadn't happened on either of my two previous hikes in walking the height of the country, twice, up the AT and the PCT: I met a girl. She sold me a pair of running shoes and we laughed and talked about the trail. I was far from Maine, far from home, and out doing a crazy thing. It made for good conversation. I'd been basically two weeks alone, riding my motorcycle and hiking the trail, and I was desperate for someone with whom to speak. She had pretty big hair and looked straight at me. She saw me. She was exactly my age, forty-one, and with no wedding ring. I paid for the shoes, and in a moment when we were alone, out of earshot of anyone else in the store, I asked if she'd meet me later. We were just like a couple of Russian spies. She agreed and suggested we meet at her favorite bar, The Twisted Vine, when she finished work. So I spent the day waiting. I felt nervous and eager. This wasn't typical trail behavior. But then, this wasn't the typical trail.

At the Twisted Vine, they served wine only. No beer, no mixed drinks. I found Jessie Gibbins sitting outside on the back wooden deck, which nicely overlooked a creek. I'd warned her in advance that I'd be sartorially out of place, as usual. I was still wearing what functioned as my hiking "uniform'" — knee-length nylon shorts, running shoes, and dry-fit, long-sleeved T-shirt. It was all I had. At least I'd showered and shaved. The Palace Hotel was kitty-corner across the street, which'd made it easier for me to steel my nerve and show up to keep the date in the first place, because if anything went wrong I could easily retreat. We sat drinking wine, talking and laughing. We were amazingly comfortable together. When acquaintances stopped by to greet her they were mostly point-blank, like, "Who's he?" So we played a joke by lying and telling everyone that we were old friends who'd gone to school together in fourth grade in Wisconsin. Everyone believed us, and we never admitted that it was a fib.

My story to her unfolded with the following essentials: born and raised in New York, now living in Maine, married once and divorced with no kids, squash coach, currently far from home on a strange hike and able to laugh at myself. Her story was only a bit more complicated: born and raised in Wisconsin, married once lasting seventeen years, no kids, divorced just one year ago, moved here to Silver City only five weeks earlier out of the blue as a friend from Wisconsin had moved here years earlier and had recommended it as a wonderful postdivorce change of scene. Her husband had left her for a younger woman. It'd been painful. She'd put him through pharmacology graduate school instead of their having children. She'd thought they were happy. She hadn't seen it coming. In Silver City, she worked part-time at the store and part-time at a horse-therapy camp for mentally impaired children. She had alimony coming in. She was also writing government grants. Whatever that meant. She'd just adopted a dog named Gus, whom she said was the kind of smelly, shaggy dog that only its owner could love. We were two divorcees, sitting on the porch.

Jessie Gibbins admitted to me between glasses of wine that she had a sex toy party that she was being forced to attend that night by a half-dozen of her new empowerment girlfriends from town. The party was for nine o'clock that night, and they'd been planning it for weeks. She couldn't get out of it. Neither of us wanted her to cancel it, actually, as it seemed that it'd serve wonderfully as an aphrodisiac. Under the mutually agreed-upon guise of my surely need-ing some off-trail comfort and computer use, she stole me away and dropped me off back at her house to dog-sit for Gus while she went to drink more and laugh and bond with her new friends over the strange toys.

Jessie had a desert mountain house outside town on a rolling, rocky, cactus-filled hillside of open land and clear sky. The neighboring homes were Adobe-style. I napped on her sofa with Gus, dozing off while wondering if this was really happening to me. She returned home after midnight and practically attacked me. That's my version, anyway. Her version went a bit differently, as she to this day reminds me. Home from the party, as she tells it, she sat down and proceeded to show me photographs of her family in an album when I ripped the album away and said, "I don't want to look at photographs," and I attacked her. It's crazy, how wildly recollections can differ. It was comfortable sleeping together. We were just two divorcees, neither having ever suspected that all our days and all our lives would land us exactly here.

We spent all that next day together. We ate in a Mexican diner. Took Gus to get sheered. We walked the sidewalks and bumped into a man who was carrying a Cockatiel on his shoulder—the bird was on Prozac, he said. The bird was wearing a tiny black leather vest to keep her from nervously biting off her own feathers. We had drinks in the Buckhorn, the Watering Hole, and the Twisted Vine. In just five weeks, she already practically knew the whole town. She could've run for mayor. She introduced me around. Everyone there came with a story. It was a town straight out of the TV show Lost, where strangers are marooned together with odd goings-on, and the viewer secretly suspects that they're unknowingly trapped in some kind of purgatory, waiting to be sent to heaven or hell. One year earlier, a Silver City woman had accidentally shot herself in the buttocks with her handgun while walking down the sidewalk. There was a Vietnam Vet who ate in the Mexican diner and had to sit facing the door due to post-traumatic stress disorder. One day a car backfired and it sent him diving under his table screaming: "incoming!" There was a Millie and Billie Ball every year, where all the men in town dressed like Billy the Kid, and the women all dressed like a celebrated prostitute. Jessie said that there was an elderly male artist in town who only painted portraits of women's vaginas. He used Silver City women as his models, and the guy'd been following her around for weeks, ever since she'd arrived in town, asking her to pose for a portrait. She'd kept refusing, but he was persistently wearing down her resistance. You couldn't make it up, what went on in that town.

Our second night together (my third straight in Silver City), we stayed in my room at The Palace Hotel. My backpack was stuffed in the corner. Jessie offered that I should quit my hike and stay with her. That I should quit my coaching job in Maine and move to Silver City. No squash courts, I told her. I couldn't do that. There was a squash club in Santa Fe, but no college squash anywhere in New Mexico. I like being a college coach, not a club teaching professional. That'd kept me a prisoner to the northeast. Which was okay because I didn't feel able to live anywhere else.

I thought of my squash teams now. I'd started coaching at age twenty-seven. I'd never studied coaching, or planned for this life. I'd just played tennis and squash forever. Had taught tennis lessons all over. Had played team tennis in Germany after college. Just always had a racquet in my hand. For me it'd been mostly tennis, but lots of squash, too. I'd tried journalism and social work, but couldn't stick with those occupations. I couldn't work a desk job. The way it'd started was like this: I'd been living in Portland in 1991 when I'd heard that Maine's Colby College had a part-time position open for men's squash coach. It was springtime and I drove up and interviewed with the athletic director. Weeks and months passed and I never heard back from the guy. I understood that I hadn't landed the job. I left Maine. But one October day many months later, while back visiting my friend Amy in Portland, I'd called Colby out of the blue, just to ask whom they'd hired as squash coach. I'd wanted to see if I knew the person. The start of the winter squash season was just two weeks away. That was why I'd been utterly shocked when they'd told me that they hadn't yet filled the position.

I'd hung up the phone and just stood there, stunned. Then the craziest thought overcame me. I'd had an idea. I set out with my wallet and car keys and drove to the nearby grocery store. I walked to produce and bought a large squash. Next, I drove to a gift shop and found a homemade card made from a squash seed package with a photograph of squash on the front. Then I drove one hour northward to Colby. I still wasn't sure how to do this. I only knew I had nothing to lose. I sat in my car outside the gym and wrote my name on the squash with a magic marker. The squash was as big as a football, and I wrote my name in large letters. I carried it inside and up to the athletic director's office. He was out. In his empty office I placed front and center on his desk the large squash with my name written on it. I set the squash card beside it. Inside, I'd written: *"Grow! Grow!,"* to show that I could indeed coach squash. I put my name and Amy's number where I could be reached. I returned to Portland and the telephone rang. It was the athletic director who asked me up for a second interview, ultimately hiring me.

That was the way my coaching career started: just a squash from a grocery store placed on a desk. Now fifteen years have flown by at warp speed. I couldn't give it up. Not for the sunshine of Silver City. Not even for Jessie Gibbins. In sixteen years I've held five different variations of college racquets coach, as my position has kept subtly changing. The first year, I was men's squash coach only. The second year, Colby fired its women's squash and tennis coach for sexually assaulting one of her players, and they gave me her two teams. During my third-to-fifth years, I became head coach of men's and women's squash and tennis, because the school had to let go its men's tennis coach for drinking in a room with his players on a spring break team training trip to Hilton Head Island in which a student fell out of a window and was permanently mentally and physically injured.

Teams had kept falling into my lap. For those third-to-fifth years, I was the head coach of four teams, had sixty-odd players, constant travel, and never a day off. I was stringing racquets around the clock and seeing balls bounc-

36

ing in my dreams. When a two-team-only position opened downstate at rival Bates College, I leapt at it. My interview was more professional this time. No squash on a desk. I ditched my royal blue clothes and bought all maroon. Starting at Bates, for my coaching years six through ten, I was coach of women's squash and tennis. Then a miracle happened when we reorganized our athletic department so that I no longer had any tennis duties at all—but fantastically in my current stint for years eleven through sixteen, and forever after, I've just been coach of Bates' men's and women's squash. This is the way that I want it. I've finally arrived. Total bliss. All through the sixteen years there's been change, including the Colby College gym burning down from arson, and both Colby and Bates building new outdoor tennis facilities and new indoor squash courts during my tenure.

Squash is an indoor sport, climate controlled, and that's the greatest thing. The sport is like racquetball, played in a room with alternating hits. Except that squash is hundreds of years older than racquetball (snob!). Squash evolved from court tennis, just as has lawn tennis (what we refer to simply as 'tennis'). A squash racquet is exactly the length of a tennis racquet. There's a strip of metal on the front wall of the squash court that's called the "tin" and is out of bounds. Players have to hit over the tin, which is similar to the feeling of a tennis player who has to hit over a net.

Change is inevitable, that's the point. It's as inevitable as death. Just when you think you've a handle on things, the picture changes. This past winter, I sat down next to a player from an opposing team after she'd just come off the court. I make an effort when possible to shake hands and say nice match to opponents, win or lose, and when I sat next to this college student, I'd told her: "Nice match, you played well." She'd looked at me and mistaking me for someone that I wasn't, cheerfully said, "Thanks. Your daughter did, too." That's my new reality. I must face it. I'm growing older. I can't run around on the court as quickly as I once could. I used to be the age of an older sibling to my players, but now I've grown to the age when I could be their parent. And I haven't even started my own life with my own children yet.

On the morning of Friday, May 13, Jessie Gibbins and I said good-bye. Our plan was that I'd hike farther north and then take a bus down and visit her from somewhere. And that even later in the summer, she'd fly up to Wyoming or Montana to visit. It felt natural. We knew that we'd see each other again.

4
Bloodied

Trail Emblem.

New Mexico is the Land of Enchantment. Its ubiquitous symbol, red on orange background, is the outline of a circle with four lines sticking out above, four below, and four on either side. It signifies the sun as well as the four points of the compass. It's on the back of the state quarter, only without color. It's on the state license plate, the state flag, and everywhere else that you can imagine. Only four states in America are larger than this one: Alaska, California, Texas, and Montana. New Mexico is so large that they've tested nuclear bombs here. So large that they have an area of satellite dishes called The Very Large Array to the east out in The Plains of St. Augustine. New Mexico has huge military bases east of the Divide, and I laughed to myself imagining that the CDTA might conceivably route our hike over there and force us to dodge machine gun fire and mortars. That'd seem appropriate for this trail.

North of town, the Gila Wilderness appears as a 3.3-million-acre splotch on the map. My route through the wilderness to the town of Reserve involved off-trail trekking. I'd be off any trail whatsoever. It'd be terrifying. Still, Jack and Mike at the Hike and Bike Shop had assured me that I'd be fine. Of course,

38

they didn't know me.

Narrow, undulating Little Walnut Road took me two hours northward from Silver City. At pavement's end, I continued walking another hour up a dirt road past a monastery and some homes. That dead-ended me at a deserted campground called Silver Park. Surprisingly, there was a CDT-marked trailhead on a tree marking a path into the woods. It was a first. On the tenth day of my hike, it was the first trail emblem I'd seen. And here was an actual path through the woods—incredible! I followed. It was just as Jack and Mike had described. Here were mountains and trees. I walked through the forest, following the CDT emblems just like I'd once followed the white blazes on the trees on the Appalachian Trail. It felt familiar. Perhaps one day the entire trail will be like this.

The CDT emblem was similar to the Pacific Crest Trail emblem in that both were rounded, upright triangles. Both read National Scenic Trail at their base, and written up and down their respective sloped sides were the names of the trails. It was only inside that they differed: the PCT emblem was green with a dark pine tree on snow-capped mountains, while the CDT emblem was sky blue with no drawing inside but just the black letters CTD. The letters were deliberately out of order so that the T was in the middle and stood taller than the others with its top overhanging the others like an umbrella (CTD: Continental Trail Divide). Compare those two intricate emblems with the simple one used by the Appalachian Trail: inside a white circle were just the letters A and T overlapped.

For the first time in ten days I had the feeling that I was on the trail. For here I was, suddenly following CDT emblems tacked onto trees. It was to be short-lived. I left the trail to follow Jack and Mike's directions. They'd told me to walk one and one-quarter miles northeastward up the trail from Silver Park, and that I should then turn northwestward off-trail into the dense undergrowth and fight my way descending cross-country down to a small river canyon below. The reason I was leaving the clearly marked CDT path was because that was the start of the undesirable, waterless, 180-mile eastern loop around the Gila. I didn't want that. Nobody wanted it. The CDTA didn't even want hikers to take it. Instead, everyone hikes up through the Gila. To do so simply necessitated piecing together a few different trails. And I first had to leave this present feeling of comfort and safety—leave the CDT emblems— and set off cross-country.

I could see my position on the Jack and Mike Bike Shop contour map. The landmark I needed to locate was a rock formation called Preacher's Pulpit. I looked out over the densely forested river canyon below and convinced myself that I could see the rocks. The brain is an incredible thing: you can convince yourself of anything if you need to. I descended into the unknown following a dried-out creek bed. I was off-trail. I easily reached the eastward-flowing Silver River below, and once there had space to walk on either side of its shores. It felt great to have water. By instruction, I was to search its north bank for a trail leading northward which would take me about fifteen miles over land to the Gila River. The trick was to find the trail, but I couldn't. I searched one hour up and down the bank and found things like discarded tires, a rusted appliance and barbed wire, but no trail. Dusk fell and I lay down to sleep next to a post with a tin box on top. It just felt comforting somehow to sleep next to a man-made object.

Sleeping and eating thus far'd had a desert quality—sand all around and room to maneuver—but that changed in the forest. I carried neither stove nor tent. I carried two lighters, and at night I'd simply been digging a tiny hole in the ground and placing two or three of the flattest stones I could find inside along the edges. I'd put a few twigs and sticks inside and rest my cooking pot on the supporting stones. It might sound appalling, as if this could start a forest fire, but it was a trick that I'd learned back on the PCT from my friend Nate. It was on a miniscule scale, lovingly monitored and perfectly contained. In the desert, micro-fires were easily made, and it'd been easy to sleep under the stars. Here, both practices felt different, with the trees and mountains encroaching upon my sense of space. Forests feel crowded by comparison.

Hermit.

Next morning, May 14, I resumed my search of the riverbank and finally found a sliver of a trail. It was so faint that I believed I might be imagining it. It led northward, though, so I followed it. After thirty minutes, the sliver widened. For many miles it took me gradually climbing northward, gaining elevation. I felt good about the route. It was surely the correct way. I grew confused, though, when I temporarily lost the trail in a boulder field of red rock where it snaked in every direction. Small rocks were piled atop each other (man-made) in several places to form rock cairns marking the way. But the twisting route confused me, so I backtracked forty yards and suddenly spied something shocking.

A house stood in the trees. I hadn't seen it on the first pass because it was well hidden. It was more of a shack: square, small, sturdy and clean. It felt strange to find it here, so far in the wilderness, with no roads. Of course, I was overjoyed to think that I might have someone to speak with, to ask my location. I called "hello!" without actually expecting anyone to answer. Before I could call a second time, the door opened and out stepped a skinny dude, perhaps fifty years old, with a long beard. He waved, so I approached and shook hands. He was a hermit. A Catholic hermit, he said. He invited me inside: cot to sleep on, wood-burning stove, cross on the wall above a small desk. Everything minimalist except for seven pairs of hiking boots arranged perfectly under the bed, and shelves stacked with cans of beans and boxes of tea.

"You have a lot of tea," I said.

"Yes, but I'm a coffee drinker."

All the more reason to offer me tea. He'd been living there for the past five years. Prior to that, he'd spent one year living in a cave about thirty miles to the northeast near a place called Lake Roberts. Looking at him, I thought to myself: If this guy could live in a cave, then anyone can live in a cave. And I firmly believe that—that anyone can live in a cave. That whole story had come tumbling awkwardly out. He was speaking too quickly. I realized that it might've been awhile since he'd had anyone with whom to speak. But then he finally started slowing down when he saw that he had a captive audience. He told me that he'd grown up in a Midwestern suburb. He'd found religion and then'd went out to California to stay with his sister and her minister-husband, but some things went wrong out there and in traveling back eastward he found himself in New Mexico. Things had kept happening, and each time it triggered another event, all of which eventually led him to the cave. It reminded me of William Kennedy's character in Ironweed who first accidentally kills a man, so he runs away, and after he finally returns many years later, he makes a go at "normal" life only to accidentally drop his baby—which was strike two for his brain and served as a final straw causing him to quit for good and live as a homeless man on the streets of Albany. I'm not saying that this guy had given up. He said that with each new stage, he couldn't find any reason to stop his continuing to go forward with it. It was a calling, to him. He felt it was god's work, and that he was on the right path. Finally, during his time in the cave, he'd met a man who owned this land and had invited him to relocate and build here to live as a hermit. This acre was the only piece of private land in any direction for dozens of miles. The man became his sponsor, and together they'd built this cabin by carting up wooden beams by ATV. His sponsor supplied him with food and mail twice a year, and dropped off items like hiking boots and winter jackets. And, apparently, tea. He had a water system and pathways, and he walked me around and showed me his compost pile out back.

"What do you do with all that tea?" I asked.

I kept referring to his tea, mentioning it, pointing to it—"Yogiing"—hoping that he'd offer me some, but he didn't. I think he was distracted by his need to talk and get out all that was stuck in his brain. He showed me a tremendous hiking stick that he'd made from a tree branch. He could see that I was greatly impressed. Some through-hikers carry a stick, others hike pumping away with two ski poles, and still others hike with only their legs and keep their thumbs hitched up under their backpack straps. Using a stick feels right to me because it's substantial. Hiking with a stick makes me feel as if I'm holding a tennis or squash racquet. It feels comfortable and familiar.

Having only recently entered actual forest, I'd picked up a stick off the ground, but it wasn't a good one. They'd sold only walking ski poles back at the Silver City Hike and Bike Shop, so I'd bought one of those. Neither my stick nor ski pole were perfect, and I'd been trying to decide which one I liked better. My hermit's stick was an awesome stick, I remarked. I wasn't trying to Yogi the stick, but was being sincere. I asked him about the monastery back near Little Walnut Road, and he said that he walks there to attend mass about once every three months. I laughed, trying to imagine that scene, how this guy must have some superior aura there when he saunters in, just that one leg up: "You guys might be monks, but I'm a hermit!"

What I desperately needed to know was: "Am I on the right track?" He knew about the CDT, and he told me that a group of three backpackers had walked by one week earlier. He'd seen them, but they hadn't noticed him. He confirmed that I was in the right place. The route north from here to the Gila River was easy, he said.

"Tremendously easy."

"Yeah?"

"Yeah. Except for one really difficult part."

It's the difficult parts that get me. A burnt-out area two miles north of here was where the trail ended and I'd have to walk cross-country to find another trail a half mile later. That'd be difficult. He escorted me outside through the red boulder field and a couple hundred yards farther to a stream, just to start me in the right direction. A bad hip prevented his walking farther. As we parted, he repeated another four times the route I should take cross-country after the burnt area. He was clearly worried. I wasn't especially pleased to need to go off-trail again, either. I said good-bye and started northward, but then he called me back. I'd known for certain that he was going to do this. He reached for my poor hiking stick and extended his fine one. I tried to refuse the offer, but he made me trade. I thanked him kindly and set out. Chalk one up for the CDT, as you just don't meet hermits on the AT or the PCT. Further evidence of the terrific lunacy of this trail.

Crawling-Bleeding.

My new Hermit-fashioned hiking stick was tall but too substantial. Unfortunately, it gave me slivers which I had to keep pulling out of my hands. My umbrella and folded-down ski pole were tied to my pack and stuck into the air like antennae. I reached the burnt area and sure enough lost the trail. The landscape was complex with hills, valleys, and mountains packed tightly together. They collided and ran up on each other, making it impossible to distinguish which ridge headed where. Dense foliage surrounded the perimeter of the burn, and I set out westward by pushing through tight undergrowth.

I couldn't make sense of where the hermit had said I should go. My goal was Sapio Creek, and I merely had to climb northward over a mountain ridge to locate the trail that would take me there. I knew that I had to go northward, of course, but I was supposed to work westward first. By compass, I descended one hundred yards westward down a slope, then fifty yards southwestward down a dry creek bed. I finally turned and climbed northward to get up over a little ridge. I kept checking my compass. It was dense bramble. I climbed, hoping to gain a view, and hoping that the landscape would suddenly make sense from up on top. Upon gaining the high vantage point, however, my heart sank and I saw that I was in trouble. My view revealed nothing but dense, rugged wilderness. I was off the grid once again. This was bad. I thought of a passage by Laurence Gonzales in a book called Deep Survival:

> *A true survivor would be attuned to those subtle cues, the whisper of intuition, which might have been saying, 'I don't feel quite safe here. Why is that so?' But most of us don't have what psychologists call* META-KNOWLEDGE: *the ability to assess the quality of our own knowledge. It's easy to assume that perception and reason faithfully render reality. But as Plato suggested and modern neuroscience has proved, we live in a sort of dream world, which only imperfectly matches reality.*

I didn't panic. I knew I was lost. I knew roughly, by compass, which way I needed to go. But this was a vast area. Connecting A to B isn't easy in dense, trailless wilderness. I looked out and picked a route. I chose an east-west mountain ridge that I aimed to end up scaling ultimately, and then I planned how I'd get from here to there. I needed to scale westward down off my current high spot and into a gulley; then I'd work my way northeastward along the downslope of a mountainside, and finally I'd climb northward up my targeted ridge. The difficulty of making necessary small alterations in order to work around cliffs, boulders, and areas of too-dense undergrowth is that you risk losing track of your overall position relative to where you'd initially wanted to go. Perspective changes, so it wasn't as simple as looking over at the ridge that you wished to end up on.

Half a mile later, down in it, I found that nothing looked the same as it had up high. Nuts that I'd gotten into this predicament. Just suddenly, here I was alone in extraordinarily dense wilderness, with no plan. My arms and legs had gotten ripped open from the branches of tough, dry bushes and trees. My ski pole and umbrella kept snagging on branches, so I had to carry them in my hands along with the hermit's stick. Still, no panic. No feeling of doom came over me. I was calm. Just not terribly happy about this. I fought my way up a hillside and tried to work laterally northward along it. It was nearly impossible. It was laughable, how dense the vegetation was here. It was a mixture of dead and live foliage—ankle-high, hip-high and forehead-high—forming a wall that I had to fight through. There was no path of least resistance. Any direction I chose was this same wall. The guidebook said:

> *The terrain is complex, and often very steep. The vegetation,*
> *although interesting, is conspicuously hostile to hikers—*
> *thorny, prickly, spiny, jagged, sharp, serrated, stabbing. I*
> *hiked here with two through-hikers who wore shorts; blood*
> *soon ran down their legs.*

It's hard to be interested in things like vegetation when you're lost. The spiny cacti here in the rocks were so dense, strong, and sharp that I believed a person could die upon falling on one. So I tried not to fall on one. My long-sleeved black T-shirt got ripped to shreds and my shorts got slashed. One water bottle got stripped from the side of my pack and was lost. That's how sharp and intrusive was the head-high undergrowth. In an attempt to find openings through the brush, I took to crawling on my hands and knees, removing my backpack and pushing it forward ahead of me and then crawling after it. Another method was crawling first and then reaching back to retrieve my pack. It was inch by inch, yard by yard. Usually, while hiking, it's merely a bother to either get lost or struggle greatly because it means that day's mileage will fall below average, but I was way past inconvenience now. I was into emergency. I was just trying to survive this. Sometimes I had to stand in one place and break all the dead branches before me, just so that the live ones would then give enough for me to push through. Sometimes I pushed through with my pack in my hands, before my face—eyes closed, pushed with my forehead against my pack with all my might while hoping that nothing would snap and hit me. My arms and legs grew bloodied. My shirt hung off me in torn strips.

A moment arrived when I found that in reaching back for my umbrella, hermit's stick, backpack, and ski pole, only my pack and ski pole came with me. My situation was so desperate that I needed to scale down, even if it meant littering and polluting planet earth for all of eternity. I could no longer lug everything. No more umbrella, no more hermit's hiking stick. The hiking stick would decompose and return to the earth; the umbrella would be found in one-hundred-thousand years by our human descendents. No more slivers in my hands. They were acceptable losses. I was extremely rough with my backpack. It was the same Gregory backpack I'd bought twelve years earlier down near the start of the Appalachian Trail at the Walasi-Yi Center in Neels Gap. It had lasted for all of the AT, then all of the PCT, and several Adirondack Mountain climbs, too. It was indestructible and I felt a close bond with that pack. I pushed, kicked, and dragged it through sharp spiny diabolical weeds. This was painful.

Still, no panic. The afternoon and evening passed with me fighting and

44

inching along, bleeding as I went. I'd thus far sustained only a myriad of small cuts, and fortunately no major gashes. I'd made my way off the face of the first mountainside and was now climbing directly north up the east-west mountain ridge I'd seen. I planned to climb to the top, where I hoped that a view down its north side would reveal a clear picture. I prepared myself for the worst, though. I knew that there was a very good chance that the top of the ridge would be densely covered and offer no view, same as everywhere else. In that case, I'd climb a tree to try to gain a view. I'd make a new plan. I'd do something. Anything. There was also the chance, though, that it would be clear. I felt that it was imperative for my mental well-being to gain the ridge before dark, so that I wouldn't have to sleep while dwelling on the uncertainty. But I couldn't reach the top in time.

Darkness fell, yet I continued for one final hour of climbing and fighting, crawling on my hands and knees, and even lying down on my stomach to wriggle through small openings like a snake. There was a moment in the darkness when I could hear my friend Toot's voice in my head. Toot now lives in Florida. He's a federal prosecutor. Prosecutes drug cases and sends little eighth-grade pot smokers to jail for the rest of their lives and off to the electric chair. I'd been best-man at his wedding. Distinctly, I could hear his voice while I was in utter darkness off the grid, on my belly, crawling forward with a stick stabbing me. As clearly as if he were lying beside me and squirming through this tangle himself, I could hear him deliver his perfect, sarcastic, deadpan pitch: "Oh yeah, I'm sure things are going to be just fine!" It actually caused me to laugh out loud. It helped calm me. There are spots in the Adirondack Mountains of New York, off-trail, that are otherworldly green and dense. If you get lost off-trail there, they'll never find you: they'll never recover your body. But this was a sharp, prickly, brown desert kind of denseness, and I'd never experienced anything like it. It was half-past ten when I gave up for the night. I forged a body-sized opening to sleep in by kicking back everything around me. I slept like a baby. Strangely calm and peaceful. I'd only a few swallows of water left. Running out of water is life-threatening.

Resuming my fight in the morning, I climbed a mere forty-five minutes — just a few dozen yards higher up the mountainside — when I hit, perpendicularly, a clear and wide trail. I rose. Untouched. I laughed! Like magic, here I'd suddenly gone from complete and utter resistance against every inch of my body, to no resistance at all. I turned left, and took off walking northwestward at over three miles per hour. I felt I was flying. This clear, wide, sandy trail climbed gradually and gently northwestward and soon crested the east-west mountain ridge. Not only that, but the top revealed a clear view northward. The trail, unmarked, continued wide, pronounced, and arrow-straight directly northward, where in twelve miles it'd hit Sapio Creek and my start up the mighty Gila River. I was totally and utterly saved. Everything made sense. I could see on my map that the trail I'd found (had stumbled upon) was on Tadpole Ridge.

I had clear sailing. I walked the twelve miles and reached Sapio Creek at the spot into which the Gila River discharged. It was the end of the Gila River—so now I just had to enter into it and simply walk upstream to its source. There'd be no getting lost because the Gila River leads northward up through a canyon that's enclosed by high cliff walls on both sides.

It'd been scary and ridiculously difficult. I probably should've been worried over my poor performance and lack of route-finding skills, for those had gotten me into the jam. But instead, I was now feeling proud of my skill in having found my way, off-trail, alone. I felt proud for having survived. Felt a renewed sense of confidence: Maybe I could hike this trail, after all!

5
Gila River

And now we arrive down in the canyon,
red rocks, down in the canyon.

—Havasupai Medicine Song

Upstream.

It was instantly clear that this was going to be worth the price of admission. Having waded perpendicularly northward across Sapio Creek, I stood at the entrance of the Gila River Canyon. On both sides—east and west—rose five-story red clay cliffs. I entered the canyon between the cliff walls, walking in water up to my naval. It felt like being down at the base of the Grand Canyon, although I can't actually say that for sure as I've never been to the Grand Canyon. The cliffs squeezed so close to the river that only tiny strips of land formed the riverbanks. My task was to follow this river forty miles upstream to a man-made dam. Halfway there, at mile twenty, I'd get a potentially fantastic pit stop at Gila Village and the Gila Cliff Dwelling Home National Monument. My issues of dehydration, foot pain, and getting lost were distant memories. The river was my reward. It was going to be one of the highlights of the summer. Everything is going right now!

The river snaked and carved back and forth, eroding the cliff walls as it's done down through eons and millennium. I walked upstream, northward, stepping out onto the riverbanks to follow washed-out remnants of little paths whenever they presented themselves. Whenever my path ended in spots where the river brushed against sheer cliff, I'd ford belly-deep through the water to

47

whatever little sliver of land I could find on the other side. I must've made at least forty crosses in the first twenty miles. I crossed with my sneakers and socks on, for stopping to remove them would have been an exhausting and ridiculous waste of time. I was overjoyed at the chance to keep my feet wet all day. It was soothing compared to the prior torture of shuffling over hot asphalt roads.

The water was warmer than I'd expected, and the current wasn't strong enough to knock me over. All I could think of was how amazing it would have been to slowly inner-tube southward downstream through the canyon on this gentle river. There were birds' nests and caves in the red clay cliff walls. Two ducks in the water spooked when they saw me and flew upstream; then minutes later I came upon them again and they took off again and flew farther upstream. The pattern repeated. On and on it went with the ducks. I always feel bad over disrupting animals. I popped iodine pills in my water bottle when I filled it and drank, to purify, just to be safe.

I stopped to sleep riverside on a beach of white sand. I built a small fire and cooked. It was the best bivy spot I'd ever had in my life. I lay gazing straight up at the stars. All that following morning, May 16, day thirteen for me, I continued up the Gila. At midafternoon I reached a bridge—the first man-made object that I'd seen in walking twenty river miles. The bridge spanned the river, carrying a paved road across it. It marked the halfway point of my river walk. It was clear on the contour map. I scrambled up to the road and walked an hour northward along it to tiny Gila Hot Springs Village—cluster of homes, RV park, bed-and-breakfast with a natural hot spring in its front yard and a small store called Doc Campbell's.

Company.

Doc Campbell's owners were curt and disinterested. They told me right off as I entered their store at four o'clock that they closed at four-thirty, so I strode the aisles and bought candy, drinks, suckers, chips, and homemade ice cream. I sat and ate outside at a picnic table in front of the store, stuffing my face and organizing my things. There wasn't a great deal of activity. The long road came in from Silver City and dead-ended here. So this wasn't a through-road. A shirtless and for some reason barefoot motorcycle rider turned into the store's gravel driveway and made a brief call from the pay telephone here before riding off again. An RV camper pulled in, turned around, and drove back the way it'd come. Otherwise, I was alone. Those brief interruptions were mere curiosities. I called Cristina and Jessie Gibbins.

"You met a hermit?"

"You got lost again?"

"You crawled on your stomach through the bushes?"

"You ran out of water?"

"Your clothes got ripped to shreds?"

The telephone calls found me walking a fine line between eliciting sympathy and triggering the ire of my friends who could at any moment grow angry and lecture me on self-preservation. I wanted to share my experience, but I didn't want them to worry. Truthfully, nothing bad was going to happen to me. Nothing was going to get me. I knew that. I've done millions of crazy things in my life and I've always been okay. We're in control until we aren't. In that way, I felt like the character from Jim Harrison's Legends of the Fall, whom everyone worries over because of all the chances he takes, but in the end he outlives everyone and it's everyone around him who's died.

Suddenly three through-hikers appeared walking up the road toward me. I can identify through-hikers with merely a glance. It was two guys and a girl. Through-hikers! It was about time. I'd been wondering when and if this was ever going to happen. On the Appalachian Trail, you meet thirty aspiring through-hikers on your first day even before finishing the eight-mile-long access trail from the Amacolola Falls State Park Visitor Center to reach the summit of Springer Mountain—but out here a full thirteen days had gone by without my meeting a single other hiker.

"Hey! I'm John."

"Weekender."

"Todd."

"Cooper."

We shook hands.

"How's it going? You guys are the first through-hikers I've seen."

"You're the first one we've seen," they said.

Finding the store closed, they sat at the picnic table beside me and emptied their packs and cooked dinner. Meeting them felt natural and comfortable, just like it always did on the AT and the PCT. They seemed an unlikely trio, but who was I to judge? Here they'd found me sitting alone in a long-sleeved T-shirt that was ripped to shreds, torn so badly that I had sunburn everyplace that there was a hole. I must've looked ridiculous. We form instant impressions. Old Man Weekender had white hair. If I'd had to guess, I would've said that he was a Boy Scout leader or a minister. Or ex-military at the very least—and I'd turn out to be right about that one. He wore his white hair in a buzz-cut, was tall, skinny and had his shirt tucked into his shorts. He wore a modest white mustache. His backpack was modest, too. He'd gotten his trail name out on the PCT because hikers would meet him there and think that he was a "Weekender." He could walk right by you and you'd never even notice. Old Man Weekender was forty-two years old. He'd seemed old to me—almost ancient—until I realized that he was only one year older than me.

"Where are you from?"

"New Jersey," Weekender said.

"Cool! I'm from New York originally, but I've been living in Maine for the past sixteen years."

Old Man Weekender was a carpenter, he said (not a pastor at all). He was quiet, but he smiled a sufficient amount.

"You?" I asked Todd.

"Oregon," Todd said, rolling and lighting a homemade cigarette.

Todd's style didn't match Weekender's. They weren't even in the same stratosphere. Todd was twenty-six years old and oozing with charisma. He was a cross between a pretty-boy and a west coast grunge rocker. It was difficult to say if he was classically handsome, but he had the hair and the body to show up on women's radar screens. He had calve-muscles like Popeye. They were his most noticeable feature. He puffed away on his cigarette. He had moussed-up hair and was quick to laugh an infectious laugh. He wore a dry-fit muscle shirt and nylon parachute pants, both of which showed his strong, wiry frame. He wore John Lennon–styled sunglasses and had a green bandana tied around his neck. He seemed like an airhead, like a male bimbo—a "mimbo," as Jerry calls it in the Seinfeld episode with the good-looking, comic-book-reading, outdoorsy-type rock-climber that Elaine dates merely for his looks, and the guy keeps saying: "Step off, George!" A creature of the Pacific Northwest, Todd had more of a So-Cal vibe, and he kept pronouncing fantastic as "fon-tostic." He'd go on and on about how this previous hike or that previous hike was "fon-tostic." And sitting there with Todd if your mind wandered and you drifted away to some thought of your own, all of a sudden you'd snap out of it when you'd catch the punch-line of one of his jokes or the tail end of a story that he was relating to the others: "… so then I was like, 'dude, i don't have any oatmeal!' "

"And you?"

"Virginia," said Cooper.

Her name was Laura Cooper. She was twenty-five years old. Cooper was gorgeous, if not entirely fit. She had a warmth about her; she was calm, relaxed and clearly very happy. She was loving life. She didn't seem like a rock-hard CDT through-hiker type, but that was okay. After an instant or two of seeing Cooper start taking things out of Todd's pack, a light went off in my head, and I realized that they were a couple. Todd was a sneaker salesman who worked for REI camping stores. He'd met Cooper when he'd spent a yearlong stint running REI shoe training seminars in Virginia. Todd hadn't gone to college, while Cooper was about to start a master's program in English literature. Todd went about his business, laughing and cracking jokes while reading his maps and sorting through their things. He was in his element. Cooper looked on adoringly at Todd, and I got it. She had her rugged, spiky-haired mountain man, and Todd was a man in charge. They made a good couple, Todd as a possible narcissist, while to him she was borderline obsequious. They were fine, giggling happily together.

Cooper had flown out to hike for just ten days, and she'd only just begun when they'd picked her up in Silver City. Todd had through-hiked the Pacific Crest Trail two summers earlier, and he'd met Weekender there. Weekender had hiked the PCT in two pieces, half in one summer, and the other half the following summer—and he was planning on doing the same thing out here, too, hiking only to Wyoming this summer, and then hiking Wyoming and Montana at some later date. It didn't matter that their ages differed, because they got along well. Old Man Weekender and Todd had agreed to come hike together. So in this group of four, Todd and I were the only two going for a CDT through-hike. And Todd hadn't hiked the AT, so I was the only one in the group now attempting to complete my triple crown.

"Man, I almost died back there," I said.

It felt wonderful to have people to talk to. Ironically, here I was finally meeting my first fellow CDT through-hikers only after having left the official CDTA route. I was thrilled for the opportunity to ask over which route had Todd and Weekender begun.

"We started at Columbus-Polomis," they said, describing a twin American-Mexican town east of where I'd begun.

"Why'd you start there?" I asked.

"It's the Ley route," Todd said.

"What's that?"

Goofy Todd explained clearly through puffs on his cigarette that Jonathon Ley was a CDT through-hiking alumnus who lived in Oregon and had personal maps of the entire trail, which he sold. Todd'd met with Ley in Portland and was now hiking with "The Ley Maps." Columbus-Polomis was Ley's suggested embarkation point. They told me that it'd been an outstanding way to start, for it'd taken them through mountains northwestward into Deming, and from there northwestward through more mountains into Silver City. They'd missed two dozen miles of trail because they'd had to skip ahead to meet Cooper in Silver City the night her airport shuttle van had arrived. They'd exited Silver City by walking northward up Little Walnut Road as I had, and they'd then hiked cross-country and up the Gila River, same as me. Except they hadn't gotten lost. And their clothes weren't torn. But they hadn't met the hermit, either. None of their starting route had been the official CDTA, and yet they'd walked through mountains while I'd walked the official trail over tedious, deadly roads.

Todd laughed so hard when I said that I was using the CDTA books, that it sent him into a violent coughing fit and triggered convulsions. He'd never heard such a thing before. To him, it clearly signaled that I was ill-prepared for the hike. Quite true! I hadn't prepared much at all. I'd been busy with squash. Plus, I don't like to prepare. Everyone chides me for that. I asked Weekender what he was using.

"The Wolf book," he said.

What the hell was that!?

Weekender was using neither the CDTA books, nor the Ley Maps; instead, he was using the maps and guidebooks that were published by a guy named Jim Wolf, an attorney from Maryland who was another CDT alumnus and had been an advocate for the trail for two decades, to the point that he'd formed something called The Continental Divide Trail Society. It was actually a competitor of the Continental Divide Trail Association. My association and Weekender's society didn't work together, didn't help each other, but were rivals. Like bickering academics. It made me think of Monty Python's The Life of Brian, with the competing anarchist groups who share the same cause but use different names. They bump into each other down in the catacombs underneath Rome and start fighting:

"We are the Judean People's Front!"

"We are the People's Front of Judea!"

My CDTA was the official trail organization. It was eight years old and empowered by Congress to establish and maintain the CDT. But now I'd found out through Todd and Weekender's explanation that all CDT through-hikers worth their salt use either the Ley Maps or the Wolf Guidebook. Great: I didn't have either of those. I may have been the only one in this group to have already hiked both the AT and the PCT, but it was clear that Todd and Weekender were far more prepared than was I for the CDT. We walked another two road miles at dusk and slept on the ground, bivied out in the parking lot at the Gila Cliff Dwelling Home National Monument.

Cliff Home.

Two park rangers arrived by car to unlock a small gate on the morning of May 17 and welcomed us to set out on a self-guided walking tour of the cliff dwelling monument. We followed a sidewalk over a bridge and through trees along a trickling creek in a quiet gulley. Shortly, at sidewalk's end, a path took us gradually up the face of a cliff to the Cliff Dwelling Homes. We were a motley crew: my shirt was torn and goofy, spiky-haired Todd wore his earphones, listening to music on his iPod. He tuned us out and played air guitar while singing some song by Nirvana:

" 'I sit and drink Pennyroyal Tea, distill the life that's inside of me. Sit and drink Pennyroyal Tea, I'm anemic royalty…' "

Built into a high cave was a multiroom home with clay walls, platforms, ledges, and landings. It was just like all the photographs of the cliff homes in the Southwest. It was perfectly constructed. Nothing like it exists back East. We fanned-out and investigated small rooms and gathering places. Sunshine radiated all through the interior. Even while bare it felt homey. I imagined that it must've been beautiful back when it was filled with potted flowers, dried decorative flowers, colorful blankets, food, corn, chickens, dogs and children running about. I could easily imagine living back then, here with my family and other families. The cliff dwelling home had supposedly been vacant since 1260, but before that the Mogollan Native Americans had a trading and farming community here. Our conception is that only a few Native Americans lived on this continent back then before the European invasion, while in actuality there were several million people already here.

The view overlooked the creek and a low cliff on the opposite bank. The first Europeans to find this had theorized that the Native Americans must've traveled up and down by vine, but surely they must've used pathways and ladders. There was a room toward the back that I believed must've been used as a nursery for infants and toddlers. The babysitting responsibilities must've been awesome.

River's End.

We parted ways after the tour. Old Man Weekender and the young attractive couple of Todd and Cooper stuck together as a Trio, taking a different route than I back to the Gila River. It was okay because I knew that I'd see them again somewhere in the river canyon, as we still had twenty more river miles to walk. I walked seven miles overland on a clear path from a horse coral off the Gila Monument Road across a high plateau and then finally descended an endless series of switchbacks that dropped me back down to the base of the Gila River Canyon. I rejoined the Gila River at a place called The Meadows which is a spot that has a natural hot spring. There, I met two kids fishing, five young men playing cards and seven old men who were professors at Colorado College, who told me that they hiked the Gila River Canyon every year. Those were the only human beings that I saw for the total forty miles in the canyon.

The others had instead walked down to the Cliff Dwelling Home Information Center to resume their way up the Gila River from there. My way amounted to a shortcut and placed me farther north up the river than they. I felt glad about that, for if anything went wrong they were behind and could come along to save me.

The second half of the forty-mile canyon walk was along the 'West Fork Gila River.' It felt fine to return to the water. I settled back into its rhythm, winding through the twisting canyon, constantly fording back and forth through the river just to find some little sliver of land to walk on. I slept alone again in the canyon, until midday on the 18, I knew I was nearing its end. I was ready for it to be over. The river canyon was exceedingly beautiful, but I'd begun to feel positively claustrophobic from being hemmed-in by the high cliff walls for so long. I finally grew so impatient that I just wanted out. I longed to have the cliffs fade away and the earth open so that I could feel space once again. I'd begun to worry that the river might never end. I'd made about eighty or ninety fords of the river in all. Finally, I came to a tributary—THE FIRST IN

FORTY MILES. It marked my exit off the West Fork Gila River. I followed it half a mile northwestward, then climbed a path up to the concrete dam of man-made Snow Lake. It was all on the map. It made sense. From there, I'd begin an overland adventure, to try to find a way northward out of the Gila Wilderness to the town of Reserve.

Gravel Maze.

Paved Route 12 arcs over the north side of the Gila Wilderness, and there stood my destination, the town of Reserve. No through-roads existed, but I'd finally reached far enough north to where I could pick up one of the dirt roads that burrow south, dropping down from Route 12 into the Gila like tree roots. Snow Lake was small and murky-brown. Picnic tables and public restrooms weren't enough to make it enticing. Not a single person nor car was about. Cows grazed across the lake. A lone dirt road led northward from Snow Lake.

Sometimes, you just want the work to be over. You want to hurry up and reach town in order to eat, get clean, recharge and regroup. I felt that now. It was my fifth day north of Silver City and my food was running low. My pack was light and that was a good thing, but I felt desperate to reach Reserve just to get a break from the route-finding turmoil. I had to solve one final puzzle first. The AT and the PCT would've both had huge blinking neon-lighted signs here with arrows guiding the way. However, here on the unfinished CDT, I had to choose a way to connect unmarked dirt roads and reach Reserve.

The way began with an obvious twelve-mile westward then acutely-angled northeastward gravel road walk from Snow Lake to a place called the Negrito Fire Base. The distance was a mere four miles as the crow flies, but I wasn't brave enough to leave the road and walk cross county directly northward and flirt with possibly getting lost in dense terrain again. I needed to safely stick to the road and take the long way. I set out for a few evening miles.

At dusk I stepped fifteen yards off the gravel road and lay down in my sleeping bag on my nylon ground cover in a sparse dry wood to cook dinner and sleep. I was halfway through eating, when by instinct I suddenly glanced over my shoulder and discovered a bear walking toward me. The ground was covered with dry sticks and dead brush, yet the bear had come within a squash court distance away without making a sound. It was a black bear, young and small at perhaps two-hundred pounds. It stopped when I turned to face it, and we simultaneously froze. A thought popped into mind, how I'd heard that it's best not to make eye contact; but I couldn't help it. We locked stares until I gained my senses and sat up. I shouted and the bear galloped away. I felt thrilled and honored to have seen it. The black bear is the state animal of New Mexico. A small one had caused me to freeze in fear. I couldn't begin to imagine how a thousand-pound grizzly bear up in Montana would affect me. But it wasn't time for Montana just yet. I lay down again and slept soundly.

Rising on the morning of Thursday, May 19, I walked the remainder of the gravel road to the Negrito Fire Base. Only two cars passed by. At the fire base was a pay phone, cabin and a helicopter landing pad. The base housed firefighters called Hot Shots who trained here and then flew away to jump out of airplanes while fighting fires all over the Southwest. It was quiet now, with no one around. There was a biology base nearby that studied the effect of the helicopters on the local owls. I could tell them the answer to that one even without doing research: *The owls don't like it!* I was up at the end of my Gila Wilderness map. I just had to get out to Reserve.

At the fire base was a T-intersection. Left was a thirty-mile northwest-ward-curving road walk to Reserve, while right was a thirty-mile northward gravel and dirt road walk which would deposit me on Route 12 for a hitchhike southwestward to Reserve. I chose the gravel walk because the others had told me that they'd be taking it. The route looked possible on the map. However, reality doesn't always match what's on paper. From the fire base, I walked four hours northeastward, then stopped to eat dinner and nap. My plan was to fully rest a few hours and then rise and night-hike. Nighttime just calls me sometimes. Night-hiking would help me avoid dehydration. I could see well enough in the dark because my Gila Hike and Bike Shop–purchased headlamp flashlight was strong. I'd also bought a new lightweight hiking stick at Doc Campbell's store, and I was pleased with it. The stick would last me for the rest of the summer. No splinters or anything.

I'm not exactly sure when it was that I began noticing that the gravel roads no longer seemed to correspond with my map. I encountered numerous forks in the road and kept having to choose which fork to take. Of course, I was painfully aware that my instincts are poor. That's meta-knowledge: the ability to assess the quality of your own knowledge. The gravel roads kept meeting tributaries of equal size, and splitting off. The wishbone forks appeared time and again. I would choose continue, choose continue. On and on it went, hour by hour.

I hiked four hours in the darkness, until half-past one in the morning. There were no homes or cars, just this maze which kept me guessing. The worst came at a spot where the road curved so much into an endless, spiral-ing descent that it seemed to be taking me down to the center of the planet. I couldn't imagine how it could possibly uncoil. My worst fear had come true. Something had gone wrong and no bit of luck was going to save me. I wasn't going to suddenly step out on Route 12. My internal emergency light flashed brightly. I suddenly stopped and climbed back up, retracing my steps in the direction I'd come. I had to admit to myself that I'd messed up. Nothing about any of my choices for the past several hours had made any sense. None of the road forks seemed to correspond to anything on my map no matter how much I wanted them to. It was hopeless and it wasn't going to suddenly get better or work itself out. There'd be no happy ending. I had to admit that.

I knew what to do. I had to cut my losses and backtrack to the fire base. I was tired. Regardless, due to fear, anger, and desperation, I couldn't stop walking now. I felt that if I stopped and slept while still in the maze I might wake up disoriented and get stuck inside it forever. Only thing I had going for me on the return was that every fork had an acute angle opening northward, so in retracing my steps I simply had to go with the grain at every fork. It was easy. Adrenaline surged through me and kept me walking until six o'clock in the morning, all the way back to the stop sign that marked the point where I'd entered the gravel maze. I lay down to sleep. In total, I figured that I must've hiked over thirty-six miles on the day.

I was still ten miles shy of the T-intersection at the fire base. I rose at nine o'clock after a few hours of troubled, tossing, turning nightmares—nightmares in which I was just walking and nothing made sense—then I staggered back to complete my retreat. I felt perfectly lousy about my skills. A forest ranger took pity on me when he saw me sitting despondently on my backpack in the road by the fire base. I knew that I made a pathetic sight. He handed me a cold Pepsi. Also, he broke federal policy and gave me a ride thirty miles northwestward to Reserve.

Green Or Red?

Dictionary definition for reserve is: "A resource not normally called upon but available if needed." That seemed about right. Reserve was the seat of the largest county in the fifth-largest state in America, yet the county's population was only four hundred people. Just seven students comprised the senior class at Reserve High School. I was best friends with the park ranger by the time we reached Reserve. That's because he appreciated my listening while he pointed out caves on the cliffs and hillsides which he said he'd explored. After finding no vacancy at the downtown Reserve hotel due to a motorcycle rally that had it rented out, he dropped me off at the only alternative, the Elk Country Café, which had a few ranch hotel rooms out back. The restaurant's walls were decorated with enormous stuffed elk heads, marbles for their eyes and antlers as big as automobiles. I felt numb from my previous night's sleepless debacle. At least I knew that the others—Weekender-Todd-Cooper—were due in shortly. I was anxious to see them again.

The café owner had quadruple duty as my chef, waitress, hotel manager, and chamber maid. She was from Brooklyn, no-nonsense, had come here postdivorce, and had bought this place. She also ran a local youth group for at-risk kids. I liked her immediately. She told me that this town was famous for having passed a law that required you to own a gun. It wasn't that you may own a gun if you live here, but that you must own a gun. I didn't seek verification, because I didn't want to find out that it wasn't true and find out that this was just an average place like any other. They'd also once demanded the return to them of 2.8 million acres of federally owned wilderness, but somehow that didn't fly: the federal government refused and the town was still mad. Local cars had antitax bumper stickers, and ones which depicted the government as a wolf in sheep's clothing.

I sat in a comfortable booth. Meals on the trail are carbohydrate-heavy with noodles, so in town you crave protein through meat, dairy, and nuts. Take away the meat and dairy and you've a vegan. I've always aspired to that, and back home I'm almost there. But out here in the trail towns I ate eggs, milkshakes, grilled-cheese, pizza. It was lots of dairy for me. I feel bad about that. It's not consistent with my beliefs. And I know that it's possible to be vegan while hiking, but that wouldn't be easy. I'd always load up with potatoes and toast, too. My Brooklyn chef–waitress–chamber maid served perfectly gargantuan portions of Southwestern breaded potato dishes, omelets, pancakes, and salads. Her chocolate milkshake was otherworldly. You try to eat fruit and vegetables when you're in town, too, just to get those vitamins and minerals—but mostly you crave just exactly this type of heaping, quasi–greasy spoon entrées. It was a feast. Quite fun to stuff one's face while pouring over trail maps.

A couple of locals spied my hiking stick and talked to me. Unless through-hikers are loud and obnoxious we always get accepted as locals. It just happens that way. It might have something to do with the way that we enter other people's towns—only slowly, on our feet. We have felt with our bodies, with our feet what their home feels like. We've earned it. We've cared enough about the place where they live to sweat walking in. It's that important to us. Coming to see their town is worth sweating for. It's the highest compliment imaginable. Sweat brought us in, so we were okay. It didn't hurt matters any that our faces were dirty and we were dressed worse than anyone. That made us nonthreatening. We had to exist and ultimately walk out on our own, too, so they knew that we had to make friends with everyone.

The conversations with strangers in restaurants are what I like best about life on the trail. One of my squash players had once said something to me which had stuck in my mind. It was an early morning on the streets of Philadelphia. We'd emerged from our hotel and were crossing a city street walking over to the University of Pennsylvania squash courts for individual nationals. A scruffy man on a bicycle had ridden up to us. He had a suit in a case slung over his handlebars (like a tuxedo rental) and was waving a piece of paper, calling out to us. I hesitated, and he'd instantly launched into asking something unintelligible about whether hotels give receipts upon checkout. My player was from Boston, and she'd rolled her eyes understanding that this guy was trying to engage us in conversation as a way to begin some kind of scam. I listened awhile and finally walked off, and when I caught up with my player seconds later she'd said with mixed condescension and sympathy, "You'd never make it in New York City or Boston." Meaning that I'm gullible, I'm a mark. But I didn't consider it that way. I'm just curious and I need information. I want to see all of life, not merely the good parts. In my defense, I'd told her: "If you want to peer into the abyss, you have to walk close to the edge!"

She had no idea of all the hundreds of people I'd met in all the crazy mountain towns up and down the east and west coasts, and all over the country. She could never know the things that I'd heard from all the people with all their mumblings and all their sharing of dreams and crazy philosophies. I sat thinking of how much I loved it. Of how much I love it when the old guy across the aisle in the Elk Country Café spies my backpack and gets a little twinkle in his eye and says, "Been out backpacking?" And I get to grin and say yes. Something inside me loves people. We're cruel, scared, needy, horrible, and worthy of pity. Einstein, Mark Twain, Kurt Vonnegut, Hermann Hesse, and others had all come to the same simple conclusion late in their lives: that our species is a curse, and we are doomed. And yet the love is there just the same.

My confidence: shattered. I'd unsuccessfully navigated the gravel maze. All I could think of now was the reality that I am not cut out for this trail. My first time getting lost off-trail and crawling through the dense bramble had been a sign, but I hadn't acknowledged that signal so the gods of the trail conspired to hit me with the gravel maze to make sure that the message got through and sunk in: I don't belong out here on the CDT. That was a fact. It'd been confirmed now. It's not that I couldn't stick with a long hike. Nor that I couldn't stomach discomfort or physically put in the miles. I'd proven before that I could do those things. And if this trail had been marked, I could do it out here, too. Or if I was hiking with a partner, I could do it out here. It's just that I'm not skilled enough to figure out routes on an unmarked trail alone. I hadn't missed an inch of the AT or the PCT, but I could no longer say that out here. I rationalized: because long sections of the CDT were unconnected, perhaps neither success nor failure was possible here.

"Red or green?" the café owner asked.

"Red or green what?" I asked, snapping out of deep reverie.

"It's the state question of New Mexico," she said. "Red or green chili sauce with your meal?"

Mountain Test.

Seated in the café in a spacious booth under elk heads with lunch spread out around me, I studied my New Mexico road atlas to see what lay ahead: apparently, more desert. Imagine that. The CDTA book for New Mexico was filled with warnings about lack of water. No surprise. It was a heat wave outside with the temperature topping one hundred degrees. The sun blazed and there wasn't so much as a wisp of cloud in the sky. This wasn't like the weather we get in New England. I went out back and lay in my room with my door open. A little dog rummaged around and kept peeking inside.

Old Man Weekender arrived and ate dinner with me. The next morning,

Todd and Cooper arrived and we ate breakfast together. The food here was the best on the entire trail. The portions were enormous and the service instantaneous. Through the course of the day, we were usually the only ones inside. It was May 21, and this would be a zero day for me. Todd and Weekender were expert hikers, but Cooper was new to this. She was out here for only seven more days before heading home to Virginia. She stared adoringly at Todd: he, of the gelled hair and tremendous goofy energy. He exuded world-class flakiness, and yet he could knowledgeably discuss the key features and personality of every "fon-tostic" mountain range that he'd ever hiked. He told us stories about his rock climbing and winter camping in the Sisters Wilderness in Oregon. He wasn't bragging, but just sharing experiences. Todd and Weekender didn't respect the Appalachian Trail. I kept explaining how great it was, but they weren't buying. They felt that hiking such a clearly marked trail would be beneath them.

I quite strangely suddenly took it upon myself to give Cooper a test of her mountain knowledge. We were bored, and I guess I'd just wanted to make her laugh. I wasn't trying to flirt with her, but I admit that it was fairly experimental, just to see whether it was even possible to divert her fixed gaze off Todd and onto something—anything—else. I wrote down twenty questions on a piece of paper and handed it to her. I told her that she was a hiker now and that she needed to learn these things. She took the paper and read the questions, laughing and writing down answers.

Tallest mountain on Earth? Its elevation, to within 3,000 feet?

Tallest aboveground mountain on Earth? Its elevation, to within 500 feet?

Does the phrasing of Question II shake your confidence any in your answer of Question I?

Tallest mountain in New York?

Tallest mountain in New England? State in which it lies? Its elevation, to within 1,000 feet?

State that contains America's tallest mountain east of the Mississippi River?

State that contains America's tallest mountain? Its name and its elevation, to within 2,000 feet?

State that contains America's tallest mountain in the continental USA? Its elevation, to within 2,000 feet?

Elevation of the tallest mountain in Australia, to within 2,000 feet?

Elevation of the tallest mountain at the South Pole in Antarctica, to within 2,000 feet?

Number of mountains in the world that are over 27,000 feet?

Number of mountains in the world that are over 25,000 feet?

Number of 25,000-foot mountains on Earth that lie outside the greater Tibet-Nepal-India-China-Pakistan area?

bonus i: Height of the tallest mountain in the solar system to within 20,000 feet?

bonus ii: Nation containing highest mountain that's north of the equator and east of the Mississippi River in the western hemisphere?

bonus iii: Local name for Mt. Everest?

The answers were: Mauna Kea in the Pacific Ocean at 33,476 feet from base to peak (thus taller than Mt. Everest!); Mt. Everest at 29,035 feet; Mt. Marcy; Mt. Washington in New Hampshire at 6,288 feet; North Carolina (Mt. Mitchell at 6,684 feet); Alaska's Mt. Denali at 20,320 feet; California's Mt. Whitney at 14,505 feet; 7,310 feet (Mt. Kosciusko); 16,067 feet (Vinson Massif); 5; 31; 0; bonus i: 88,000-foot Olympus Mons, on Mars; bonus ii: Jamaica (Blue Mountain Peak at 7,402 feet); bonus iii: Chomolungma ("Goddess Mother of the World"). Cooper failed the test miserably, but it gave us all something to laugh about. "That test was fon-tostic," Todd said. It was all just for shits and giggles.

The AIDS.

We walked a mile up to the center of town and washed laundry, then returned and organized our things in our rooms. We spoke with a hiker named Scott who'd been camped at our hotel for five days already. His room had a lived-in feel (and smell) and was cluttered with dirt. He was through-hiking, he told us. He'd been featured with a photograph and small paragraph in the April edition of Backpacker Magazine because he was going to through-hike the CDT and he was living with what he called, "The AIDS." He showed us the tremendous amount of pills that he had to take daily. Some looked like horse tranquilizers.

Scott had a ponytail and pockmarked face. He had translucent blue eyes, a natural smile, and a friendly demeanor. He was small, but had thick, heavy hiking boots, a colossal backpack and a substantial amount of heavy things to put inside it. He was the type of novice hiker typically found at the start of the busy Appalachian Trail. I myself had been that way back then. Scott had no prior through-hiking experience. This was his first time on a distance trail. He'd picked a doozy of a trail to begin with. No one should start and learn on this trail. He told us that he'd lived in New York City with hippies for three years outside on the green in SoHo before Mayor Rudy cleaned up the city streets and had kicked them all out. He was originally from Texas. He had a steady girlfriend waiting back home whom he called his wife. He told us that he'd gotten sick from a needle. Along with the pills on his nightstand were two quarts of Southern Comfort. He asked if we wanted to smoke a joint or take some shots. We declined. Scott said that he'd intended to start his CDT hike in Silver City, but that he'd then hitchhiked from there to here and would set out shortly. So he hadn't actually walked an inch of trail yet. He was clueless. None of us would've taken any odds that he'd make it.

6
Fire & Ice

What matters most is how well you walk through the fire.

—Charles Bukowski

Death.

My hike had changed, for now I had company. Todd and Weekender were terrifically competent, and Cooper would be heading home soon. I needed to stick with their group. I needed the help and camaraderie. I was grateful to them for letting me glom on. They had every right to suggest that I piss off, but they didn't. Normally on the trail, you at least give the new guy a chance. It's common decency that way. Scott with The AIDS was welcome with us, too, but he wanted to stay behind in Reserve for one more day.

Pie Town was our next trail town and was halfway up the state, so reaching it'd mean having finished one-eighth of the trail. It'd validate our feeling of having progressed well so far. Road walks would take us there. It was Sunday, May 22. One-hundred-degree heat kept us prisoners in Reserve all day; then we hitchhiked out at dusk. Our pickup truck ride dropped us off at the side of Route 12, at its CDT road crossing just beyond a gas station called Apache Creek. It was where I'd intended to pop out from the gravel maze. Here lay the official CDT. It was making a celebrity appearance. It was such a rare sight that I felt I should ask the trail for its autograph.

The Weekender-Todd-Cooper trio and I hiked ten miles up a dirt jeep road (the official trail, here). The full moon shone so brightly that it cast our shadows

61

on the ground before us. We talked and laughed as we walked, pretending that werewolves were lurking in the shrubs, all of us trying to scare Cooper. Just because guys enjoy trying to scare girls. Why is that? We stopped at midnight and slept on the ground at small, deserted Valle Tio Vences Campground.

A worried, nervous emotion caused me to set out alone before the others that next morning. Or perhaps it was overconfidence. Or my solitary instinct. There was no great reason for it. I think I'd merely just wanted to get ahead simply so that I wouldn't fall behind. It's the type of anxiety that makes people crave money, horde belongings, or frame things to their own advantage. Instead, I should've been nurturing the relationships at hand. I assumed that I'd see the others shortly. I hadn't planned on staying ahead of them. I climbed a side dirt road from the campground to a fire tower on a wide, forested mountain. Then I promptly got lost. I'd noticed a turnoff, but I hadn't thought it was the right way so I'd continued past. Ultimately, I doubled back when my straight route petered out, and then I noticed the footprints of the others descending down the turnoff. They'd come up and gone on while I was off searching for the way, so I set out behind them trying to catch up. It never would've happened if I'd stayed with them in the first place. I think it's a character flaw—I'm such a loner. I never like to jog with others or train with others. I pay the price at moments like this.

I soon got lost a second time, adding a few additional miles of needless hiking. Nobody ever counts up all the extra miles that you hike. I got saved that second time when I came upon a tall guy named Jon who was out hiking his native state of New Mexico. His father was in jail, he told me. But we didn't talk too much about anything else. I was too mad at myself to feel social. Also, if it's someone that you know won't be in the picture for long and that you won't see very much of, then it tempers your enthusiasm to fully bond. He helped steer me right. It was inexpressibly helpful simply to have a second opinion. Hiking alone on the AT and even the PCT works fine, but it's important to begin the CDT with a partner. You just don't meet many people out here.

We reached a foreboding tall metal fence holding a no trespassing sign. We opened the fence and walked through. Strangely, that road never dead-ended like I'd expected it to, but it just kept going, and off we continued walking northward for miles along the dirt road. We'd come far down off the wide mountain leaving the pine trees behind and returning to the desert with its miniature trees and bushes, and no water. The day became all about pain. What matters most is how well you walk through the fire, but I wasn't walking through the fire well. My pace slowed to a shuffle as my feet turned raw once again. They hurt with each step. The slow going was okay for tall Jon, though, because his right knee hurt. The two of us limped along, dragging ourselves through dust toward Pie Town.

A quintet of five old men on dirt bike motorcycles came up the road one by one, trailing dust clouds in their wake. I flagged them down and asked for water. They were old hippies from California. They'd flown out and had rented these bikes. They wore knee pads, elbow pads, gloves, goggles, and motocross jerseys. They climbed off their bikes and sat in the road with us. They gave us water, brewed hot coffee, and offered us pot. We passed around two bowls. They were doctors, lawyers, and two CEOs. Rich hippie dudes. It was hilarious. They laughed about everything. Then on they went, motorcycling away. Their water had saved us.

We stopped for the day a mere eight miles short of Pie Town. As much as I'd wanted to reach town, I couldn't take even one more step. I was sorely disappointed not to have reached town because I'd have staked my life that Weekender-Todd-Cooper had all made it in. Lying bivied out that night, looking up at the stars, native New Mexican Tall John said that down there it's natural to gaze up at the stars at night. I'd spent my life in suburbs, towns, and cities with lights everywhere obscuring the night sky. When my mother was a child in rural Georgia, one of her favorite things was to be taken outdoors late at night to see the constellations. But I hadn't grown up that way. Something's lost without that view. Not a single person anywhere on Earth should be denied that view. It's the most incredible sight of all.

Tall Jon taught me the wonderful trick of identifying the North Star. To pinpoint the North Star (Polaris), you first locate the Big Dipper (Ursa Major), which is always tremendously easy. You take the outer edge of the Big Dipper's pan and trace up the two stars that make its far edge. Extend an imaginary straight line and you come to the North Star. It isn't the brightest star in the sky, but you know it when you see it—it stands alone and is the only star that appears in the same place throughout the night. The constellations rotate slowly around it imperceptibly across the sky (of course, it's the earth that's turning!). It shows the way north. If you need to walk north, just find it and walk toward it. If you reach the north pole, then you're actually underneath it.

At three-thirty in the morning, I awoke and couldn't fall back asleep. I was impatient and determined to reach Pie Town for breakfast. That feeling just came over me. Tall John stirred and I told him I'd see him in town. I rose, stuffed my pack, and set out alone up the dirt road in the darkness. The others wouldn't be taking a zero day in Pie Town, so I needed to catch them in order to stick with them. I was desperate to keep up. But all I could manage on tremendously sore feet was a painful, limping, shuffling gait. It took me forever. I finally reached the outskirts of Pie Town at daybreak. I spied an old man outside his house watering his garden with a hose. He looked at me but didn't say anything. I nodded and limped silently by.

Pie Town's population was fifty people. There was a public park, some box-type homes and two restaurants, both of which served pies—the Daily Pie and the Pie-O-Neer Café. There was a longitudinal highway here, and truckers detoured into town for food, for pie (John Steinbeck: "Lesse...Gimme piece pie."). I left my pack outside on The Daily Pie's porch and sat at a large table and ordered breakfast—eggs, potatoes, toast. In walked Weekender-Todd-Cooper. They'd indeed reached town the night before, and they'd slept in the public park. They weren't surprised to see me.

An unhurried breakfast turned into lunch, as we all just kept eating and talking. The café filled with locals and an occasional trucker. Tall Jon arrived. All of our backpacks, hiking sticks, and ski poles stood out on the porch. We read our guidebooks. My book for New Mexico said that Pie Town had gotten its name from a local gas station owner who liked to bake pies. In 1927 the government had proposed a post office and they'd asked for the name of the town. The gas station owner said: "It's either going to be named Pie Town, or you can take your post office and go to hell." The inclusion of that fact alone made carrying the CDTA's heavy book for New Mexico worthwhile.

The hillside home of Nita Lorrande had pop art in the form of old toaster ovens and silverware hanging by wire like wind chimes from the branches of the desert trees all over her yard. We'd been given her name as a home where hikers were welcome. We walked two long country blocks, found her home with the hanging toasters, and discovered that she had a deliciously long, wide wooden porch in the shade, with cushioned benches and Adirondack chairs. She had cats, bottles, plants, painted rocks, and millions of little trinkets everywhere. Nita was gone for the day, but her door was unlocked. We took water from inside and used the bathroom. It was a warm, cluttered house with nothing discarded, everything saved. The house could've been featured in a knickknack magazine. I had food enough to last me to the next town of Grants, but the others had gotten PO food drop boxes here and sat organizing and packing.

We spent the afternoon on the shaded porch waiting out the one-hundred-degree heat of another day when suddenly we heard a terrifically extended tire screech followed by a shattering crash. You hate to hear a crash after such a telltale tire screech. The others leapt up and ran two blocks down to the main road that was just out of eyesight below the trees from Nita's house. My shoes were off and my feet hurt too much to run down, so I waited. It was a full ninety minutes before the others returned and told me the news. But I already knew the news. Neighbors whom I'd seen scurry down the street hadn't come back. Sirens had eventually sounded, headed to the crash. The whole world, going to the crash. I could see blue- and red-colored rays from emergency trucks lighting up the treetops. It turned out that an elderly woman in a van, blinded by sunlight, had pulled out in front of an eighteen-wheeler. The crash had killed the woman. The truck driver was okay, but the collision was so violent that even his mighty eighteen-wheeler was twisted and had careened down off the road. Initially the woman was breathing, but she died before they could remove her from her flattened van. She'd lived on Nita's street. Her husband had been one of those who'd run down on foot to the crash site, and he was there with her when she died, even though she'd never regained consciousness. Pie Town's population dropped from fifty to forty-nine during the time that we sat on Nita's porch.

Human Caboose.

The route to Grants was more road walks. Go figure. Qu'elle surpris! There had to be something more to this. But such was life on the CDT. It just hurt my feet so much. I longed for the snow and high peaks of Colorado. I needed to hurry up and get there. We left Nita's porch at four o'clock on Tuesday, May 24. It was my three-week anniversary on the trail. I'd been out for twenty-one days. Nita hadn't come home, and so I never had the chance to thank her. I quickly found myself limping along and bringing up the rear. I was the human caboose.

My feet caught fire. We crossed flat, treeless desert. There were only slight undulations in the land. We took dirt road A-56 to a fork and picked up dirt road A-83 which we'd follow for a whopping twenty-five miles. The sun burned down. My feet hurt with every step. Old Man Weekender disappeared in the distance, racing away. I could still see Todd and Cooper ahead. Cooper was limping from knee pain and was practically dragging her right leg. Despite that, I still couldn't catch them. Just the opposite, for soon they, too, disappeared in the distance. I couldn't walk faster. I felt too much pain. I used my hiking stick like a crutch, grinding it into the ground for support, which in turn gave my hands blisters. The pain in my feet was incredible. I finally had to stop walking. I sat down and waited for the sun to set. I wanted to cry. Then I rose and set out again, determined to catch Todd and Cooper. I wanted to catch them for their company.

Night fell and the sky was clear. I looked up at the North Star. I felt grateful to Tall John for having taught me how to identify it. He was staying behind a few days in Pie Town. I trudged laboriously on. The entire plain lay at seven thousand feet. Distant mountains visible to the north never seemed to get closer. I was moving—shuffling forward on sore feet—yet it felt as if I was making no progress. Hours passed and nothing seemed to change. I think I even dozed off while I was walking, maybe just for a second or two, if that's even possible. It was at this bewildering moment when the strangest sensation overcame me. It was due to the combination of the sky filled with stars, my slow motion, fatigue, darkness, the featureless landscape, and the evenness of the dirt road that an overwhelming sensation suddenly washed over me that I was walking on a treadmill in the middle of a planetarium during a star show. I felt that I was about the most insignificant being in the cosmos. I thought about Cristina, my ex-wife. How I missed seeing her with her baby.

I never caught Todd and Cooper. I kept hiking slowly and reached paved Highway 117 at one thirty in the morning. I gave up the chase and flopped

65

down on the ground to sleep, unable to take even one more step. Barbed wire lined both sides of the road and a couple of trucks went by at night. They woke me up and caught me disoriented, snapping awake, scared, and thinking that maybe I was lying in the road and they were about to run over me. In the morning, I faced walking thirty-one miles up Highway 117 to Interstate 40 where lies Grants, but I felt so damaged that I stuck out my thumb and hitch-hiked up the road. I skipped the highway walk. My feet hurt so much that I could barely stand. A van picked me up, and as I gazed out the windows, I saw Todd and Cooper walking northward up the highway just one mile ahead of where I'd slept. If I'd been able to make it just the slightest bit farther that previous night, I would've caught them. Then five miles beyond them, I saw Weekender walking up the highway. I hadn't been far behind him, either. But now I'd get to Grants more than one full day ahead of them. I felt guilty, like a cheater. But I was mad at the trail. Mad at the awful route options. Mad at how many times I'd been lost already, and mad at the way it hurt my feet. I was missing a highway walk, but walking a highway is anathema to what a trail should be. This, too, made me angry. Mad, mad, mad. If I'd wanted to walk highways, I could've stayed home in Maine and walked up and down the Turnpike. What was happening to me?

Badlands.

To my left out the van window, south of Grants, was a vast area called El Malpais—the Badlands (not to be confused with the Badlands of South Dakota) —an area of dry volcanic ash. I looked out the window and remembered how the others had spoken of taking a detour inside it. Badlands tourist maps contain illustrations of cinder cone volcanoes, lava flows, and lava tubes. All were volcanic remnants, geologically recent. The 8,372-foot-high Bandera Crater was a mountain until it'd erupted ten thousand years ago, which left an eight-hundred-foot-deep hole inside it. Outside it ran a long-since hardened lava flow twenty-three-miles long. They called this "The Land of Fire and Ice" because there was an ice cave in which tourists trekked down wooden stairs to see a natural spot where frigid air was trapped inside. An ice sheet twenty feet thick remained year-round down there, even when surface temperatures topped one hundred degrees. The ice dated back to AD 170, and it gave off an eerie green glow. Also in the badlands was a seventy-foot-high natural sandstone arch, as well as sandstone formations dating back two hundred million years. The official CDT route looped westward around El Malpais, typically avoiding everything interesting and scenic. Through-hikers must detour to explore the lava fields.

The Spanish had named it El Malpais in 1540. Ponce de Leon had reached America in 1513 by landing at what he called La Florida. The Spanish were the first Europeans to reach the Appalachian Mountains, the Mississippi River, the Grand Canyon, and the Great Plains. Cristina's ancestors had explored half of America by the time of the first English colony at Roanoke. Spain's town of Santa Fe, New Mexico, predates Plymouth. Spanish settlements arose at San Antonio, San Diego, San Francisco, and Los Angeles. Before the Spanish, there were Native Americans. Those first Americans were here for over twelve thousand years. At their peak, there were twelve million Native Americans on this land. Then the Europeans came and wiped them out.

Grants.

Grants had ten thousand people, about the same size as Silver City. It was an I-40 exit just west of Albuquerque. My ride dropped me off six miles south of Grants at a Suckey's Restaurant, and I walked the final way in. I was in the top half of New Mexico. Grants rested in a giant valley which I could see spread out before me. A wall of mountain rose up at the north end of town. I headed straight for the chain hotels on the outskirts of town. I took a room at the Best Western and spent three nights intentionally cut off from all thoughts of the trail. I needed time to heal my feet. I'm such a complete idiot, though, that I soaked my feet in hot salt water instead of doing the opposite and icing them. I bathed in the hotel's hot Jacuzzi, too. Sometimes I just can't make sense of things. Sometimes I just don't think straight. I spoke with Cristina on the phone. I also spoke with Jessie Gibbins. No matter what, I always called Cristina first: I loved my ex-wife so much. I was supposed to go down by bus to visit Jessie Gibbins from here, but I couldn't do it. I couldn't risk disrupting my flow, because then I might never reconnect with my ragtag group. I finally left town, alone, on May 29.

Prisoners sartorially matched in orange jumpsuits waltzed about playing basketball and lifting weights on the grounds outside the Western New Mexico Correctional Facility north of town. It was a maximum-security prison. They looked over at me as I walked past, saw me from behind their barbed-wire-topped chain-link fence. Armed guards manned two-story lookout stations with rifles and binoculars. The CDTA guidebook humorlessly advised not to hitchhike here because no one would pick you up. I walked by, on Lobo Canyon Road, watching the flow of the basketball game. Squash, basketball, hiking, life, breathing, tides, waves, volcanoes—all such things ebb and flow.

Beyond the prison, I followed a gap through a two-thousand-foot-high wall of mountain and began to climb. The high land north of Grants was called Horace Mesa. It was a vast pedestal of land 8,200 feet high, forty-six miles long and twenty-three miles wide. The CDTA New Mexico guidebook described it to be "conspicuously remote and uninhabited." As if all else that we'd come through so far *wasn't* ?

67

Mt. Taylor.

Volcanic 11,301-foot Mt. Taylor rose just north of Grants. The peak dominated the landscape for fifty miles in every direction. The CDT didn't summit Mt. Taylor, but it led close enough to touch it. My dread wasn't the mountain, but was having to face a series of alternate routes to get past it. Three routes led northward around Taylor's western side. A fourth route went up and over the summit. Todd and Weekender would be summiting Taylor, I knew. They'd both professed interest in climbing America's Fifty High Points. It's a club that you join once you've climbed the highest point in each of the fifty states. Everyone leaves Alaska's deadly 20,304-foot Denali for last. A few of the spots are ridiculously low such as Florida's high point, which is an unnamed 345-foot hill behind a gas station; and Rhode Island's high point, which is 812-foot Jeremiah Hill, on private property on which the owners don't allow anyone.

Todd and Weekender had many hiking goals which they were always discussing. On their way to the start of the CDT, they'd met in El Paso and had climbed Texas' high point of Guadalupe Peak, at 8,749 feet. Guadalupe's relative medium-high elevation was caught in a purgatory of elevation status, between the truly high points in the west and the smaller peaks in the east. Present Mt. Taylor wasn't the high point of New Mexico—that being 13,166-foot Wheeler Peak, dozens of miles to the northeast—but Todd and Weekender would climb Taylor in the simple spirit of peak-bagging. Back on the PCT six years earlier, I'd bypassed summiting Mt. Whitney when I'd had the chance, because I'd wanted to stay on track and keep hiking to get home to Cristina. Likewise, out here I'd no interest in detouring to summit Taylor, but just wanted to make progress northward. My feet hurt and I just wanted to take the shortest, quickest route possible to reach Colorado's high snowy mountains and make it on to Canada.

A CDT sign two miles beyond the prison marked the trail that climbed eastward up through desert rocks to the top of the mesa. An hour's climb and I came to a bluff where I stood and looked southward two-thousand-feet down over Grants and out over the southern lava fields. To my great surprise, here sat Todd and Weekender. They were startled to see me. They'd gotten lost for one hour, they said. So it could happen even to them, even while they were together! They hopped up and we set out together. Todd's girlfriend Cooper was gone. She'd flown home to Virginia, so it was just we three now. I was sad to lose the only woman we had in the mix. She was very nice and a great sport. It seemed like she and Todd could possibly get married one day.

We came to a series of forks on the jeep roads amidst woods and trees, and we couldn't figure out where to go. It was all dirt roads leading northeastward across the high mesa. My CDTA book for New Mexico was no help because it read like indecipherable hieroglyphics. Imagine trying to follow this while

68

you're tired and sore, thirsty, and hot, and nothing makes sense and everything looks the same:

> *The CDT heads east across the mesa's flat top, following a dirt track through open pinon-juniper forest. Travel east for about 3 miles until you cross the heads of two small drainages with stands of ponderosa pine, and approach Horace Mesa's eastern rim. Here the route swings northeast, climbing gradually and then more steeply just before reaching the junction with the Forest Road leading 0.4 miles downhill to Big Spring. The CDT crosses this junction and continues northeast uphill through increasingly frequent ponderosa pines, following an old two-track that after a mile becomes trail.*

That book seemed to correspond to nothing. Its large-scale maps gave no perspective. It was numbing stuff. Given the choice of reading it or poking my own eyes out with a stick, I'd have to flip a coin. Reading it felt like someone was standing beside me and hitting me with it until my brain fell out. The CDTA books weren't made for through-hikers. They were possibly helpful for day hikers doing bits of the trail, but four-fifths of the text is packed with irrelevant through-hiker knowledge including information on horse-travel, llama travel, side trails, as well as glossy photographs of all types of flowers. Todd derisively called it a coffee table book. No, the CDT wasn't easy. Here were four possible routes and nothing marked any of them. It was the reason why only twenty-five people attempted to through-hike the CDT each year. It was because this wasn't something fun to do, to come out here and face this nightmare. It's almost enough to send you packing for home. But you tell yourself to stay with it. You tell yourself not to ask why. There will be lows, but the highs are so very fine.

At ten-thousand-feet elevation, we stopped for the night upon the western slopes of massive Mt. Taylor, after having taken the easternmost dirt road and then climbing up the volcano all afternoon. Todd and Weekender both wore altimeters that they had to constantly recalibrate. I hadn't planned to climb Taylor, but I'd wisely kept with Todd-Weekender, and now here I was almost on top. We were two miles short of the summit. White-haired Weekender set up his tent and then pulled out a can of lukewarm Budweiser beer and sat on a rock sipping it slowly. It was a little tradition he had—he'd carry one (and only one) can of Budweiser into the woods and drink it on his first night out of town. It took the edge off the pain of leaving the comforts of town. It was a muscle relaxant. It was carbohydrates. And the empty can would then sit crumpled in the bottom of his pack until he could recycle it in the next town. Faint beer smell on his gear, like the morning after a party. It was brilliant, something that only an old, wise person could figure out.

We spent a cold night high on the volcano's slope. Early that next morning, Monday, May 30, day number twenty-seven for me, I peeked out my tent to find Old Man Weekender already up, dressed, and packed, sitting on the same rock from the night before, only this time drinking coffee instead of his can of beer. It was his quintessential pose in the morning, up early and wearing a green fleece vest and drinking his coffee while looking out over one gorgeous view or another. He was a pastor, Boy Scout, military early riser, having his Mr. Rogers quiet moment alone. Me, I'm not an early riser. I'm a terrible riser. We zigzagged climbing two miles up switchbacks to the summit. Here was our first snow of the trail. We passed deep mounds of the white stuff.

Mt. Taylor's pointed, cyndrical-cone summit had a hole six feet deep. It was the actual caldera of the volcano. It was blocked, though, so you couldn't look down into the bubbling center of the earth or anything. Cold wind blew and we stood on top practically freezing to death, so we climbed six feet down into the hole, inside the volcano, and scrunched down out of the wind to get warm. We laughed about that. You never imagine that your life will lead you to a moment when you'll be sitting inside a volcano. Todd began smoking a cigarette. None of us were big into photographs. It was the tallest mountain that I'd ever climbed. I'd climbed higher than that several times previously—like up over 13,100 feet on Forester Pass, and over five other passes in California's High Sierras on the PCT. But those weren't mountains, they were passes. I'd also climbed higher than that on Switzerland's Matterhorn, too, but I hadn't reached the top.

Finally, we climbed out of the volcano and trotted northward down off the mountain through deep snowdrifts, often postholing through the surface and sinking up to our waists. We left the snow and dropped down into the trees where we passed a radio tower and felt warm again. We descended farther and got baked by the roasting sun. It was nothing but extremes out here.

Long Breaks.

I struggled to keep up with Todd and Weekender. I needed their navigational skills to keep me on track. North of Taylor, we picked up dirt roads. That'd become second nature. Then off they'd go, walking swiftly at "four-plus"—hiking at greater than four miles an hour. Todd was young and strong, with calf muscles the size of watermelons; while Old Man Weekender was tall and lanky, calm and focused. It wasn't time to put him out to pasture just yet, at forty-two. No, white-haired Weekender was the strongest hiker among us. He was all legs and hips. He was a machine. I'd have hated to have had to play tennis against the guy in junior tournaments when we were kids. He'd run high school cross-country long ago, and for the past two decades he'd run three miles every day. He was amazingly fast on the uphills.

Todd and Weekender had planned this hike. They'd researched it and had thought about it. They'd carefully chosen their routes and maps. They'd even been spending time checking upcoming weather conditions from the computers in the libraries of the small towns we'd passed through. Todd was an adept winter hiker. Also, he'd once taken a survival training course in New Jersey from a legendary cult figure named Tom Brown. There's a subculture of extreme survivalists who idolize him. They'd made a movie about him that starred Benicio Del Toro. He'd been raised by a Native American tracker. At age eighteen, he'd lived undetected in New York City's Central Park for six months in a hole in the ground called an Apache Scout Pit. Tom Brown, I'm talking about—not Todd. If it'd been Todd in that Apache Scout Pit in Central Park, then he'd have been detected by the cigarette smoke wafting up out of the hole. And by the sounds of Todd singing out loud to himself. And by Todd's stumbling back to his Apache Scout Pit drunk after a night of Jager Shots. I was impressed that Todd had met Tom Brown and had studied under him. Weekender was no slouch himself—he'd once kayaked around the island of Manhattan, and he'd lived for several years in Alaska both during and after his military service there. They were good at this. They were both expert with maps, compasses, and their instincts. And they hiked like bats out of hell.

I'd lag far behind the pair of them while walking the desert roads, just because my feel hurt so much that I couldn't keep up with their lightning-fast pace. But then I'd always catch up because they stopped frequently to compare Wolf's book with the Ley maps. They were impressive. The dynamic between them was different since Cooper's departure. Neither was boss: they read their papers to see which of their trail-guides made better sense for each particular situation, and then they agreed. In their presence, I didn't even pretend to look at my CDTA book for New Mexico any longer. There was no sense faking it. I'd just stand off to the side and kick dirt with my sneakers while waiting for their route decisions.

Old Man Weekender had a compulsive need to always know the location of the next water source: crazy survivalist! Our water sources ran the gambit of being nothing more than stagnant cow troughs with dead mice in them, to perfect cold springs. Ahead was Ojos Des Los Indios. I never would've found it on my own. Todd and Weekender found the spring down off the trail in a crevasse between cliff walls, and we sat there for an hour, drinking water and eating lunch. Then off we went again.

It was becoming an epic New Mexico desert day. After eating, we spread out and walked cross-country through thin woods where Todd saw a bear. Then we picked up a dirt road and emerged from the trees. The land flattened out. We could see far up the dirt road ahead. The sun blasted down causing us to sizzle like meatless vegetarian tofu-sausage in a frying pan. Todd and Weekender walked so fast again that they disappeared out of sight. I limped and dragged behind. What saved me from being left behind was that Weekender and Todd had no deadline. Weekender was only hiking two of the four CDT states, and he'd plenty of time to reach the Wyoming border before heading home to his carpentry job. And Todd had no deadline at all. His REI store in Oregon was crazy about him and they'd left it open for him to return anytime at all.

So—what'd happen was that I'd limp along bringing up the rear, but then later I'd come upon them sitting by the trail, resting. Sure they hiked fast, but they were actually casual hikers, in that they loved to sit and take long breaks. It was their style. I'd come upon them and feel very glad for the fact that this'd give me the chance to catch up, but then we'd just sit there for such uncomfortably long breaks that I knew that this pace wouldn't get me to Canada on time. It left me bewildered at first, not knowing what to feel. For out would come Todd's cigarettes. The stop-start jerkiness of it felt jolting to me. My feet hurt, but I would've actually preferred to keep right on going.

And I had that option, of course. I'd the option of walking right by and carrying on alone. But that'd be lonely. And I liked Todd and Weekender. They could laugh at themselves. I laughed loads with them. Mostly it was just me sitting there listening to their same stories told over and over of their time hiking on the PCT with two guys called "The Angry Brothers." It was Angry Mike and Angry Jim, who'd apparently hiked along getting worked up about everything. The best was once when they'd gotten separated and everything was going wrong. Angry Mike for some reason had nothing to wear but a cotton sweater, and it'd begun to rain when he'd come face-to-face with a park ranger who started lecturing him on hypothermia and proper attire. Weekender had to hold his side when recounting that, for he'd hiked with Angry Mike on the remainder of that day and had to listen to him swearing for hours on end about how badly he'd wanted to punch the park ranger in the face.

By evening, we stood on the edge of a massive cliff and looked a thousand feet down over a low, red mesa. It felt like gazing down into the Grand Canyon, or like being a god and gazing down on the surface of Mars. A dried-out riverbed snaked through it. We painstakingly scaled down the cliff wall, and once below found ourselves crossing open desert. It was an obstacle course. There was no trail. We negotiated our way northward by using the giant stone monolithic landmark of Cabazon Peak as a guide. It rose unmistakably like a nipple from the flat ground, and we kept it to our east. We slept on the mesa under the stars near cows penned in a scrub brush field. We'd been seeing lots of cows. We'd been seeing deer everyday lately, too. It was springtime, and I saw mother cows nursing and protecting their calves, and mother deer escorting and protecting their fawns.

My feet hurt terribly. We walked as a threesome that next morning until we reached the end of the mesa at midday. There, we split, and I experimentally followed new and clearly visible CDT emblems on posts, to follow a trail that led to the eastern side of easily identifiable Twin Deadman Peaks. Todd and Weekender went straight, following their Ley maps and Wolf book. I was okay for the break. I was okay to take a teeny, tiny break from them. I didn't know what it'd mean, but I assumed that I'd see them again soon enough. I just wanted to get to town.

I followed my trail into the eastern mountains and hiked until after dark, then spent the night alone. That next morning, Wednesday, June 1, it took me several hours to descend to low ground and follow a dirt road eastward to Highway 550. I stuck out my thumb and hitchhiked nine miles northward into the small town of Cuba.

Coma.

Cuba, New Mexico, had a population of only one thousand. It'd gotten its name from soldiers who'd returned there after fighting in the nation of Cuba. This red rocky landscape had reminded them of that Caribbean island, so they gave it that name. There were very many Mexican-Americans here. The town was tiny and modest. I entered the first cheap hotel I could see. A diner sat directly beside it. I needed calories. I needed to relax and rest my feet.

I awoke that next morning to my one-month anniversary on the trail, Thursday, June 2. I took a zero day. I was a month in, but I hadn't yet finished New Mexico. I was behind schedule. I tried to relax about that. I told myself that it was okay, because CDT northbounders can't set into Colorado's South San Juan Mountains too early in the season due to the lasting summer snowpack there. As consolation, I knew that at least every day that I delayed embarking into the South San Juans was another day for the sun to melt the snow. That'd make passage easier.

I rested and organized my things, bought food and a newspaper from the gas station next door. A newspaper article hit me hard by describing the saddest thing—a Virginian in her midtwenties named Rollin-Torres was a researcher at the National Institute of Health, was pregnant, and had gotten cancer and then suffered a massive stroke when melanoma had spread to her brain. She was being kept alive on life support long enough for doctors to deliver her child. She had a husband and a son. Her husband had quit his job and was spending every night in a chair by her bed. I couldn't imagine that. For certain the baby knew that something was wrong—the mother's not moving, walking, talking, or laughing. She needed three more months on life support and then they'd attempt to deliver the premature baby at the beginning of August.

Being without Prozac was hard on me. I put the newspaper down feeling overwhelmed by that article. That baby would be born and not have its mother. There are such personal, heart-wrenching experiences that people must live through. I've often wondered what makes me leave civilization to hike. I'm strong enough to hike over mountains. Strong enough to hike for months on

73

end. Strong enough to push myself and laugh at discomfort. But I don't know if I could ever be strong enough to handle anything like that. As a husband, as a father, I didn't know if I could make it. Perhaps that's why I come out here—to simulate crises but not to actually have to face such things. Perhaps it was why I loved being an uncle and wasn't a father—because if I had a child and anything went wrong, I'm not sure I could handle it.

At the Cuba post office, I picked up a drawing from my young nephew and niece: it was a hiker with the acronym H.I.K.I.N.G. written vertically, while laterally reading across the page were each letter's symbolization: Hit the dirt! Ice your feet! Kick the dirt! Ice your feet again! Notice Nature! Go! It went a long way toward buoying my spirit.

I'd been constantly thinking about babies, ever since Cristina'd had hers. I was forty-one, without kids, but perhaps, yes, ready to be a father. I'd be getting a late start, but that was okay. In watching Cristina with her baby, I always felt I was witnessing a miracle. That I was witnessing a magical, artful thing. From Spain, it was her Mediterranean nurturing way. Cristina'd treated her body like a temple her entire life for the inevitability of having this child. All her life, she'd eaten no meat and had taken no drugs. She'd taken no pain killers during childbirth, and she and Steve had given their child no immunization shots and were raising him as a vegan. It wasn't an easy road to go down, but I respected her so much for that. Her boy Francis was an extraordinarily confident, happy, healthy, and outgoing kid. I loved Cristina so much that by extension I loved her child. I was absolutely crazy for Francis. He could sense that, too, and he knew there was something special about the way that I acted toward him. We had a special bond. I watched the way cow calves kept to their mothers out here on the trail. How the mothers walked with their calves and stepped between them to shield them from strange backpacking bipeds, even as we walked by at a distance. It amazed me to see the communication between mother cow and calf, between mother deer and baby fawn out on the mesas, in the woods, and on mountainsides. It was glorious. Motherhood amazes me. I find no greater miracle in the world. And when it's done right, when it's done just right, then life is perfect and beautiful.

7
The Faraway Nearby

The idea of the north was taking him;
he needed something to brace against.

— Annie Proulx, *The Shipping News*

Butchers.

Hollywood's most delicious cinematic sports quote comes from Ferris Bueller's Day Off, when the high school kid Ferris tries to weasel out of a gym class and goes to scam the gym teacher, only to find the guy sitting in his office polishing bowling trophies. Bowling trophies are scattered around the office, and the guy's wearing a bowling shirt and bowling wrist guard. He looks up at Ferris and reverently preaches while polishing away, *"It's the ultimate sport: one man, ten pins, sixty-two feet..."* It's kind of the way that every coach feels about their sport. We each believe that our sport's the greatest one ever invented. Well, here's another movie quote, from the remake of The Fly, when Jeff Goldblum's scientist-character tries to impress a female reporter at a cocktail party in the movie's opening scene by telling her that he's working on an invention that will change the world as we know it. She tells him that two other people have already told her the same thing that night. He says, "Yes, but they're lying." Like that, other coaches will tell you the same thing that I do, that their sport is the greatest. But they're lying. Forbes Magazine in 2003 ranked squash as the number one sport for cardiovascular workout. Nothing else compares.

Intercollegiate Division I men's tennis currently has international students making up over half its top-fifty-ranked players, and the Association of Tennis Professionals has only nine American men ranked in the world's top-hundred. American squash is even more marginalized. Intercollegiate American squash currently has just three natives ranked in the men's top-twenty, and the men's professional squash tour has only two American players ranked in the world's top-hundred. No American has won the men's intercollegiate singles title since our conversion to the softball standard of the game fifteen years ago. The best American athletes diffuse and participate in a wide variety of sports, while many of the best athletes in other countries are on the squash and tennis courts. At some point Americans will do better in squash on the world scene because we're growing familiar with the softball game and coaches are coming from around the world to teach in well-paying American clubs.

Many our intercollegiate coaches are international, too: the Dartmouth, Amherst, and Smith coaches are all Canadian, the Harvard and Colby coaches are both Pakistani, the Brown and Rochester coaches are Scottish, the Wellesley coach is British, the Wesleyan coach is Welsh, the Penn coach is Australian, the Cornell coach is Kiwi, the Williams coach is Israeli, the Tufts coach is Malaysian, the Mt. Holyoke coach is Zimbabwean, the Vassar coach is Bermudan, and the Bowdoin coach is Mexican. I take solace that the top three men's teams are Trinity, Princeton, and Yale, and all have American coaches; while the top three women's teams are Princeton, Penn and Yale, and they all have American coaches, too. The Bowdoin and Colby coaches, my two rival coaches in Maine, both played on the professional squash tour. I never did anything like that, but my teams have consistently beaten theirs. My two rival coaches in Maine are back running squash camps at this very moment. It's what they're supposed to be doing. It's how they put food on the table. Meanwhile, I'm out here on this impossible trail. Heading for Colorado.

Friday, June 3—my thirty-second day on the trail—I walked northward out of Cuba alone and walked four miles up a dirt road to a dirt parking lot and the start of a trail that'd take me high into forested mountains. I climbed the trail alongside a creek up into the San Pedro Mountains, stopping occasionally to stand in the freezing creek to let the icy water numb the residual foot pain I had left over from the desert. The top of the climb deposited me a few hours later up at ten thousand feet on a flat expanse lined by woods. It was bitterly cold. Ten-foot-high snowbanks lined the woods around the field and the wind blew snow-cold air across the open to chill me. It was just like putting a block of ice in front of a fan. The field was underwater, topped by a cover of ice. I sloshed through it, crunching ice as I went, thoroughly happy to have my feet cold and wet.

I followed the route description outlined in my CDTA book for New Mexico, but it took all my concentration. The tricky route led me across a succession of four wood-lined, frigid, watery plains, each one the size of several football fields, all of it high up at ten thousand feet. Occasional posts marked the way, but they were great distances apart and hard to spot through passing fog banks. Some of the old posts were so decayed that they'd toppled over and lay on the ground. Sometimes I had a groove of trail to follow, and other times there were multiple grooves leading all different directions. By some stroke of luck, I seemed to be staying on track, sloshing through the tremendously wet, icy fields.

Suddenly I saw movement in the trees to my left. Huddled in the trees against the cold sat Todd and Weekender hovering over dinners of hot noodles before their little trail stoves. They were again surprised to see me. I was glad to have company, to have someone to talk to. I couldn't get lost now. Or at least if our threesome got lost, it wouldn't matter so much because my two hiking partners could figure things out. I imagined to myself that they must've been impressed that I'd found my way alone across the high fields through the wet and the cold and the fog banks. They were freezing. They packed up and we set out. All across the high fields we saw elk. The elk didn't know what to make of us. Finally, we began to descend northward off the cold, snowy plateau of the Sierra Nacimiento and San Pedro Mountains down into dense woods where we were sheltered from the wind.

The going was easy and the trail, clear. Still, no single moment stays danger-free very long out here. Enjoyment of our easy downhill was soon shattered by a sky that grew dark, threatening to storm. Thunder rumbled, but there was no lightning. No rain fell, either, but all indications showed it'd come. We shuffled quickly, with urgency, and stopped at dusk in a clearing recently used by butchers. There were deer parts littered nearby, together with horse shit and horse prints in dusty chewed-up dirt. There were chin-high beams nailed between trees on which to tie horses, and also much higher ones on which to hang butchered deer and elk. Weekender pulled out and sipped on his first-night-out-of-town can of Budweiser Beer.

Todd and Weekender both used tents, but I had only a tarp. I was trying to be an ultralight hiker whose pack weighed nothing, enabling me to race along. But by now I'd experienced enough cold nights even in New Mexico to understand that I'd need to alter my plan and send for a tent. We were approaching Colorado, after all. I also didn't have a stove, but had been making small fires on which to cook my dinners. I'd need to buy a stove, too. I'd do both immediately in the next town. I just had to get there.

Light rain began to fall, so I scrambled over and strung a line of nylon rope between two trees. I draped my tarp over it and used rocks to hold down the corners. I lay beneath it, but still got wet from even this very light rain with water somehow hitting the ground to find its way under my tarp. A heavy rain would've drenched me. Todd picked up the small fire I'd built, and he carried it over to me at my new tarp location under the trees. He worked to get it going again so that I could cook dinner. It hadn't gone completely out, and he blew it into form. Todd had a thing for fire—he loved it. Suddenly, the rain turned to hail, and for thirty minutes we got pelted by hail chunks the size of golf balls. They turned the ground white and we laughed in amazement.

Pink Ribbons.

Seasonal conditions on particular sections of a trail can be so prohibitive that they force a hiker to temporarily skip the spot and return to hike it later. Skipping a spot and returning to hike it later is called flip-flopping. It's a legitimate part of through-hiking. It doesn't matter how one completes a through-hike as long as one hikes the whole trail in a year. One common CDT flip-flop is to hike northbound up New Mexico to the Colorado border, then skip to Canada (by car, bus, plane, train, hitchhike) and hike southbound through Montana, Wyoming, and Colorado. That's done because early summer snow mass in Colorado's South San Juans can be substantial so they save it for last.

Todd and Weekender had learned from the Cuba library computers that a small group of northbound through-hikers who were ahead of us had done this exact flip-flop due to huge amounts of snow that'd fallen in the South San Juans over the winter. The online computer journals of those hikers said that they hadn't even attempted to enter the South San Juan mountains. But I didn't want to flip-flop. I hadn't flip-flopped on either the AT or the PCT, and I wanted no disruption out here, either. Call it a bit anal on my part, but I liked to always be heading in the same direction.

Departing under calm skies in the early morning from the deer- and elk-butchering clearing, Todd and Weekender were in disagreement over which route to take. There was a dirt road that appealed to Weekender, but Todd wanted us to take a barely perceptible herd path. We took Todd's way and we soon encountered overgrown foliage that was so thick we had to push through it. Then the path ended. We stood on a hillside with a view out over rows of mountain ranges to the north. My partners took out their maps and discussed what they saw. Todd pointed to a ridge here and a ridge there, calling them by name and showing how we'd walk through. He looked down at his map and then up at the mountains and analyzed which topographical lines corresponded to the complicated landscape ahead. For me, I just looked out and saw mountains. I stood and waited for them to figure things out and agree. Todd took us forward, hiking off-trail—off any trail. Of course, I went with them.

Todd walked us two miles across thin-wooded hillsides, sticking together, picking our way, forging our path, when quite surprisingly we suddenly came to a string of pink ribbons that were tied to bushes and trees, spaced out about thirty yards apart. There was no trail, but just the pink ribbons. As they seemed to lead in the direction we wanted to go, we started following them northward from ribbon to ribbon. They were the markings of a future trail, where they were going to route the future CDT. I couldn't believe that Todd had found this exact way in such a vast wilderness. Just a few dozen yards to the east or west and we wouldn't have found this. Hitting this exact spot was the most impressive mountaineering feat I ever saw Todd do.

We followed pink ribbons for one mile, crossed a desolate paved road which gave us our exact location, and then we climbed northward up a dirt road that led steeply up a wide mountain. We got strangely competitive here and began practically racing each other. I must stop for a moment to describe Todd's calves. They were so pronounced and unavoidable that one could get intimidated just by looking at them: "This guy must be strong, this guy must be fast." In trucking up this mountain trying to keep pace with these guys, it was hard to keep going and not just give up or back down when confronted with the size of Todd's obtrusive calves—because no one could beat that guy up a hill, a guy who possessed such calves.

Hiking isn't about beating anyone or winning anything. But competition is a funny thing: once you start the competitive faucet gushing, sometimes it's hard to turn off. We compete constantly for mates, food, jobs. I've lived a life of competition and it even follows me out here to the woods. As usual, Weekender, at forty-two years old, was out in front. But then Todd and I caught up. It was partly because my feet finally felt okay after having healed them all that previous day by walking through ice water. My heart was pounding, but I stuck with them like glue for the hours it took us to get up and over the mountain range. I could do it because I play squash. I knew how to deal with lung pain. That surprised them. I was in better shape now then when I'd started in Mexico.

Our road led down the north side of the mountains and then we followed a path across one final dry mini-mesa to reach the Chama River Valley. We slept on the riverbank. Our issues of dehydration were almost over for good. Rio Chama offered a parklike setting. It felt heavenly to have fresh water and lush greenery. The river ran two hundred miles southeastward where it fed into the Rio Grande. A dirt road paralleled the river, offering designated camping spots and a public restroom. We awoke riverside that next morning, feeling calm and relaxed, as this was to be a town day. We were ten miles shy of our next trail stop. It wouldn't be a town but was a 21,000-acre oasis in the desert called the Ghost Ranch.

The Ghost Ranch.

We hiked five miles up the dirt road along the Rio Chama, on the morning of Sunday, June 5; then Todd took a compass bearing, and we set out westward, cross-country, off-trail, over high sand dunes, and down to Highway 84 in the distance. We walked two hot highway miles to a defunct, boarded-up natural history museum, then one mile cross-country to the Ghost Ranch.

The Ghost Ranch compound was instantly visually stunning. Billowy willow trees dotted abundant water-sprinkler-nourished manicured grassy lawns and were interspersed with small Abode-style tan buildings. Everything still and quiet. Most spectacularly of all was that bright red cliff walls rose towering over one thousand feet above the northern edge of the green oasis in the desert. The cliffs showed geologic demarcation lines in the layers, and a handy stratigraphy chart on a placard at the ranch identified different epochs of time corresponding to color variations on the cliff walls: late Cretaceous, early Cretaceous, Jurassic, Triassic.

Geologists salivate and their knees wobble here. Geologists and fossil hunters from all over the world flock here. Nearby were fossil-rich quarries where've been discovered thousands of dinosaur fossils. In 1947, they discovered an enormous accumulation of Coelophysis bauri skeletons. Those were Velociraptor-like, eight-foot-long, fast-running, carnivorous bipeds with crazy sharp teeth and claws. You wouldn't have wanted to run into one. They were the State Fossil of New Mexico. There was a dinosaur museum at the Ghost Ranch with a large sign out front sporting a drawing of Coelophysis bauri.

At the main lodge they rented us rooms for the night in one of the many small buildings that were spread out across the compound. There was a library, outdoor pool, Laundromat and cafeteria-style dining center. The receptionist was nonplussed to see us standing before them wearing backpacks. It didn't matter that we'd walked there from out of the desert. Through-hiking didn't mean anything to her. They'd a wide variety of people in here for various reasons from all over the globe. Not too many through-hikers came here. It was a natural, convenient, and terrific spot, but there just weren't many through-hikers in general.

Locals called it "Rancho de los Brujos" due to ghosts tales associated with the ranch after ancient hangings there. The king of Spain had given this area up in a land grant in 1766. Privately owned for a while, it'd then been donated to the Presbyterian Church in 1950. The place was famous because painter Georgia O'Keeffe was a Southwestern icon and had lived here for forty-one years and had died here in 1986 at age ninety-nine. She'd been born and raised in Wisconsin and had then studied art and lived for many years in New York City. It wasn't until she was thirty years old that she'd first visited New Mexico. Her second trip was twelve years later when she'd spent a whole summer here. It'd happened for O'Keeffe accidentally like that. She suffered a nervous breakdown in New York City at age forty-six, and then she spent every subsequent summer here. She moved here for good at age fifty-eight. She bought a house in neighboring Abiquiu and spent the rest of her life painting New Mexico's flowers, mountains, rocks, bones, and red landscapes. There's an O'Keeffe museum in Abiquiu, and another in Santa Fe. Her paintings sometimes auction for millions. Visible from the Ghost Ranch was 9,862-foot Mt.

Pedernal, which she'd painted hundreds of times. She'd designed the Ghost Ranch logo, which is a frontal view of a steer's skull. She'd adored the Ghost Ranch. She'd called this region "The Faraway Nearby." New Mexico's stunning red beauty can overwhelm a person like that.

A corner table in the cafeteria allowed us to huddle over our lunches in a room filled with college students here on a midsummer archeological dig. We washed our laundry and made telephone calls. With my credit card, I ordered a tent, stove, and snowshoes over the phone. I arranged for my purchases to be mailed to the next town, Chama. I'd pick them up there in a few days. A little piece of plastic in my hand and needed things would be waiting ahead up the trail. What an amazing thing is a credit card. What a change from old-time through-hiking. Grandma Gatewood back on the AT in the 1950s with her shower curtain and Keds sneakers hadn't had it so good.

Todd and Weekender exited the Ghost Ranch without me on the morning of June 6. They set out hiking up into the cliffs heading for Chama, the last trail town in New Mexico, which sat at the Colorado border. We were almost done with this state. I'd told them to go ahead. They were well motivated and eager to hike, but my feet and my heart just weren't in it. My feet were hurting once again. My psyche was low. It was due to a combination of things: of not having a trail to follow, not having helpful maps, and always having to tag along. I needed a break from my dependency on Todd and Weekender. My pride couldn't take it. I formulated a different plan. I'd make my own way to Chama. They were following the Ley route, a four-day roundabout northeast-ward loop into high mountains and snow across the Colorado state line and then back westward to a landmark spot called Cumbress Pass. From there, they'd hitchhike fifteen miles southward to resupply in Chama. My CDTA book for New Mexico listed the "official" route as a fifty-mile road walk up Highway 84 into Chama. So that's what I'd do—head up the highway. I just wanted to reach Chama as quickly as possible.

It seemed fitting to end this state the same way that I'd begun it, by road walking. The road walks had been murder on my feet. So I decided to hitchhike it. I felt awful because of that. I was a hypocrite and a pretender. So many times on the Appalachian Trail and Pacific Crest Trail, I'd thought poorly of others who took shortcuts or hitchhiked. Now here I was, hitchhiking to Chama. New Mexico was beautiful, but I wanted my time in the state to be over. If the trail had been marked, clear, and connected, then I'm sure that I could've hiked it. But we were just winging it, town after town. And that gets old.

I walked away down the Ghost Ranch's long dirt road. It felt fine to have a moment alone. The world was quiet and still. Suddenly, up the road toward me walked a backpacked young man. He was tall, broad, and wore long cotton tan-colored pants and an unbuttoned long-sleeved tan-colored shirt. He wore running shoes and had a confidant, powerful stride. His backpack was tiny, and he carried neither hiking stick nor ski poles. Just had his thumbs hitched up under his shoulder straps. Clearly a through-hiker. Someone new! Quite incredibly, his demeanor and gait were such that it appeared he wasn't even going to slow down to say hello let alone stop to chat. I had to practically step in front of him.

"Are you through-hiking?" I asked.

"Yes."

"I'm John," I said, extending my hand.

"Pony Express."

Twenty-one-year-old Pony Express had a swagger to his step. He was solid as a tree.

"Oh, we heard of you," I said, remembering this now. "The two guys I'm with, Todd and Weekender, read about you on your Web site. We knew you'd be coming up behind us."

"Where are they?"

"They just set out north."

"How long ago?"

"They just left an hour ago."

"I'll catch them," he said.

This guy had started long after we had, but was hiking huge daily mileage and was tearing up the trail. We'd known that he'd overtake us. He'd be taking the Ley Alternate Route to Chama, right behind Todd and Weekender, he said. Now came something strange. Here I was exiting the Ghost Ranch and yet he asked me nothing about it. Usually, a through-hiker will ask about what a place offers in the way of laundry, food, telephone, lodging. Pony Express clearly wasn't the type who liked to stand still. And he didn't really look at you so much as look past you. He looked beyond you, looking for something else that must be more important. Unless you asked about him, which I did—and then you could tell he was interested.

The young redwood tree named Pony Express had already been through both the AT and the PCT, in the summers after his sophomore and junior years of college. He'd just now graduated from the College of William and Mary, where he'd been on a track scholarship and so he'd be finishing his Triple Crown by age twenty-two. Having run cross-country and indoor and outdoor track in both high school and college, he'd thus spent the past eight years doing nonstop running, often averaging eighty miles a week. I asked about his feet and how they were holding up on New Mexico's hot road walks. It'd been a mistake to ask him that, though, for he answered that he was holding up perfectly. Entirely immodestly, without self-effacement, he said: *"My feet are as hard as rock."* Okay, it was unpleasant to hear a guy say that about himself and then walk away, but I also had to admit that it was pretty bad-assed what he was doing, hiking out here alone, apparently without any issues or problems.

82

Galloping Goose.

New Mexico had been a beautiful state, but I was ready for something different. I was ready for snow and high peaks. It felt fine sitting here in Chama at the end of the state. My ride up the highway had been with an ice cream distributor. What a new and novel way to through-hike: if you like to spend time in the trail towns as I do, then you just hitchhike to town and rest. On the other two trails, I'd never had to wait for anyone else. The routes on those trails were so clear that you could always set out alone and find the way. Here, I wasn't about to start northward into the South San Juan Mountains without Todd and Weekender.

Chama became my home for four days while waiting for Todd and Weekender. I slept in the Shamrock Hotel from June 6–9. I found three others waiting here for them, as well. And Pony Express, too, was headed in. A bunch of us were assembling. Chama on the CDT was the equivalent of Kennedy Meadows on the PCT—it was the spot where hikers transitioned from sand to snow, changing into winter gear and leaving the desert behind. The AT doesn't have such a spot. But out West, the mountains are high and you have to be careful. I had to heal up and steel my nerve.

Chama was tiny with a population of twelve hundred people. They'd billed it as a center of outdoor activity and recreation, but I found no evidence of that. The town didn't even have a backpacking store. What Chama had was a railroad station which brought tourists in and out. The big talk in town was of the once-every-four-year appearance of a train called The Galloping Goose, which was a makeshift contraption—part school bus, part train, and with a big goose painted on its side. People from town rushed down to see it. The Shamrock Hotel stood across the street from the train station. The hotel sold train memorabilia in its lobby, like posters and clothing. There was a café next door where I ate all my meals. I mailed home my CDTA book for New Mexico and cracked open my CDTA book for Colorado. Then I lay about my room, trying to research the trail. I found to my horror that the Colorado book was written for southbound travel. Different authors had written the CDTA's four books about the four states, so the style of each one differed. Ideas and suggestions differed. For instance, the first paragraph of the Colorado book said that hikers should travel with a llama. Except that I didn't have a llama.

The Shamrock had a computer with Internet access on the second floor. One night at ten o'clock (late night for through-hikers, unless they're out drinking in bars), I spied a young shirtless man surfing the Web with the lights off. Next morning in the hallway, I noticed that a door was ajar. I looked in as I passed, smelled a ripe odor and spied the night Web-surfer and two others who were crashed out amidst filth and hiking gear. Junk all over the floor. Through-hikers! I met them hours later.

83

Porno-Sausage-Mule: they were all twenty-six years old (same as Todd), and were three friends from California. Actually, they knew Todd. At least Porno knew Todd, and that was good enough for the rest of them because Porno was their trio's leader, and he was the only one of them that'd through-hiked a trail before. Porno was the experienced hiker of their group. The other two were just following his lead, right down to the way that they dressed (in long kaki clothing), and didn't shave (because he didn't shave). Porno had through-hiked the PCT in the same year as Todd. They'd met there and had kept in touch and had been planning on bumping into each other out here. Now, I suddenly remembered having heard Todd talk about being on the lookout for this group—but I'd forgotten about it because he'd only said it once and then I don't think he'd ever brought it up again. I guessed that these must've been the three northbound hikers that my hermit friend had seen walk by a week before me down in the Gila.

That was about as much as I learned, for they kept mostly to themselves. I only caught glimpses of those new guys those few days in Chama, and I didn't speak with them much. I felt no need to force it. I figured that talk would come later if need be. I told them that Todd and Weekender were due in imminently. They'd wait. I wondered what that'd mean for my hike. Would we form a hiking group of six or seven—Todd–Weekender–Porno–Sausage–Mule–Pony Express and me? That'd change the dynamic. The others certainly realized that the dynamic of their hike was about to change, too. Maybe that was why they were quiet. Weekender didn't know Porno, but any friend of Todd's would be a friend of his. And Weekender was easy to get along with. I was anxious to get started again.

American Thunder—*Burning through the night!* Porno sang and played air guitar. He said, "Only nine northbounders are ahead of us. This guy Raw Food has a Web page that says they all skipped around the South San Juans because of the snow. They flip-flopped all the way to Canada and they're hiking southbound to here."

Porno's threesome had done research on the Internet. He said that we'd be the first ones to enter the South San Juans. There'd be no trail. Just snow. I felt nervous, yet eager to begin. My new Hilleberg tent, my Jetboil stove, and snowshoes arrived at the Chama post office. I was glad to have them. Change was certainly afoot. Nobody'd used snowshoes in the High Sierras on the PCT, and I hadn't intended on using them out here in Colorado, either, but Todd and Weekender had mentioned getting snowshoes, and so I'd thought as per usual that they'd known something I didn't. So I'd ordered the snowshoes. It'd turn out that I didn't need them—but an ice axe should've been mandatory.

I sat waiting for Todd and Weekender, but Pony Express with his "Hard as Rock" feet arrived first. He was a guy who didn't take rest days. He didn't stay over in town. He didn't get sore feet. He wouldn't take a rest day here.

"Did you see Todd and Weekender?" we asked.

"I passed by them like they were standing still."

It wasn't exactly the answer I'd been looking for. He wasn't modest. He didn't need any of us to like him or want to hike with him. He'd been expecting to hike this trail alone. That was rare for someone so young. He didn't care a rat's ass what impression he made—but we had to wonder if he even knew that his words were repellent. He ate a quick meal in the café, collected a package at the post office, and was instantly ready to go. He wouldn't sleep even one night in the Shamrock. Todd and Weekender would arrive momentarily, but I made the decision not to wait but to set out with Pony Express. I was going to follow Pony Express, a guy whose pace was dramatically faster than any of the rest of ours. It was like I'd done earlier—setting out ahead so that I wouldn't fall behind. For if anything went wrong, I'd have five guys coming up from behind. Pony Express had been planning to enter the South San Juans alone, but he said he'd be glad for my company. He expected this section to be treacherous.

I checked out of the Shamrock. I stood wearing my backpack and holding my new snowshoes. The woman co-owner of the hotel noticed my snowshoes and commented on them, as she'd been following the saga of our readiness to tackle the snow. From Chama, one can look northward and see the foreboding, snow-covered, monstrous spiked peaks of Colorado. It's a daunting sight. Pony Express walked up, wearing his backpack. The woman noticed that he didn't have snowshoes, so she pointed to mine while telling him:

"Well, you can follow his snowshoe tracks."

Pony Express answered, "Actually, I will be out in front and he will be following me."

We knew that this was true, yet it seemed like an odd thing to say. I'd never walked with him a day in my life—not even one inch—so how, really, did he *know?*

Midmorning, June 9—day number thirty-seven for me—I rode with Pony Express up to Cumbress Pass in the owner's truck. The truck pulled away, leaving us standing alone. My Rocky Mountain High journey was about to begin. I'd one state down and three to go.

8
South San Juans

The rain to the wind said,
"You push and I'll pelt."
They so smote the garden bed
That the flowers actually knelt,
And lay lodged—though not dead.
I know how the flowers felt.

—Robert Frost, "Lodged"

Vestibule.

In all the walking and hiking I'd done, my feet had never before touched
Colorado soil, so I felt overjoyed to step out of the truck at Cumbress Pass at
ten thousand feet and look up at the snow, knowing that I was about to climb
and hike through that entire state. John Denver's mountain ballad, which I'd
known all my life, echoed in my ears: "Colorado Rocky Mountain high, I've
seen it rain and fire in the sky. Friends around the campfire and everybody's
high. Rocky Mountain high, Colorado." As a summer camp kid in the Adirondack Mountains of New York, I'd sung that song. I'd believed in it. I'd always
heard that Colorado was a state that a hiker could visit and then never want to
leave. Now here I stood, expecting greatness.

National Geographic had topographical maps for Colorado: map 142 was for the South San Juans. They were available in stores, but Chama with its lack of hiking stores didn't sell them. So I didn't have map 142. The Ley route, the Wolf route, and the actual groove of the CDTA all coincided in this section. My new hiking partner Pony Express had a contour map that he'd gotten from the government, or some such thing. I had only a few indecipherable pages from my CDTA book for Colorado, written for southbounders, and of course they wouldn't help. No, I wasn't even going to fake it: I was flat out unapologetically going to follow twenty-one-year-old Pony Express eighty miles through this overly snow-filled stretch of the South San Juans to a place called Wolf Creek Pass. I told him so. He was okay with it. From there, we'd hitchhike to resupply in the Colorado trail town of Pagosa Springs.

It was June 9. In four days Jessie Gibbins was to drive eight hours up to meet me at the Pagosa Springs Resort. It was a hotel that she'd found on the Internet which had a riverside backyard terrace filled with natural hot springs. It was something to look forward to, powerful incentive to get me through this section. The next four days would take us through deep snow up at twelve-to-thirteen thousand feet, through an area so wild and isolated that as recently as 1970 they'd found and shot a grizzly bear here. That'd been decades after grizzlies were long-since believed to have been exterminated from everywhere south of Wyoming. I wasn't overconfident. My having walked through California's snowy High Sierras at high elevation six years earlier didn't trick me into a feeling of invincibility. Experience can better prepare one for the future, but past success can also cause overconfidence. You can never take wilderness lightly. Each experience is unique.

We set out midday from Cumbress Pass—Pony Express leading the way—and within half a mile of climbing up out of the parking lot we got lost. Or at least, confused. I'd later learn that all the others would have trouble here, too, but they'd begin a day behind us. We twisted up streambeds, up densely forested steep slopes, until Pony Express announced that he knew our location. Beneath our feet was snow, but occasionally we caught some bare ground and trail. We were the first two northbound CDT through-hikers in the South San Juans that summer. We kept our heads down and motored as fast as we could.

Pony Express stopped occasionally to check his contour map and identify landmarks. He hiked swiftly, but in stopping to check his map he was patient and methodical, unfolding it fully, and then afterward fully refolding and replacing it in a ziplock bag in his side pants pocket. His father was an army ranger, he said, and had taught him everything about navigating by contour map and compass. Pony Express had hiked in the South San Juans before. He'd grown up in Colorado and had lived there through junior high school before his family had moved to Virginia. On long climbs he'd get out ahead and then stop to rest a moment, but as soon as I'd catch up he'd set out climbing again, so I never got a rest. We never paused for long. We didn't stop for lunch. We never sat down. Pony Express munched all day long, but he ate on the go. He carried a massive bag of mixed chocolate, peanuts and raisins, and he pawed into it, stuffing his face midstride. We passed the Dipping Lakes and hiked well past dusk. We set up our tents in a snowless patch of grass behind some bushes on a high plateau. It was the only dry spot that we could see in any direction, excluding the vertical cliff walls on the sides of the thirteen-thousand-foot peaks scattered about. Dinner was cold for me, as I had no fuel for my new Jetboil stove. I hadn't been able to buy its specialty Lindal Valve fuel canister in hiking-store-less Chama.

June 10, I left my snowshoes behind in the morning, out of desperation. I'd only tried using them once that previous day, and all they'd done was slow me down. I had to keep pace with the track star. Circling and searching for small landmark Blue Lake, midmorning of our second day, was a frustrating waste of two hours. We finally found it after a great deal of backtracking and searching. It was crucial because it pinpointed our location. We continued, hiking strongly the whole day. I was weak from not eating much for dinner or breakfast, but I knew the threes of survival: you can survive three weeks without food, three days without water, and three minutes without oxygen. Don't violate those rules and you can live. I snacked on candy bars and crackers, knowing that a few days on low food wouldn't kill me. Getting separated from Pony Express, on the other hand, probably would.

All day, it was steep climbs and descents up and down terrific cliffs and through trees. It provided an unequalled chance for athleticism. We felt like kids in a candy store. We took long snow slides down steep icy slopes on our rumps. On those, it was important to concentrate, plan ahead and keep the slides controlled, for unseen cliffs always lurked below, out of sight. Trees factored in prominently: we'd use them to help stop slides—but you never wanted to hit a tree too hard. It was risky, chancy, and wonderful. There were no rules here. Usually in assessing the route for a quick descent, I'd visualize the slide and double-check my own thoughts to plan and make sure that what I thought would be safe actually probably would be (meta-knowledge: the ability to assess the quality of your own knowledge). Here lay risk. Here lay an adrenaline rush. Pony Express used his ice axe constantly, but I had none. I had my hiking stick, but no true ability to self-arrest. I held my own with Pony Express on the free-for-all descents, except that once I chose what I thought was the fastest route, but I looked down and saw him standing at the base of a river valley eight hundred feet below me, looking up and waiting.

We crossed back and forth over the Continental Divide. There was grooved trail here—the CDT—and there were even side trails. It's just that all of it was buried in snow so we couldn't see it. Pony Express plotted our course. We were the only two people on planet Earth. The only two people inside a playground the size of Manhattan. We had hundred-story-high rock buildings for toys, whose windows we'd climb out of and slide down steep ice flows to Broadway and Park Avenue below before climbing again. Several of our descents were dangerous, and we could see evidence of avalanches. Suffocating under packed snow would be an absolutely ghastly way to go. Avalanches had wiped out a broad patch down one slope of a ridge all the way to a river basin. Trees were piled up at the bottom, sticking out of the snow after having been snapped off like so many toothpicks.

We tented in the river valley that second night in the South San Juans. We found a dry patch. We knew our location. So far, so good. June 11, we rose early and crawled on hands and knees across a snow bridge over the valley's swift river, hoping not to fall through. North of the river, we climbed to a high plateau thousands of feet above it, and once up there our path undulated at 12,500 feet, with the rocky peaks of Mt. Summit and Mt. Montezuma jutting up beside us like nipples to heights of 13,300 feet. We spent an exhausting day climbing and hiking through snow, trying to avoid avalanches, trying to choose our routes wisely.

Hours later, the sky darkened as black clouds rolled swiftly in out of nowhere. It was five o'clock. We were high on a rocky patch. Thunder roared and a lightning bolt struck in the distance. The electrical storm moved on, but thick clouds remained. Then it started to snow. We sat on the ground and waited to see if the clouds would blow past to create visibility again. There were few hours of daylight left, so we didn't set up our tents. We curled up on the ground against our backpacks at twelve-thousand feet and draped jackets over ourselves. I closed my eyes. Drifted to sleep. But the storm never passed. It settled overhead. The snow fell harder.

When we finally roused ourselves forty-five minutes later, we were buried in a white out and pinned down. We couldn't proceed. We shook ourselves off and set up our tents to stay put for the night. We had no choice. We'd come sixty-five miles in three days and were only twenty-five miles shy of Wolf Creek Pass, but we couldn't hike farther. Our day had been cut prematurely short. We'd need to haul to make it all the way in that next day in order for me to meet Jessie Gibbins on time. I worried about that. Alone in my small new tent, I ate my cold dinner of dry snacks. The snow continued falling. We were getting hammered. The wind picked up. I could hear it howling. It's a glorious noise to hear when you know that you're okay in a warm sleeping bag in a strong tent. I closed my eyes to sleep. Next thing I knew, I was awakened by the sound of yelling.

"*HELP!*"

What was that? Had I heard something?

"*HELP!*"

It was Pony Express. It took me a groggy instant or two before I was able to register that he was calling me repeatedly to wake up and give him a hand. A quick check of my watch showed it was three-o'clock in the morning. Shit.

"What is it?"

"*COME HERE! HELP ME!*"

Our tents were beside each other, but we had to scream so that we could be heard over the extreme whipping wind. "Come here" wasn't something that I relished hearing just then. But I owed him. I owed him for having guided me through this high rugged wilderness for three days. I'd told him face-to-face and eye-to-eye on a couple different occasions in no uncertain terms: "Do not lose me. I will not be okay out here if I end up alone." And on the couple occasions when he'd gotten too far ahead out of sight and I'd had to search for the route, when I caught up with him I'd told him that I wasn't pleased. I wasn't trying to be his friend. I was old enough to be his father. I needed him to know that I was unqualified to be out here alone. To get that point across, I'd told him: "I am unqualified to be out here alone." Now, he needed my help. The wind blew frenziedly. But I couldn't imagine what was wrong. I threw on my socks, shorts, wet shirt, jacket, and sneakers. I unzipped my tent and peered out. The cold wind hit me like a baseball bat. Suddenly, I thought I was starring in a movie, like some kind of Mt. Everest disaster cautionary nature film.

Pony Express' tent was a sheet of plastic—just a lightweight tarp that he'd tie down at the corners at night, for he was an ultralight big-mileage hiker. Usually, it was held down on four corners, but now it was held down on just two while the rest of it was flying, flapping, and snapping impressively, horizontally in the wind. It was dark, but I could see. It'd stopped snowing, but the wind had blown snow into drifts, and great heaps of it had found their way underneath Pony Express' tarp. I stumbled a few feet over in the snow and grew instantly cold. I could see he was lying on his back and was reaching back to hold down two corners of his tarp-tent with his hands. If he let go, it'd blow away in a heartbeat.

"HELP ME! I CAN'T HOLD MY TARP DOWN ANY LONGER!"

His belongings were buried in white.

"GRAB MY TARP AND HOLD IT WHILE I PACK MY THINGS!"

I did as I was told. He grabbed and stuffed his snowy things into his pack. He groped around in the snow, feeling to make sure he had everything.

"I CAN'T FEEL MY HANDS!" he shouted. *"I'M FREEZING! CAN I COME INTO YOUR TENT?!"*

This was life or death.

"Of course! come in!"

My tent was very small. But what happened next was utterly amazing, in that he came inside my tent but instead of lying down inside his sleeping bag, he spent the next three hours sitting scrunched up in a ball near my feet. My 1.5-person Hilleberg tent from Sweden was tiny, but was easily the best tent I'd ever owned, and lying down next to me to gain body heat was just what he needed right now. I'd had to convince him even to come inside my actual tent, as it had a vestibule and at first he'd suggested that he just sit in the vestibule, until he realized the temperature difference. Inside, I lay as far as I could against the right wall of my tent and created space for him to lie down next to me, like two cigars. Instead, though, he curled up in a seated position near my feet, hugging his knees and shivering, his head crumpled under the low tent cover.

"Dude, lie down," I said. I tried to reassure him, "It's okay if we lean against each other."

"No, that's all right."

"What, you don't want to impose?"

It actually would've been the best way for me to get comfortable under the conditions, as to accommodate him I'd wedged myself so far to one side that my balance had me falling back, and it would've helped me to lean. But Pony Express stayed put. I wasn't going to force him. He just sat there. I loved my tent. It was the same brand and model that Weekender carried—a Hilleberg Akto Solo, weighing three pounds. That's how I'd known to order it when I'd used my credit card over the phone back at the Ghost Ranch. I'd seen how well it'd worked for him, and I loved the vestibule and had asked him about it. The tent was remarkably easy to use: only one pole needed. And the vestibule was convenient because you could put your pack there and have it covered from overnight rain. The tent, combined with my warm heavy sleeping bag, created complete protection from the cold. The tent weighed under three pounds. I felt great security knowing that cold couldn't penetrate me, so that if anything ever went drastically wrong I could always curl up in my sleeping bag inside my tent and be fine.

Leaping The Rapid.

Homophobic Pony Express was a magnificent hiker. He roused us early in the morning. He hadn't slept much, sitting up. He was as anxious as I to make quick time and race to kick out our final twenty-five miles and get into town on that day. We had different reasons. Mine was to reach Pagosa Springs as soon as possible to see Jessie Gibbins. I feared that she'd worry if she reached town and I didn't show up that evening as planned. She'd no way to contact me, no way of knowing if I was on the way or if I was okay. She didn't know through-hiking, didn't really know how these things went. That was mostly why I wanted to finish and get out and not spend another night in the woods. Pony Express had a different reason—for him, it was just that he'd spent a crappy night freezing his ass off and he needed to dry out his things and get a warm night's sleep.

June 12, we set out in an eye-blink, racing away. Conditions were fine. Visibility was good, and we made our way through the snow. We had a chance. We just needed to hike strongly. Pony Express had done a masterful job getting us this far, and now we just had to finish. The worst was behind us. A large part of me relished this time, hiking with someone who didn't take breaks. That was how I liked to hike. That made sense to me. It echoed my time on the AT and the PCT. It was different than hiking with Todd and Weekender, who took very long breaks. Problem was that I liked Todd and Weekender. They could laugh at themselves. I laughed loads with them. Meanwhile, Pony Express couldn't see the lighter side of this. He was no more expert a navigator than was Todd, yet he took himself far too seriously. In four days, he hadn't once laughed at our situation. And our situation had been ridiculous. We'd been through some sketchy spots, like long ice slides on our butts, and laterally crossing steep ice slopes while hoping that we wouldn't fall to our deaths. I wanted to send him the Nicholas Cage voice-over in the opening scene of Charlie Kaufman's film, Adaptation:

Do I have an original thought in my head, my bald head? Maybe if I were happier my hair wouldn't be falling out. Life is short. I need to make the most of it. Today is the first day of the rest of my life. I'm a walking cliché. I really need to go to a doctor and have my leg checked. There's something wrong, a bump. The dentist called again; I'm way overdo. If I stopped putting things off I'd be happier. All I do is sit on my fat ass. If my ass wasn't fat I would be happier. I wouldn't have to wear these shirts with the tails out all the time. Like that's fooling anyone—fat ass! I should start jogging again. Five miles a day; really do it this time. Maybe rock climbing. I need to turn my life around. I need to fall in love. I need to have a girlfriend. I need to read more, improve myself. What if I learned Russian or something? Or take up an instrument? I could speak Chinese. I could be the screenwriter who speaks Chinese and plays the obo. That would be cool.

In praise of mediocrity! Why not laugh at life? There's no real point in taking oneself too seriously. We'll all be worm food soon. The rest is silliness. We hiked swiftly and silently for hours. It was wonderful, hard work. True hiking. We got to within eight miles of Wolf Creek Pass when suddenly the sky turned black under a rush of dark clouds, just as had happened yesterday. They were the same black clouds threatening snow and a lightning storm (well, not the same clouds: History never repeats itself, but sometimes it rhythms). We stood exposed up at 12,600 feet. This storm was going to catch us and pin us down high on the ridge just like the night before. We couldn't afford it. We were too close to town to settle for that. Pony Express whipped out his map and found a way for us to bail off the high ridge. He showed me that we needed to push ahead a bit farther to reach a place called Bonito Pass, and from there we could descend eastward down to a dirt jeep road. Down there at low elevation we'd be able to head northward to reach our destination, Highway 160, just east of Wolf Creek Pass. The bailout would put us three miles east of there.

We rushed to Bonito Pass, hoping that lightning wouldn't strike. Then we turned and dropped eastward off the high ridge. The ground was all snow, so if our descent was on a side trail, we weren't aware of it. We picked our way cross-country, loosely following a snow-covered stream. We descended three-thousand feet, picking our way. Finally, we gained low ground down at nine-thousand feet and stumbled onto a half-buried (in snow) dirt road. We followed it northward a few miles to within sight of the highway. There was just one problem, as an obstacle stood in our way: a whitewater rapid.

It was a narrow, jet-fast rapid—one last hurdle to leap, one final test. Nothing came easily on the CDT. There were constant tests to see if we'd crack. The rapid was so intimidating that we actually checked our map and contemplated walking two-and-a-half miles northeastward to reach a bridge where we could cross it. But we were just too close to the highway for that. We were exhausted from our four-day concentrated effort. We just wanted it to be over. We'd survived so much that we just said, screw it. And here I found the Kryptonite of Pony Express. I hadn't been looking for it, and I wouldn't have imagined there'd be any, but here I found it: water. Or, more specifically, terrifyingly fast river-rapids that one must leap across.

We scaled down to the water's edge, which was low in a brutally narrow ravine. We searched up and down the bank for a place to cross. We spent thirty minutes looking. That was how much respect we gave this, anxious as we were to leap to its opposite bank and scramble up to the highway. We couldn't possibly walk through it but we had to jump over it. I finally found a spot that was especially deep and fast, but its saving grace was it narrowness. There wasn't room enough to take a running start because we were down in so narrow a chasm, so we wouldn't be able to jump the river's width; but a standing broad jump could, if executed correctly, land us beyond the surging water and into a slower-moving survivable spot. The trick would be to land in a forward-leaning position and hit the river while stumbling forward through the relatively slower-moving shallower water to the opposite bank. Landing and falling forward face first to get wet was in order. Then all would be fine. But landing and falling backward would not be okay. I went first, leapt, and made it, still wearing my backpack. It took quite a large amount of coaxing to get Pony Express to make his leap. But then, I'm a coach. It's what I do for a living. I get paid to motivate and encourage. As I waved him in, willing and motioning him toward me with my hands, I stood in the shallow ice-water feeling my feet go numb.

"Just land and lean forward and fall—even if you have to do a face-plant."

It took a long while, but Pony Express finally jumped. He leaned backward a little upon landing. His arms began to flail and do the backward tightrope-walker's twirl. I was on it, alert. I grabbed his shirt and pulled him toward me. Otherwise, he might still be floating down that rapid. We climbed two hundred feet up to the highway, which was at ten thousand feet just east of Wolf Creek Pass. We hitchhiked thirty miles southwestward down out of the mountains to lower elevation, getting a ride from the second car that passed. The ride to Pagosa Springs brought into relief the extreme height of the land that we'd come through. The auto descent was a twisting, turning, switchbacking affair through long auto tunnels carved through the rock. It felt like coming down out of the sky. Had we really been up that high? The engineering feat of building that road up and over Wolf Creek Pass was impressive. We got dropped off at the Pagosa Springs Resort. Pony Express took a room across the street at a cheap hotel while I walked inside the resort and at the front desk asked for the room for Jessie Gibbins.

Pagosa Resort.

Jessie opened the door in a negligee. I'd known for certain that it'd be this way. The lights were off and she had candles burning. Just like a movie scene. Bottle of wine on the counter. Soft music playing from a portable CD-player that she'd brought with her. Now here's my crazy admission: I had to ask her to please not be offended but to please, please dress and come with me to a restaurant immediately, or else I would die.

"I need to eat."

"Right now?"

"Right now. I just walked eighty miles without food."

At dinner, I realized that I hadn't shaved or changed my clothes, including my underwear, in four days. You know it's bad when you can smell yourself. People at the other tables started inching away. I was poor company. I cleaned my plate and then I started eating all the food off Jessie's plate, too. I asked, "Having fun?" I felt bad about the turning on of the lights and the changing out of the negligee. It was supposed to be a vacation for her. For me, it was like a hospital stay. I should've prepared her more fully as to the state in which she'd likely find me; but I hadn't wanted to talk her out of visiting. I hadn't completely misrepresented things, for I'd been calling her weekly from telephones in all the little trail towns that I'd been passing through, and I'd been complaining about how difficult it was. What a fun guy I am.

Jessie's big plan for Pagosa Springs had been to bring therapeutic oil and give me the world's greatest foot massage. That was because I'd been telling her all along how badly my feet hurt. So I'd known she was going to bring oil. And I guess I'd just figured that was going to morph into wine and candles, too. It was like what'd happen back when I was married, how I'd return from long four-day competitions all cranky and tired, and Cristina'd be waiting

94

for me with a romantic mood set. That's what couples do. A normal person would be flattered and grateful, but all I'd been able to think of back then at those moments was my overwhelming need to just shut down and turn off completely and escape from the world.

Back at our room, I shaved, showered and then pretty much passed out. I was an old guy, what can I say? Those four days of hiking through the South San Juans had been terrifically hard. We slept late in the morning and we lounged in bed and made love and got reacquainted. I was feeling better now. It was good to see her again. At least up until the moment when she accidentally peeled off one of my toenails. The toenail had already died several days ago and had been hanging on by a thread. So I didn't actually feel any pain—but Jessie didn't know that, so of course I teased her. It was during her long-awaited and much-promised foot massage, which made it extra funny to me. I pretended to be a tough guy who was taking the pain.

"Shit! Ow! You just peeled off my toenail!"

"Oh my god!" she screamed. "I'm sorry!"

"No it's okay," I said, really milking it. We'd calmed down by now, but not wanting to let it end, I said: "Please don't worry about it. Thank you so much for the foot massage. You're really excellent at it."

"Yeah?"

"Yeah. Except for the part with the peeling-off-of-the-toenails..."

We walked out back in our bathing suits (hiking shorts for me), along with white slippers and white cotton robes from our hotel's closet. On the terrace behind the resort were natural hot springs that they'd fashioned and gloriously corralled into eighteen tiled and sculpted tubs on multiple levels, interspersed with tables, lounge chairs, and umbrellas for shade. Flowing alongside the bathing tubs was the wide, shallow San Juan River. From the terrace, you could look across the river and see the backs of the town buildings. A footbridge led across the river to stone steps which climbed to Main Street. All of it under a backdrop of snowy Colorado high peaks. The peacefulness of the scene was most outstanding. Heaven for a sore through-hiker upon emerging out from a grueling winter wonderland is a good hot soak. For that reason alone, I'd rate Pagosa Springs the best of all the Triple Crown trail towns.

Each of the eighteen hot spring tubs had a name and distinct personality: Lobster Pot was the hottest at 114 degrees, Cliff had a waterfall flowing into it, and Serendipity was accessed by walking across a sunken wooden bridge that lay inches under the thermal mineral water, so you soaked your feet even while walking to the tub. Several of the pools—Paradise, Treasure, Venetian, Marco Polo—were riverside, so you could reach out your hand into the cold water. A placard called this the world's largest and deepest hot mineral spring. To the Native American Utes, Pagosa meant "Water That Has a Bad Smell." For centuries, they'd used the springs for healing purposes. They'd fought bloody battles against neighboring tribes for control of it. A bathhouse, massage studio, juice bar, café, and salon were at the resort now. Locals could pay for a hot spring membership, and tourists could pay for day passes. Only hotel guests could remain on the back terrace to soak in the mineral pools past ten o'clock, though. For hotel guests, the hot springs were open all night.

We lay in the pools through the early afternoon, sunbathing, soaking, and watching river kayakers and inner-tubers paddle and float by. It felt like something close to heaven. Everything peaceful as could be. A few children pranced around. In the late afternoon, we took a break and Jessie drove me around town to buy groceries. Pagosa Springs had sixteen hundred people, but there was a growing population outside town, swelling the county with retirees who'd moved here for the golf courses. The town had an excellent Switchback Mountain Gear hiking store which sold me an ice axe, a Lindal Valve fuel canister for my JetBoil stove, and National Geographic maps 139 and 130 for the upcoming next two sections of trail. I wasn't about to set foot in the mountains again without an ice axe, and I'd have warm dinners from now on. Things were shaping up.

Todd and Weekender found us at the resort. They'd spent the previous night across the street, drinking at the hotel bar with Pony Express, who'd told them where to find me. It was good to see them again. Jessie told them she felt like she knew them. They sat outside on the back terrace with us, soaking their legs in the mineral hot springs.

"How's my friend Pony Express?" I asked.

"He's good," Todd said; "He told us about your little adventure, hiking on the ice slopes with no ice axe."

"Yeah, that was crazy," I said.

Todd and Weekender told me that none of the others had made it through the South San Juans. I was surprised to hear it. Todd and Weekender had gotten separated from Porno-Sausage-Mule on the first day. On the second day, they'd bailed out of the mountains and descended eastward down to low jeep roads. The other three had done the same thing. Except the other three had kept on going and were walking low roads straight northward all the way to the next town, Creede. I admitted that I'd just followed Pony Express the whole time. I said that he was an excellent route-finder, but that I hadn't had fun hiking with him.

It felt strange to digest—that Pony Express and I were the only ones who'd made it through the South San Juans. Todd and Weekender had to view me at least a little bit differently now. They had to grudgingly gain at least a tiny bit of respect for me. Sure, they knew that I'd already through-hiked the AT and the PCT—but up until now in their eyes I'd just been the pathetic limping guy who'd dragged himself across the roads of New Mexico, tagging along while just trying to keep up. I was even the guy who'd taken a couple pathetic hitchhikes. Now, at the very least, I was the lunatic who'd kept pace with Pony Express—at least for a few days—and had hiked through the South San Juans

96

with no ice axe. I still felt bad over the rides that I'd taken into Grants and Chama. I was still feeling like a pretender. But now the South San Juans had put some hair on my balls. I could hold my head slightly higher now.

"Are you taking the Creede Cutoff?" Todd asked.

That's how it went out here. I was always just accidentally hearing about important, strategic things in just such off-hand ways.

"'What the hell's *that?*"

"The Creede Cutoff. It's going straight north from Wolf Creek Pass into Creede instead of looping five days westward through the Western San Juans."

"Jesus," I said. "What are you guys doing?"

"Western San Juans," Todd said.

"Creede Cutoff," Weekender said.

"Dude, if you're doing the Creede Cutoff, I'll go with you," I said to Weekender.

So it was settled just like that: the following morning, Todd would set out with Pony Express for a five-day westward swing, following the Divide through the Weminuche Wilderness and the Western San Juans in what was supposed to hold the most majestic scenery in Colorado. Weekender and I would hike two days northward into Creede and wait for them there. Porno, Sausage, and Mule were apparently already hiking straight to Creede where they'd wait for everyone else to show up. Creede would be our point of convergence. Because Todd and Pony Express would take the longest to reach there, it'd give me a day or two to rest upon arriving. That was good news. I was exhausted. I was being pulled by opposite needs: I needed the rest days—I enjoyed the rest days—but I also needed to make quicker progress. My September 1 deadline was weighing on me. I was behind schedule. I'd have killed to be able to take a week to just stay in town and chill and do nothing. Having all of us together in Creede would be fun. It was a fission-fusion social structure on the trail—groups and friends split up for brief periods of time only to rejoin later.

At midnight, Jessie and I soaked in a hot tub out back. We looked up at a clear night sky filled with stars. Lightning flashed to the north in the distance from clouds that hovered over the snow-covered Rocky Mountains. The water was warm. We sipped some wine. We leaned back, closed our eyes. I asked her sweetly whether she was planning on peeling off any more of my toenails that night. We heard distant rumbles of thunder. I thought about being up there, pinned down and afraid.

9
Team Locust

When you hear the sound a coming,
Hear the drummers drumming,
I want you to join together with the band.

—The Who, "Join Together"

Forty-Year-Olds.

I've just had my four-hundredth win. That's a lot for a coach. It's a lot if you coach only one team, like football, and you play just twelve games each year and on average win half. It's even a lot if you coach one basketball team and play twenty-five games and win twenty every year. Then there are coaches of sports like track, skiing, and swimming who have meets and carnivals instead of dual contests, so they don't compile wins and losses. A few of the squash coaches in the Ivy League coach only one gender—either men or women— and their level of play is so high that they play only a limited schedule and compete against only a small number of the other best teams, so those coaches don't actually get too many wins a year that way. But each of my two squash teams play twenty-two matches a year, and since my teams usually win most of those, my numbers have added up quickly. And then there'd been the years when I'd been the head coach of four teams back at Colby. I'd tacked on lots of wins there. It's been sixteen years, and I can imagine coaching another twenty years, easily. If someone now offered me an easier job and said that I needed to coach only one squash team instead of two, I might turn that down because it'd mean fewer chances for wins. I've always been obsessed with crunching the numbers.

The tennis coach at Bates was a gifted instructor. It's quite something to be gifted. Very few people are. There are no degrees to it. You can't be very gifted or extremely gifted. It's just that you either are gifted at something or you aren't. The guy could take any player at any level and instruct that person on how to get better. He could do it with a tour pro, and he could do it with a beginner. He saw things. He could teach a rock how to play tennis. He'd played on the pro tour and had earned a nice world ranking. He'd been practice partners with Ivan Lendl. Now he was a division-III college coach. He had a house and kids, was living a healthy life. My friends and rival squash coaches in Maine—at Colby and Bowdoin—had both played professional squash. All three have moved on with their lives now. They both have children and homes. They have balance in their lives. Me, I still care about the level of my own game. I play tennis and squash tournaments. Still compete against the young guys. I'm still trying to win. It's unbalanced, I know. I recognize that. Recognition's the first step toward recovery. I only hope that I can take the next step.

I really don't mind losing. I once heard someone say that a defining characteristic of a champion is that the person hates to lose. I don't know about that, as I've never really been a champion. And maybe it's different for a coach than a player. But I don't hate to lose. Sometimes it hurts to lose, but I don't hate that. And I've never made my players feel bad about a loss. Everybody is going to occasionally lose. For me, it's just that I love to win. And I love the pursuit of attempting to win. I only teach my players to never be afraid to try their hardest. And not to be afraid to take the pain that comes when you try your hardest and it doesn't work out. That pain means you care. And it's nice to care about something. That's all. I never claim to have all the answers. I just do what I can to support them, and I wish them well.

Lots of coaches make their players call them, "Coach." They don't tolerate disrespect. They're sure of themselves in every decision they make. Me, I'm like Hamlet, because I'm never really sure about anything. Sometimes I don't want to act, and don't even want to lead or take a stand. I'm curious about life. Who am I to be sure? Sometimes I just want to observe. I make my players call me by my first name. Whenever anyone calls me coach, I cringe. I can't explain it—I just don't like it. I'm me, that's all. Call me by my name.

Saying good-bye to Jessie Gibbins was difficult, bordering on tragically stupid. For what could possibly cause a person to leave this luxury and happiness to go off and stagger through high mountain wilderness? Or take a more extreme example and ask what could cause a person to go off and die in a war? Why do we do the things that we do? Early afternoon, June 14, Jessie drove away back to Silver City. Weekender collected me and we two forty-something-year-old guys hitchhiked up to Wolf Creek Pass.

Since those ahead of us had flip-flopped around the South San Juans to hike southbound from Canada, it left only nine of us who were attempting direct northbound through-hikes in the summer of 2005, and six of us were now bunched together: Todd, Porno, Sausage, Mule, Pony Express, and me. Our ages were twenty-six, twenty-six, twenty-six, twenty-six, twenty-one, and forty-one, respectively (Weekender, only hiking half the trail this summer). The three remaining were people that I'd never meet: a guy from Belgium, a young guy named Hans Solo who was way up ahead of us and was trying to set the CDT speed record (whatever it was), and some other guy who was also trying to set the speed record. These days, everyone who goes out on any of these trails is always trying to break the speed record.

Weekender and I felt no rush in facing the easy Creede Cutoff. We hitchhiked up climbing, twisting, switchbacking, tunneling Highway 160 to Wolf Creek Pass at ten thousand feet. It was Weekender's first time there. I followed his lead in hitchhiking a bit farther eastward down the highway to the community of South Fork, which had a new golf course and dozens of McMansions under construction popping up on the surrounding hills in the Rio Grande National Forest. The Rio Grande originated a few miles west of town, so here it was just a little thing. It ran through South Fork and proceeded out of Colorado, down through New Mexico and along the Texas-Mexican border to the Gulf of Mexico two thousand miles later. I'd been west of the Rio Grande my entire hike. Now, I crossed a small bridge to its northeastern side and bid it good-bye.

Hiking was what I'd come out here for, so to set out hiking again sent positive electrical currents through my brain; it told me that I was fulfilling my purpose. That I was on track. I don't know whether enjoyment or happiness are words to describe that, but it was a start.

Weekender was quiet. The totality of his talking on the trip so far had been mostly limited to his rehashing and laughing about old inside PCT jokes with Todd. I'd heard their stories a dozen times. I learned more about Weekender now. He was decent and friendly. He'd served in the military as a decoder stationed in Alaska across the Bering Straight from Russia as a teenager during the cold war. For fun, he took long kayaking trips. We walked northward up a dirt road past Hanson Mill, then turned onto a trail leading into forested mountains. That unmarked trail was visible on our maps and easy to follow. We were figuring on two and a half easy days to reach Creede. The temperature was mild. Our packs were light.

Weekender hiked incredibly fast, so I took the lead and hiked out in front just so that we could keep together. Otherwise he'd have taken off and I'd never have seen him again. Our first night, we stopped at dusk in the middle of enormous Silver Park plateau. We set up our matching Hilleberg tents, and in the morning discovered elk bones littered around us. There was hair and the stench of decay. We simply hadn't noticed that the night before. Weekender guessed that the elk had been killed by lightning. Lightning was an issue here.

100

We were finding that out the hard way. Weekender sipped his town-departing Budweiser.

Where Lightning Lives.

National Geographic map 139 was my prized possession. It was easy to read. I felt joyful to have it, especially after having hiked the entire state of New Mexico using only a road atlas. From the skeleton-filled plain, we walked northwestward along trail 790 and came to dirt road 600.4 which we followed two miles to the southern entrance of the Wheeler Geologic Area. There was no entrance fee. There was nobody in sight. It'd once been a national monument until they'd removed its statues because it was so remote that no one ever came to see it. It lay in the middle of the wilderness, far off the beaten path. We'd reached a spot east of Creede, and a short day's walk would find us descending easily in. We were due to reach there before the others so we felt no hurry. We had all the time in the world. Weekender was keen on investigating this six-hundred-acre geologic anomaly, so in we went.

We climbed a path up through pine trees until we emerged on a sandstone ledge where we looked down at an otherworldly sight. What we saw didn't make sense, didn't match the surrounding landscape. Here, thirty million years ago, a volcanic explosion had blown the mountaintop into the atmosphere, leaving behind La Garita Caldera, the basin of which we stared down into. Inside were strangely eroded, Gothic-looking spires and pinnacles — tan spikes that rose hundreds of feet and were crammed closely together in white and beige layers of lava and ash. It was wonderfully out of place, tucked away and sunken inside that pit amongst pine trees. It had a different color, shape, and texture than anything else in Colorado. It matched more what we'd seen in the Gila River canyon or at the Ghost Ranch in New Mexico. It thrilled us to take photographs there.

Instead of backtracking, we climbed steeply up and out the north exit of the park, popping out above tree line. We climbed two miles westward into deep snow beneath a ridge, and then we scaled the ridge at landmark Halfmoon Pass, up at 12,725 feet. We were up in the clouds again. And I dutifully got us lost. The trail was prominent and I hiked in the lead. Weekender, trusting me, followed behind. The person behind never thinks to concentrate much. That was the problem. Weekender had grown accustomed to following accurate and reliable Todd, but now he found out the hard way what it was like to follow me.

Three trails intersected on Halfmoon Pass. I checked my map and took what I'd thought was La Garita Stock Driveway. It took us crossing to the eastern side of the ridge that divided Mineral from Saguache County. That was a mistake. We dropped down through deep snow and traversed along the eastern side downslope of the snow-filled bowl of La Garita Mountain Range.

We struggled for two hours, laboring to walk through waist-deep snow before we finally caught on and realized that we never should've crossed over to the eastern side of the ridge. Todd, where he here, would never have allowed this to happen.

Angry and dejected, instead of retracing our steps back to Halfmoon Pass, we turned westward off-trail and climbed straight up the steep cliffs to the top of the 12,800-foot ridge. We picked our way up through loose rocks and snow. It helped that I'd gotten an ice axe. The going got steep. We crested the ridge safely and peered westward down over a complex cross-country descent down through a mix of blown-down trees, woods, cliffs, glacial ponds, and deep snow. We carefully descended and finally emerged upon the vast open plains of Wason Park, down "low" at eleven thousand feet. There, we suddenly stumbled upon the clear groove of trail that would lead us to Creede. Our getting lost and the extra hiking had placed us out of striking range of town. Just a handful more hours would've done it, but the sky was darkening already. In getting us lost, I'd turned a leisurely Creede Cutoff stroll into an ordeal. We were exhausted.

Thunder rumbled and we raced westward with urgency, trying to reach a spot called Inspiration Point, which was a cliff that hovered two thousand feet directly above Creede. Unfortunately, we had to quit the race because we couldn't beat the storm. Tremendous lightning bolts struck in the distance, and we could watch the storm approach. We were terrifically frightened. My Halfmoon Pass mistake was now going to cost us our lives. A herd of one thousand elk temporarily distracted us. We laughed watching them curve gracefully across our high open plain at a distance. They were as afraid of the storm as we were. They were racing to escape the lightning.

We ducked inside the only area of small trees we could find and we set up our tents and waited for the lightning to kill us. It was going to be bad. John Denver's song refers to "rain and fire in the sky," but he fails to mention that the fire is lightning and that in Colorado you'll very likely be killed by death bolts. Nikola Tesla had moved for a year to Pike's Peak, Colorado, to conduct electrical experiments. A scene from the movie, The Prestige, finds Tesla's assistant in Colorado exclaiming, "God, I miss New York." "Then why are you here?" asks a friend. "This is where the lightning lives," he says. I liked that—it was a nice way to put it. There was no shortage of lightning here. This was where the lightning lived. We peeked out our matching Hilleberg tents and watched bolt after bolt strike down in the Western San Juans. Todd and Pony Express were somewhere out there up on the Divide. They'd probably been struck and killed already. Or maybe Todd had been killed and Pony Express was happily eating Todd's body for sustenance. You know: the show must go on and all that.

Ferocious bolts zapped down from the sky and we wondered if those two had been able to escape the high ridge and get down to safe ground. We counted strikes. They were great, thick, multipronged monster bolts: eighteen, nineteen, twenty, twenty-one—they lit the night sky. We counted the seconds elapsing between the peals of thunder and the rips of lightning, and the lag time got shorter and shorter. That wasn't good. Soon, the storm would be overhead. We watched it come eastward straight toward us, until finally it just didn't help to watch any longer. I went in my tent and cursed to myself, bracing for the worst. But somehow the lightning passed around us, off to the north. I lay awake thanking my lucky stars that I wouldn't die.

Next morning, alive, tired and frustrated, we hustled down the trail to Inspiration Point. From there, we looked down over the rooftops of miniscule Creede, tucked down low in between cliffs. The buildings looked like pinheads. We got lost one more time while searching for the descent down the cliffs; then we spent hours descending a switchbacking dirt road until we grew impatient and turned off for a cross-country tumble down a steep, grassy, animal-hole-littered hillside. We reached town exhausted, our legs numb, shaking like jelly. It was Thursday, June 16.

Street Creed.

Creede was an old mining town in aptly named Mineral County and was quite fantastically wedged between two cliff walls in East Willow Creek Canyon. The town's elevation was 8,852 feet, but it felt like sea level because the close cliffs dwarfed it. We climbed gradually to the town's northernmost narrow quarters where it was greatly confined. The city was a mere one-hundred-feet wide up there. That top part of town was almost in the cliff wedge, and held two cafés, two small hotels, an old mining museum, and not many people around. The whole place had an old-Western feel, like a relic from the past. You felt like time stood still there.

We took a room at the Firehouse Café and Hotel. The building dated to 1892, as did just about everything else in the mining boomtown. The ground floor held a clean café and had firefighting equipment decorating its walls. Interior stairs in the café led to a carpeted loft where there were sofas and three computers. Across the street stood the Creede Hotel and Restaurant, much larger than ours but less cozy. Beside it was the Creede Repertory Theatre with nightly shows in the summertime since 1966. That top part of town wedged between the cliffs held the center of the action.

Creede's current population was fewer than one thousand people, but in the peak of its bustle, when Nick Creede discovered silver here in 1890, miners had flocked in skyrocketing its population to ten thousand citizens. Back then, tramcars had carried a million dollars of silver ore monthly down from the cliffs to railcars in town. The town'd had saloons, gamblers, dance hall girls, and even gunfighters like Bob Ford, who'd killed Jesse James. They liked to say that in those days the city never slept. There was a Creede town song written in 1892 by the newspaper editor:

Here's a land where all are equal—of high or lowly birth,
A land where men make millions, dug from the dreary
earth.
Here meek and mild-eyed burros on mineral mountains
feed,
It's day all day in the daytime,
ALL SING: AND THERE IS NO NIGHT IN CREEDE!
The cliffs are solid silver, with wondrous wealth untold.
And the beds of the running rivers are lined with the
purest gold.
While the world is filled with sorrow, and hearts must
break and bleed,
It's day all day in the daytime,
ALL SING: AND THERE IS NO NIGHT IN CREEDE!

The squeaky-clean Firehouse Café served me delicious Caesar salad, Coca Cola, potato skins. Weekender and I sat stuffing our faces while talking with our waiter and waitress who were both teenagers from Germany. They were here on a summer work exchange: *"Bitte shon, noch ein Weiss Bier!"* I told them that I'd lived in Germany and had played team tennis there. They were only mildly interested. So I got to practice my German.

We walked down the street to buy groceries. The Porno-Sausage-Mule trio wasn't due to arrive for another day or so, and Todd and Pony Express wouldn't be arriving for at least two days. Or so we'd thought. That was why we were utterly shocked when Todd emerged from a bar onto the sidewalk right in front of us and ushered us inside where we found all the others sitting there, too. what? They'd all just arrived, he said. It was a catastrophe! I was devastated. How could they be here? I needed nothing more than to rest, but now this put my rest time in jeopardy. We sat and drank beer for an hour.

"We almost died of lightning last night," Todd said, smoking away.

"Jesus," I said, ignoring that and still not wanting to believe this was happening: "How did you guys get here so quickly?"

"We bailed out," Todd said.

Bailing out means dropping off a high ridge to low ground, and taking a low route to a road or a town. Todd and Pony Expresss'd had such a bad lightning scare on their second night that they'd dropped eastward down off the high ridge of the Western San Juans, and Todd had refused to climb back up. Part of that, I couldn't help but imagine, was that Todd probably hadn't been enjoying himself hiking alone with "my feet are as hard as rock" Pony

Express, as I hadn't enjoyed hiking with that guy, either. Todd'd then told Pony Express to go ahead and do whatever he wanted, and to climb back up and continue on alone if he pleased, but that he was heading to Creede. Pony Express thought the better of it, so he'd relented and stuck with Todd. The others had just come straight in.

I felt sick and achy, like a fever was coming on. I had chills. I walked back to the Firehouse Café, climbed to the loft and lay on a sofa with my jacket over me. I closed my eyes and tried to relax. I tried mentally preparing myself for the immanent announcement that our big group was heading back out. I wasn't ready, but I'd have to drag myself up and go. I drifted in and out of sleep. The others came and went—washed laundry, ate meals downstairs, used the computers beside me. Hours passed. Then Pony Express climbed to the loft and announced that he was leaving. And did anyone want to go with him? There was silence. So off he went to hike the entire rest of the way to Canada alone. It'd been fast hiking with Pony Express, and I realized quite clearly that sticking with him would have gotten me to Canada by my September 1 deadline. But it wouldn't be fun. I'd no desire to hike with him ever again.

Team Locust Is Born.

I still felt guilty over my hitch the final day into Grants and my hitch into Chama, but now things were at least somewhat partially evening out because the others had all missed spots, too. Todd and Weekender'd hiked only one day in the South San Juans, and Todd had hiked only one day in the Western San Juans. Even mighty Pony Express had spent only one day in the Western San Juans. There's a badge of honor associated with never taking shortcuts, never skipping even a mile. I'd lived by that code on my previous two hikes, and I aspired to live by it out here, too. But none of us seemed able to. It was just the current state of the trail. We were all doing the best we could, trying to connect places and towns. Many hikers loved the CDT precisely because there was no trail and there were no rules. But it was the walking and hiking I liked, not the course-charting and route-finding maze, not the walking along paved roads. The CDT's elusive and inconsistent nature had unfortunately made me dependent on the others. I kissed good-bye my solitary tendencies and tried to make the best of it. I tried bonding with the new guys.

Porno-Sausage-Mule. They dressed like clones, all wearing identical long tan pants and tan shirts, so they all looked like Fidel Castro. None of them shaved, and so that only heightened the Fidel-Effect. I hadn't gotten to know them at all back in Chama because they'd kept to themselves there, but I made an effort here.

"Why do they call you Porno?" I asked the muscular one, the leader of the group.

"Because my last name is Porto."

That was a relief.

"Why do they call you Sausage?" I asked the quiet, political one.

"Just before the hike, I got horrible poison ivy on my legs. My legs looked like sausage. Call me Brett."

Another relief.

"Why do they call you Mule?" I asked the nervous, bobble-headed one.

"I don't know. Call me Gabe."

Porno, Brett, and Gabe.

Porno was the leader. With brown hair and growing beard and mustache, he was stocky and borderline barrel-chested with an upper body like Perry's in Truman Capote's In Cold Blood. His appetite was insatiable, and he was perfectly crude. He wasn't afraid to fart, stuff his face, or say whatever came to his mind. He was smart, and he was consistent. I could tell right away that what you saw was what you got with Porno, and I liked that about him. He was upbeat and cheerful. He was a rare breed and one of the most uncynical people I'd ever met. He ate the most, drank the most, farted the most. Porno hadn't met Old Man Weekender on the PCT, and their personal styles weren't going to mesh—but they'd have Todd as their go-between, so that'd work out. Besides, Pastor Weekender was accepting of everything, and Porno just wouldn't have cared one way or another. Porno carried the heaviest backpack of us all. He did most of the planning for his trio, and when I saw him kneeling before row upon row of organized food like power bars, prepackaged dinners, tuna fish, and all manner of things, then I couldn't believe that those three were going to be able to eat all that tremendous amount of food in just the five days it'd take us to reach the next trail town. That was why it surprised me when I'd asked him about all that food for his trio, and he'd answered, "Huh? What? No, this is all just for me."

Porno wore a yellow "Cal" baseball hat. Brown-haired Porno (noisy) and black-haired Brett (quiet) had been fraternity brothers and house roommates together at Cal-Berkeley. Muscular Porno had an electrical engineering degree, while Brett had pursued environmental studies. Both were marketable, they admitted. Both were fit and athletic. They were the same height, just slightly shorter than me. Unlike Porno, Brett wasn't the least bit crude. He had more artifice to him. Brett wore a mesh, nylon, runner's jogging cap. He had impeccable manners and he seemed like the deepest one of us because he was mostly so quiet that he seemed to be brooding. Taciturn Brett was a suave, pensive, and polished son of a lawyer. The strange thing was that frat brothers Crass Porno and Smooth Brett didn't seem to talk much to each other. They went way back together, and it seemed either that they didn't feel the need to chitchat or that they'd simply exhausted all that they had to say to one another. But you could tell that they respected each other and that if push came to shove, then they had each other's backs. They got along well, if only by silent communication.

Gabe was the odd one out, all jiggly and filled with neuroses. You looked at him and thought: bobble-head toy. Gabe was just barely the tallest of their trio. He had curly hair under a green barrette, which made him look especially like Fidel Castro. Gabe's saving grace was that he at least made some effort to cut back his facial hair. Gabe, it took about fifteen seconds to witness, followed Porno's lead on everything, so that if Porno audibly farted for comic affect, then Gabe would be there to belly laugh and then immediately fart back as quickly as he could. Gabe was from Virginia and was a Virginia Tech graduate who'd studied photography and had then moved out to California where he'd met the others while working in a bicycle shop. Gabe was the least athletic in our group, but he had the highest IQ. You had to watch what you said to him as he was defensive and mercurial like me, and no one could more quickly or lethally whip something back. Meanwhile, Gabe giggled constantly with Porno. And whenever he could, Gabe seemed to take little swiping jabs at Brett—tiny digs here and there—as if to try to draw a wedge between the old fraternity brothers and then crawl down into the opening to get himself in tighter with Porno. Brett, very much to his credit, rose above it in that he never punched Gabe in the face. Brooding, taciturn Brett never said a word in return, but just took it. He carried himself with great dignity and pride, and you could tell that nothing Gabe said actually bothered him in the slightest.

So that was the CDT—if you had a trio like the Fidel Castro communists Porno-Brett-Gabe, or even a partnership like Todd and Weekender's, you could stick together and keep your cool and plan and figure things out and not get lonely (and laugh when you're lost). It was harder being alone. My plan was to stick with that group. I didn't know what it'd mean—if we'd hike six of us all together, or if we'd remain as two groups of three. Nobody talked about it. There wasn't any real plan. I didn't have any say in the matter. I was just hoping that they'd let me tag on.

By late afternoon it'd become clear that we'd be staying overnight in town. The young guys walked down the street and ate hotdogs from a street vendor. Then Todd, Porno, Brett, and Gabe sat in an empty baseball diamond and discussed arranging a place to sleep. They knew they could stay at the Firehouse Café with Weekender and me, but the weather was mild and the town was quiet so they considered saving money and sleeping in the baseball dugout. Todd turned silly. He said: "I'm going to sit here and wait for something good to happen to me." Thirty minutes later, a woman came along and invited them to sleep in her trailer. They accepted, and that night the woman took them drinking at the bars. Weekender went to meet them while I slept alone back at the hotel with my sore throat and chills.

The trailer home woman had spent all night trying to molest Todd, they told me that next morning, Friday, June 17. While drunk, they'd invented some new trail names. Todd had become "Noodle," and for me they'd invented the trail name, "Cave Dweller." It wasn't meant to be flattering. But I liked it. I

107

was Cave Dweller because they said it was clear that I'd rather stay back at the hotel and dwell alone inside my cave than hit the town and go out drinking with them. I loved the name. Little did they know how accurately they'd hit the nail on the head. I was out here on the trail without my Prozac, just wanting to hole up alone in my room. Dwell in my cave. Pull down the shades. Block out the sun. Block out the world and never come out. I was Cave Dweller on the CDT!

The others all had hangovers. We went grocery shopping at the market down the street. Then Todd announced the greatest news in the world, that we'd take a zero day. I was overjoyed. I couldn't have heard any dearer news. I needed this zero day in Creede. We'd all just realized that this town was too special to race away from. We lounged in the loft above the restaurant.

"Hey, read this," Porno said, ushering us over to his computer screen.

It was the Web page of a CDT through-hiker from a prior summer, who'd written of hiking the CDT in Montana's Glacier National Park. He'd written that Glacier's park rangers get angry over boorish behavior, thus warning us not to go in there with "AT attitudes." He explained that having an Appalachian Trail attitude meant being an "Amateur Asshole." Somehow that touched a nerve, because all the rest of the day we kept joking and laughing incessantly about having AT Attitudes and being Amateur Assholes. It just seemed funny to us at the time.

"What do you expect, we're just Amateur Assholes," Porno said.

"Dude, don't sell me short," Gabe said, parroting Porno, as always: "I'm quite majorly a professional asshole."

"That's true, actually. We're *professional* assholes."

"Totally."

"Professional assholes." We all nodded.

"We suck the life out of the trail."

"We suck the life out of all the trail towns."

"And all the bars."

"And all the women."

"We suck the life out of everything good and decent in the world, all the way from Mexico to Canada!"

"We invade trail towns like a pack of locusts."

"Like a swarm of locusts."

"We're Team Locust," Todd said, puffing away on his hand-rolled cigarette.

"TEAM LOCUST!" we all agreed.

He'd coined a phrase.

"Our motto is: 'What can YOU do for US?'"

"What have you done for us lately?"

"Careful—that's an 'AT Attitude.'"

It was the birth of Team Locust: Todd, Weekender, Porno, Brett, Gabe, and me as the Cave Dweller.

"We're team locust—sucking the will out of America."

"Sucking the nation's will to live."

"We need matching Team Locust T-shirts."

"A yellow bolt of lightning on the front."

"A swooping locust on the back."

"With outstretched talons."

"A swooping locust that looks like an eagle, with eyes bugged out."

"And outstretched tentacles."

"American Thunder!" —Porno sang, playing his air guitar— *"Burning through the night!"*

Lumberjacks In Love.

The Creede Repertory Theatre, across the street, suddenly figured into our stay. I'd met a young woman named Renee Prince who'd stood buying ice cream in the Firehouse Café. I'd overheard her mention something about "the show," so I'd asked her about it. She was an actress who'd moved there from Chicago, she told me, and she also ran the youth acting troupe for local children. She was so nice that I could easily imagine her working with kids. I'm sure that all the kids in that town must've loved her. I told her what we were doing and she became intrigued by the concept of through-hiking. She said that she'd have six free tickets waiting for us at the theatre counter for that evening's performance.

That night we watched the play Lumberjacks In Love, a farce about four lumberjacks, one of whom is secretly a woman disguised as a man. The woman falls in love with one of the men, but she doesn't want to give away her identity and risk losing her job. Things get awkward when he (she) begins to flirt. It was a comedy, but we felt touched and almost moved to tears during the plaintive solo of one of the lumberjacks who began singing about how he was a dirty person due to his having lost a bar of magic blue soap when he was a child. He hadn't been able to adequately wash and clean himself since. That resonated. We could feel for the guy. We could identify. The guy was ever-hopeful that his magic bar of soap would one day turn up. It was his greatest wish in life. He sang:

> *I will be clean, I will be clean,*
> *I will be clean someday.*

We practically gave Lost-Soap man a standing ovation. Renee took the others out drinking that night. She introduced them to the cast. While I slunk back to dwell in my cave. We were going to leave in the morning, and I wanted to be ready for it. The others stayed out late and even got free lodging thrown into the deal. Renee's fiancé owned the Creede Hotel adjacent to the theatre, and they invited the group to sleep in his house behind the hotel. They accepted. Except that Todd disappeared for the night.

Early morning on Saturday, June 18, Team Locust sat waiting on the sidewalk in front of the Creede Hotel waiting for our missing link, Todd the Noodle. Todd was the preeminent cigarette-smoking barfly among us. He would bide his time on bar stools, surveying rooms while drinking his vodka tonics. His hair sticking straight into the air and his green bandana around his neck. He hadn't come home and now wasn't answering his cell phone. We had no idea where he was. All but me were badly hungover. Nervous Gabe clumsily threw on his backpack while tinkering around on the sidewalk, and his ice axe smacked a hanging potted plant knocking it off its hook so it shattered on the pavement—little dying flower lying at our feet in spilled dirt and broken clay. The flower'd been adding beauty to Creede, but now it was ruined. That flower had become a statistic, murdered in cold blood by insensitive brutes. It symbolized everything about us. We looked down and realized that Team Locust had officially overstayed its welcome.

10
Cave Dweller

This is a perfect *day for Bananafish.*

—J.D. Salinger

Through Creede's Crack.

Squash is chess at two hundred miles an hour. You play in a four-walled room. A shot hit down the line along the wall is called a rail, and that's your rook, moving any number of spaces in a straight line. A crosscourt shot is the bishop, moved any number of spaces diagonally. A short little drop shot poked into the front corners is a pawn, and an all-powerful, rangy, aggressive volleying player who hits anywhere to any length is the queen. The only three-dimensional chessboard piece is the knight which can pass through pieces without knocking them over or capturing them, and the squash equivalent of that is called a boast, which is a wild card. It's a shot that you hit into the side wall nearest you—hit at an angle sufficient enough to cause it to ricochet to the front wall where it ricochets again to the opposite front corner. That shot's needed from the back corners, for when a ball gets behind you, you'll soon run out of room to keep chasing it, so instead you simply turn your body to face the back wall or the corner and you hit the boast. Squash is a game of positioning, like chess. It's a game of hitting shots that keep the ball out of the middle, for that enables you to hold the middle of the court with your body to be in the best possible position to run and retrieve your opponent's next shot. You want your opponent behind you, stuck in the back corners where he can't hurt you.

Great physical conditioning is essential, and one beautiful thing about the

111

sport is that you can play it in order to get into shape to play it. It serves as its own conditioning. When you're a squash coach and you want to get your players amazingly fit, you can send them onto the court and tell them: "Go play squash." The players who take this sport seriously and achieve do the crazy conditioning things like running star drills for ninety minutes without pause (running back and forth to six different spots on the court), and sprinting fifty times up a steep hill just for kicks. There was a Swedish guy who once rode his bike to Tibet, climbed to the summit of Mt. Everest without oxygen, then rode his bike home again. That guy was a squash player.

Tennis players pick up squash quickly, as the sports are closely related: both evolved from the very old game of court tennis. But tennis players aren't used to contending with walls, so they have a hell of a time in the back corners. You plug away hitting shots into the back corners, until ultimately you stick one in there so well that it forces a weak reply which comes to the middle of the court. At the moment your opponent gives you such a loose ball, you can put it away in the front with a drop shot. Or do the opposite, by pressing forward with an offensive drop shot early in the rally to put your opponent under pressure, and then close in behind and cut off the reply with a winning volley to length.

College coaches teach patience, teach hammering away at the back corners. They utter Zen-like strategies such as: "Don't try to end the rally—the rally will tell you when it's time to end." It might win matches, but sometimes that leads to play that's so conservative it's not fun (the United States Naval Academy guys just stand muscularly on the T and hit endlessly into the back corners). Sometimes you have to take chances. Sometimes you have to shoot for winners or throw in short stuff simply to see how your opponent reacts. Hit offensive boasts. Create chaos. Stir the pot, simply to see what rises up. It might be undisciplined, but at least it's fun!

Badminton players convert well to squash because they're wristy and they lunge. Alpine skiers as well as dancers convert well because they have focus, leg strength, and balance. They have good training habits, too. But the best converts are hockey players because they're so aggressive and physical. They, too, have strong legs and great balance. They have excellent hands, and if you bump into a hockey player, then you just bounce right off. The natural motion of squash is a gliding movement around the court, very much like skating. Both sports are similar in that they require never-ending flow. Only difference is that hockey games can end at 0–0, while in squash you must actually tally points.

A standard drill is called Rotating Rails. Two players move to the right wall and keep a continuous rally of deep rails going, hitting down the line with alternating shots (later, do the same on the left wall). There's no keeping score and no hitting drop shots. You have to clear out of the way for your opponent every time. You can do this drill endlessly. You can hit hundreds and thousands of rails along the wall, and no matter how seemingly perfect you make them, no two rails will ever be exactly the same. No two points will ever be played exactly the same. It's like waves coming ashore, or snowflakes falling. No two waves are identical—but there are patterns. Patterns emerge. There are rhyming patterns, familiar patterns, and sequences of shots during squash points that grow recognizable to the expert player. The game is gorgeous to watch. It simply doesn't televise real well, and that's kept it from being in the Olympics.

There are lobs and drops in squash, so it's not just a matter of smashing away. Service aces and service winners don't occur. That's the best part of the game. It's what distinguishes it from tennis, where service winners are routine and disrupt flow. You get only one serve in squash, and the serve is slapped almost perfunctorily into play and is always returned. The rallies are long. And when a rally ends, the ball is nearby (perhaps even rolling toward you!), so it's effortlessly gathered up and the next point is served. Traditional scoring is to nine points and you only win a point when you serve. Whoever wins the rally serves the next point, so if you keep winning rallies, then you keep serving. Three out of five games wins a match.

There's remarkably little downtime in squash. In that regard, it's different from tennis. An experiment once showed that in an hour's time on the tennis court during a segment of the Wimbledon final with Becker playing Edberg in 1995, they dissected film of the match and determined that only eight minutes were spent actually playing tennis during that hour. The rest of the time was spent walking around, changing sides, adjusting strings, arguing over line calls, or missing first serves. Granted, that was on fast grass with two serve and volleyers and not two baseliner dirt-ballers on slow red clay at the French. Still. In squash, though, in an hour's time, a full forty-five minutes or more are spent playing. It's a better ratio. It's a better workout in a shorter amount of time in a more social setting. Your opponent is right beside you, and you can joke with the person if you want. It's a perfect city sport. That's why there are more squash courts than tennis courts in Manhattan. It's the perfect lunchtime sport on Wall Street.

Amazingly, when Todd finally arrived on the sidewalk on the morning of June 18, with all five of us waiting and ready to leave, he walked past us and inside the Firehouse Café to order and eat breakfast while we waited longer, still. How brazen! And none of us moved. We didn't leave without him. I would've left early just for the insult, except that National Geographic map 139 showed a confusing area back in the mines north of town through the cliff wedge, and I didn't wish to get lost. We needed Todd's navigation skills. I was itching to leave, though. Todd finally finished and we all set out—six of us—through the cliff crevasse at the northernmost end of town.

Beyond the mountain crack at the northern tip of Creede, we climbed a dirt road up past dozens of old, historic mines, switchbacking into the mountainsides. The dirt road ended in a small lot where we picked up a trail which took us higher still. We climbed gradually, steadily, for four hours without a rest. It felt like a race. There was definite testing going on. It was our first time hiking all together and it was like we were all trying to prove ourselves to each other. Nobody wanted to back down or be exposed as the weakest link. Todd brought up the rear, but that was only because he seemed to be operating on no sleep. He reeked of cigarettes and beer. It was on his clothes and came out in his sweat. He hadn't hiked nearly as strongly as he normally would've, but to his credit he kept his head down, his mouth closed, and kept up. Porno'd already known that Todd could hike, from the time they'd spent together on the PCT, but Brett and Gabe hadn't yet seen the real Todd and didn't know the extent of his considerable skills. They just thought he was a burnout.

The climb from Creede at 8,800 feet took us up above tree line to 12,800 feet where we stood on top of San Luis Pass. We were back under way, back on the Divide. The whole world lay spread before us. Todd bent over with hands on his knees on top of that pass after our four-thousand-foot climb. He was having a lousy day. He coughed and yelled: "That's it—I quit smoking!"

"For good?"

"Forever?"

"Well, no—but at least until we finish the entire rest of Colorado," he said.

Swimming.

Mt. San Luis marked the beginning of Colorado's "Fourteeners." There are fifty-two fourteen-thousand-foot peaks in Colorado, and we were climbing into them. North of San Luis Pass was a snowy winter wonderland inside a giant bowl. Mt. San Luis rose 14,014 feet high across the bowl, to the north-west. Weekender led us for three miles, dropping into the snowy bowl and traversing and postholing across it. Weekender paved the way, and the rest of us followed in the path that he cut through the snow. We came to a side trail that climbed to Mt. San Luis' summit, and Todd began salivating to detour and climb up it. Even in his damaged, sleepless, beer-smelling state, he begged us to detour and climb San Luis, but we wouldn't. We kept to the task at hand. Todd'd used up our collective patience by keeping us all waiting earlier that morning back in town. This was payback.

Four peak-bagging hikers descended off the prominent side trail from San Luis' peak and asked us questions, expressing concern over their having to walk southward through the three-mile snow-bowl that we'd just traversed and climbed out of. They'd climbed San Luis up a snowless route, and now they were heading for Creede. Their group hadn't yet experienced postholing. We assured them that they'd be fine. We'd walked through so much snow in the past two weeks that we no longer even gave it a thought. At dusk we saw two

114

elk on a slope beside the trail. We were seeing deer and elk constantly.

We slept beside Cochetopa Creek, on Skyline Trail 465, which showed clearly on National Geographic map 139. The National Geographic maps were remarkably helpful. On the back of each individual map was a Colorado map divided into boxed sections that were numbered to correspond with the maps. Another beautiful thing about the National Geographic Colorado maps was that they marked the Continental Divide Trail. To hike Colorado, you could look at the back grid on any of the individual maps, and see that you needed (in order, progressing northbound): maps 142, 140, 139, 130, 129, 110, 109, 108, 104, 103, 102, 106, 115, 118, 117, and 116. Each map cost about ten dollars, which was just another expense on the trip. That National Geographic had tremendous contour maps for Colorado had nothing to do with the Continental Divide Trail Association. That made me want to curse the CDTA even more.

It's a rare pleasure and a gift from the hiking gods to be able to start a hiking day with a long gradual descent, which was what we had here, on June 19. We casually descended for several hours alongside Cochetopa Creek. We reached level ground and the creek widened and deepened, offering swimming and fishing holes. A few trucks were parked here, having come down from the north on a dirt road. We swam awhile and did backflips off the riverbank, but then quite unfortunately the others lay down for a very long rest. I tried to be okay with it. I tried to relax. But the pause felt disruptive. Track star and homophobic Pony Express with his Hard-as-Rock-Feet never would've stopped here. Neither would my old PCT friend Zoomsteen or many of the other PCT crazies with whom I'd hiked.

In Team Locust, I was the only one in the group with a deadline. My need was to zoom up the trail and hike big miles in order to reach Canada in time to return to my job at the college by September 1, but I wasn't going to get any big miles if I stuck with this group. That sealed my fate, and I knew it. My emergency wasn't their emergency. Facing a deadline feels antithetical to the wilderness experience, yet mine was a reality. Hikers love to be carefree. And I needed to learn to enjoy such moments as this in life. But all I could feel was panic and rage. All I could think of was that I couldn't afford it—swimming, lounging, and sunbathing weren't going to get me to Canada in time.

Team Locust was strong and was easily capable of hiking big miles, but they just weren't interested. It all came down to that. Yet along with my deadline came the simple fact that I just like to be on the go. Through-hiking isn't merely about the wilderness experience, after all, but it's also very much about motion. I like to keep moving. I enjoy the flow. So during the break I kept quiet. I sat listening to their jokes and their Carmen from South Park imitations: "I'm Jennifer Lopez, I like tacos and kesses." The length of the break was excruciating for me. I tried not to panic, tried not to think about Canada. Tried not to think about how at this rate I'd never meet my deadline. I didn't say anything to them about it. There was nothing that I could say: "Excuse me but could you alter all the plans that you've made to have a leisurely CDT hike, and instead stop taking all these breaks and start busting it and start speeding up so that I can reach Canada?" That wouldn't have gone over well.

One option existed. That was for me to simply stand up and walk northward alone. Leave Team Locust behind. Not a single thing was stopping me from doing that. Except that I wasn't Pony Express. I'd get lonely and I'd get lost. The National Geographic maps for Colorado were so good that I would've been able to negotiate this state—but then I'd be mapless and lost for Wyoming and Montana because National Geographic didn't make maps for those two states (or New Mexico). And if I was going to be eaten by a grizzly bear in Montana, then I least I wanted to have company while it happened. No, I stayed put. My fate was sealed. I was screwed. I was shit out of luck.

A dirt road took us northward off the river across exposed, featureless ground. John Denver'd never sang about this. The others all wore iPods and listened to music, except Porno. I hiked up alongside him and remarked that we were the only two not wearing iPods. I was about to ask if he agreed with me that listening to music while hiking distracts from the experience, when he told me how mad he was that his iPod batteries had died. I felt like a Luddite.

Weekender assumed the lead as per usual and sucked us swiftly along, as if to make up for our long river pause. It was surge hiking: pause-race; pause-race—repeat all summer. It didn't make sense to me. But there was nothing I could do. They were the ones who'd planned to meet and hike together. I was merely the guy who was crashing the party. I was just clinging onto their coattails.

The next day, June 20, I set out ahead alone that next morning, but that was only because the route was clear. I climbed a steep, heart-pounding, lungs-heaving dirt road up to The Spanish Divide. The others caught up, except for Gabe. He was the slowest one in our group. Jason and Brett would take turns lagging behind to wait for him. That kept Todd, Weekender, and me always at least a little ahead of the trio of hairy, tan-clothed communists.

Patterns Emerge.

Like during squash points, patterns began to emerge: Porno-Brett-Gabe would stop for long breaks through the course of the day, and Todd and Old Man Weekender joined them by stretching their own already long breaks just that little bit longer. They'd take a one-hour midmorning break, a one-hour lunch break, and a one-hour dinner break. It was three hours daily spent sitting by the trail. That could've been ten extra miles every day. That was the difference between hiking twenty-mile days and hiking thirty-mile days like I'd done on the second half of the PCT. It wasn't heroic. In olden times, hikers'd grab just an apple, a hunk of cheese, and a loaf of bread and hike all day without stopping. It wasn't purely that I needed to hike like a speedster,

116

but also I simply enjoy continuity.

Something had to give. On our third day past Creede, my threesome again got far out ahead of the bearded, hairy communists. We climbed over the summit of 11,685-foot Middle Baldy Mountain, and for ten miles eastward after that I leapfrogged through rolling woods hour by hour with Todd and Weekender—me, alone as the tortoise who kept going; and they, together as the hare who'd swiftly catch up but then sit to rest while I continued ahead. The trail was easy to follow. Those past few days, we'd been seeing occasional CDT emblems. It felt startling, almost disorienting to see them. If the entire trail had been marked this way, then I could've gone on alone and sped up. Others would've been out here, too, if this trail was connected and marked. That would've allowed me to continue alone and meet new and different people. And meet my deadline.

Todd and Weekender caught up with me again near the summit of 11,885-foot Windy Peak. Todd removed his pack and climbed cross-country over boulders up to Windy Peak's summit. I didn't wait, but set out alone descending three miles northward to the low point of 10,882-foot landmark Marshall Pass with its paved road, park, and small cement restroom. I sat at Marshall Pass waiting for the others. I was expecting Todd and Weekender to catch up. I was just ten miles south of Monarch Pass and Highway 50, from where we'd exit to the town of Salida. I was anxious to get there. Just ten more miles would do it. I was right where I needed to be. I felt strong. But the others never showed.

I waited thirty minutes for Todd and Weekender. A storm swiftly built, again, as per usual: you could set your watch by it. Every midafternoon—lightning. The sky turned black. Six motorcyclists rode into the park, about to get drenched, but there were no cars. It wasn't the imminent rain that I feared, but lightning. Thunder began to peal. I couldn't wait any longer. I didn't want to get trapped in the restroom. Instead, I jumped up and raced northward up the trail. It began as a jeep road through forest; then it narrowed into a single track and popped out of the trees and across a boulder field beneath the western base of the cliffs of behemothian 13,971-foot Mount Ouray. My heart began pounding in my chest, for down came the rain, and then sure enough out came the lightning.

I raced across open ground. It wasn't smart to continue, but I crouched down—as if that would help! —and pushed forward across the boulder field and back into trees. Again came the now familiar fear of dying by lightning. It's absolutely terrifying to know that if a bolt strikes you, it'll be too late. You won't even be around to know that it's happened. You'll just be gone—deceased—that's all. The lightning passed, but rain continued falling periodically. I hustled through another brief forest and then across two vast, open, snowy plateaus. I climbed a mountainside covered by a deep snow bluff. The packed snow was easy to walk on. I made excellent time. In a ten-minute span, I saw a deer, an elk, and a fox. The final three miles were an easy descent down a mildly graded trail to Monarch Pass at Highway 50. I'd hiked roughly thirty-two miles on the day. That was more like it. That was the way it was supposed to be.

No Bathtub.

Monarch Pass had a huge concrete slab parking lot as its central feature. There was one building, a gift shop. All that up at eleven thousand feet and with Highway 50 crossing over the mountains here to connect all the people on one side with those on the other. I stumbled into the gift shop to buy ice cream and sign a register. The place was filled with automobile travelers out stretching their legs and buying postcards of the mountains. Everyone clean and nobody noticing me. My body was muddy and dirty. I was wet and wearing my backpack. Still, I could've been invisible for all anyone cared.

My body'd begun to shut down. It wasn't anything serious, just that my back rapidly stiffened up. I couldn't blame it, though, after all that I'd put it through that day—the carrying and the climbing over mountains. I needed to hurry and get to wherever it was I was going before I crashed. I needed to get off my feet. For days, I'd been dreaming of soaking in a warm bath. I felt overjoyed knowing that it was about to happen.

Outside, I stuck out my thumb. I got a ride almost instantly, twenty-three miles eastward down off the mountains to the low trail town of Salida at seven thousand feet. I stepped out at a strip of hotels outside town. Salida was good-sized by trail-town standards, with six thousand people. It was just barely an EEP town, with its Elevation Exceeding its Population. That meant that it wouldn't be owned by huge chain-store conglomerates. No vacancy at the first hotel, nor at the second. I was walking to a third when a woman in a compact car with a baby in the back pulled over and kidnapped me, taking me back to her house for dinner with her husband and kids. It was well-intentioned and generous of her, but it turned out to be a mistake. It'd all just happened so fast.

I ended up spending two hours with that woman. I'd been initially thrilled for someone to talk to—for someone to take an interest in me and give me the chance to learn local knowledge and gain information. But once in her car and later in her house, waiting for dinner, waiting for her eldest child to return from karate, I realized that I was in trouble. I was trapped. I'd no need of a family meal. I couldn't find the strength to force myself to be gracious and polite. Instead, my only need was to shut down. I needed to crash. I felt physically horrible in my aching skeleton. I felt mentally terrible, too. I desperately needed to slink into Cave Dweller mode and escape from the world. Take a long, warm bath. Wash with soap. Shave. Eat chocolate. Drink ice water. Lie in a comfortable bed. Make my few telephone calls. Call my ex-wife Cristina. Maybe call Jessie Gibbins, too.

118

My hostess had hiked the Appalachian Trail twenty years earlier, she told me, back when she was nineteen. It was why she'd pulled over to kidnap me in the first place. She'd seen my backpack and had identified me as a CDT through-hiker, then rushed in to help. She hadn't completed the AT, but almost. She said that she'd always wished to go back. It was still there, I told her. Their small house sat on the bank of the Arkansas River, which flowed southward into and through Salida. Whitewater kayakers flocked here and mingled with the local hippies.

Downtown had bars, coffee shops, kayaking outfitter rental stores, and an outrageously well-stocked backpacking store. There was Laughing Ladies Restaurant, Bongo Billy's Café On the River, Dakota's Bistro, Cornucopia Bakery, Dot Candy, Pizza Works, and Maicas Wood Fired Pizza. A professional kayaking course hung above the river beside a downtown park, with gates dangling from trees branches. Spectators watched from the park or from a bridge that led over the river. A huge S made of white stones lay 550 feet above downtown on a mountainside just across the river to the north, and signified Salida.

I sat at my family dinner and my back ached. I couldn't bare it any longer. I knew clearly that I needed to escape and lie down. My father had once incredibly asked me what was the benefit of getting diagnosed with a mental disorder, as opposed to living with an undiagnosed one. He was okay. He'd never had one and just didn't understand. Still, he lived with my mother. So it baffled me that he either couldn't or hadn't bothered to think it through. The answer is that knowing takes the fear away and makes the episode less toxic. Gone is the panic. It's replaced by a simple understanding. The next step is to act. I tried to stay with it. But when my hostess invited me to set up my tent to sleep in their backyard by the river my inner voice screamed: no, I don't want this! I excused myself. For she had me confused with someone younger. With some broke kid on the trail. I was older. I wasn't trying to save money.

"Please," I said. "I need a hotel room."

The Thomas House Bed and Breakfast opened its door to me thirty minutes later. It was downtown, fourteen blocks down from my host home. I'd walked over after having first reached them by phone. I'd called the two inns that were downtown. Both were expensive, both had one vacancy. The Thomas House won my heart because they'd answered affirmatively to the very pressing question that I'd asked: "Does my room have a bathtub?" They'd said, yes it does. That was all I cared about. Thomas House had four rental rooms, and the only vacancy was their luxury suite. I took it. The room was fantastic. I set down my things and undressed for my bath. However, to my utter confusion and disappointment, I entered the bathroom and inexplicably found a shower but no bathtub.

That couldn't be true. I couldn't get my mind around it. I'd asked them so clearly, "Does my room have a bathtub?" It was the only question that I'd asked. It hadn't been a complicated question. And they hadn't given me a complicated answer. They'd immediately said, "Yes, it does." Now, I found out that it wasn't true. Imagine having your heart ripped from your chest. I wish that I'd felt only as bad as that at this moment. I lacked the energy to cause a scene. My scenes aren't pretty, so my lacking energy was a good thing.

I called Cristina. My ex-wife. My friend. My inspiration and life savior. She was the only one who could help me get through this. I was crashing. Then disaster struck again. For I'd just missed her. She'd just left on a three-week vacation back home to Spain. I'd been dreading that. I needed to hear her voice. There was nobody else that I wanted to talk to. Strange how that works, once you've been married to someone.

I couldn't sleep. I had racing thoughts, and I couldn't shut down my mind. I was perfectly physically able to hike this trail. Even the difficult CDT climbs felt easy for me. Except for when I'd had sore feet on the hot roads down south, I could keep pace with the youngsters. No, my mind was all that was causing me fits. No bathtub, no Cristina, no Prozac, no guidebooks, no larger community of through-hikers. The crippling part was knowing that I'd no chance to finish the trail if I stuck with Team Locust. They were the only group, but sticking with them would mean not finishing. We were only in central Colorado, but I already knew that reality. I could see the writing so very clearly on the wall. Our twenty-mile-a-day pace would find us reaching Canada long after my deadline.

All I had to do was step forward alone. But there was no way I wanted to hike three states all alone. I hadn't been alone on the AT, and I hadn't been alone on the PCT. I'm a loaner, but not a hermit. Still, I wanted to reach Canada, and to do that I'd need to step ahead and bid this group good-bye. I kept waiting for the decision to come to me. Once it hit me, I'd lock my jaws down onto it like a wolverine or a pit bull dog. But it never came. It was like when you're a tiny kid and you stand at the end of the diving board and tell yourself, "Jump!" and you can hear everyone around you saying "Jump!" And you try willing yourself to jump, but you just can't do it.

Everything seemed to be falling apart. I couldn't get over the missing bathtub. It was an overwhelming disappointment. And such a clear case of miscommunication. Quitting never entered my thoughts. I didn't want that. Maybe instead I'd just crash. That my group should name me Cave Dweller spoke volumes. It occurred to me that I should go back on Prozac. I wasn't doing well off it. More than ever before on my hikes, I felt in true danger of a breakdown. Long hikes are emotional. What was I doing here? Why was I off Prozac? Why had I left my job and everything that I loved? I lay awake until daybreak, until five o'clock in the morning, paralyzed with anxiety.

I can adapt and change the structure of a squash practice in the blink of an eye without missing a beat. I can plan a full practice three minutes beforehand and have everything go perfectly. I can handle any situation seamlessly. It'd never been that way for me as a tennis coach. It was just the opposite, which is why I don't coach tennis any longer. Back when I was a tennis coach, practices would go badly. At least it felt that way to me. It didn't matter how carefully I prepared. I could intricately plan things only to see my tennis drills crumble and disintegrate before my eyes. But with squash, I feel like I carry a magic wand. My players are happy; practices are fun; matches are fun; weekend trips are fun. The exercise does something good for their brains. I'm not saying that everything does go right, but just that it feels that way to me. It's comfortable. I feel like I have a dial from 60–100, containing degrees of intensity and that I can incrementally hit any number on any day at any moment based on specificity of need. I can dial upward or downward to exact numbers all through a practice, change on a dime, blow my whistle, wave the wand.

Student evaluations bear me out. Student-athletes at the New England Small Colleges evaluate their coaches after every season. They also evaluate their professors and deans. Soon they'll be evaluating the dining staff and custodians. It gives the students the feeling that we work for them, as if we're their employees instead of our working for the college that they currently attend. Established professors and coaches ultimately stop reading their evaluations. I've reached that point. It just hurts too much to read anything negative after we pour our hearts and souls into our work. I know what mine'll say. I used to read them religiously year after year. The categories include: "Runs organized and efficient practices;" "Cares about the academic well-being of the student;" "Coach displays highest ethical standards;" "Communicates well and effectively with students." For these particular categories I get high, medium, perfect, and low marks on a scale of one to ten.

I disagree only with their perceived sense that I have a mere lukewarm level of caring about their academic well-being. Of course I care. I encourage them to take full advantage of the semester abroad programs, even though it'll take them away from the team. I assure them that it's okay if they miss a practice for academic reasons. I talk about issues with them—about their classes and current events. I don't quite get how I rate medium on that. The only category in which I've hit perfect scores in every year with every team at both schools is that on ethical standards. I'm certain that has something to do with my driving them crazy by always promoting vegetarianism. The low marks I get for communication are deserved because I'm damaged goods. I try counseling my players and try helping them, but I have my own overwhelming issues to deal with.

I awoke from two hours of sleep in Salida's Thomas House to begin the Summer Solstice on the morning of Tuesday, June 21—the first day of summer and the longest day of the year. Things are always better in the light of day. I sat at a communal breakfast over coffee, bread and fresh fruit with a few other lodgers. I heard them refer to "the Jacuzzis out back." Whoah: *WHAT?!* The owners came and verified to me that indeed there were two Jacuzzis out on the back deck that were for guests to use. I almost fell out of my chair, almost choked on a piece of cantaloupe. It would've helped me to have heard that little tidbit the night before. A perfectly delivered line by Adam Sandler in a movie called Wedding Singer suddenly came automatically screaming into my head: "Once again, things that it would've helped me to've known *yesterday!*" I guess when they'd said that there was a bathtub in my room, what they'd really meant was that there were two Jacuzzis out back. The owner said that I'd looked so haggard upon my arrival that he'd assumed I'd just wanted to sleep. So he hadn't given me the tour. He'd planned on waiting until the morning for that. Miscommunication is the story of my life.

I took a zero day in town. I walked a few blocks to a pharmacy and got their fax number. The pharmacist told me that he could fill a prescription. But when I called my famous-surgeon older brother to have him write me up for Prozac, he refused. I was startled by that. It was for a small dosage, and he knew I'd been on it. He knew our family history. Despite that, he said that he didn't feel comfortable and that I should contact my family doctor to get the Prozac. Shit! I didn't want to have to work that hard. I forgot the whole thing. Never mind that I'd barely made it through the night.

I walked past Moonlight Pizza in town and heard:

"CAVE DWELLER!"

They where drunk. It was the five of them, Team Locust, sitting at an outdoor table in front of the pizzeria—huge pizzas and multiple pitchers of beer on the table. They were a good group. I sat with them briefly. They were planning on hitting Salida's bars later. And was I going to join them?

"I can't."

"WHAT?!"

"COME ON!"

"TEAM LOCUST, DUDE!"

They were drunk and were unintentionally shouting.

"DUDE, JAGER SHOTS!" Todd said, no cigarette in front of him for the first time.

"WE'RE SUCKING THE WILL OUT OF AMERICA'S MOUNTAIN TOWNS!"

They toasted and clinked their glasses together, calling: *"TEAM LOCUST: KEE-ARR! KEE-ARR!"*

"No, I'm just going to head back and dwell in my cave."

I returned to take the first of three Jacuzzi soaks that day. My final Jacuzzi came late at night, alone, out back under a clear sky and stars. Jacuzzis don't rate as high for me as warm baths, but it'd do. I stayed up all night again channel surfing on the TV, unable to sleep. If I'm not careful, during the summers when I'm not coaching, I'll shift my sleeping pattern and start staying up later and later. I nervously tossed and turned.

11
Gold, Silver & Guts

Where are all the good men dead,
In the heart or in the head?

—Grosse Point Blank

Group Reforms.

I needed my Team Locust group to reform its ways and speed up the pace, but instead we just reformed, reassembling as a group. It wasn't until late afternoon that I spied the rest of them and descended switchbacks down a cliff to meet them at a lake. We hadn't planned an official rendezvous. I'd slept late at the inn. Then, after only a couple hours of sleep again, it'd taken me forever to motivate, organize, and walk to the edge of town. There, it'd taken me longer than forever to land a ride in hitchhiking back up to Monarch Pass. Todd's ride up, I'd later learn, had been from a model from Los Angeles. She performed in something called The Living Garden, where she'd dress to blend in with hedges and trees for public display or photographs. She'd given Todd her business card and had made him promise that they'd get together the next time that she was in Portland, Oregon. Todd was always striking gold like that. It was his calves. And his spiky hair.

Weekender'd hitched on his own and had met Todd up in the Monarch Pass parking lot amidst thousands of spandex-clad bicyclists who were there on a cross-state tour. A man had approached them, identifying himself as a CDT through-hiker. He hadn't started his hike yet, but was to be a southbounder and was just then on his way driving up to Canada to begin hiking down to

Mexico. He'd sat talking about the trail with Todd and Weekender for two hours. His name was Uncle Green Bean.

I'd been amazed by the mass of bicyclists on Monarch Pass. They stood in twelve lines, each twenty people deep, waiting for their turn in the Port-O-Lets. I'd found a CDT marker on the northern side of Highway 50, and I'd climbed up the slopes of the Monarch Ski Resort. Random ski paraphernalia like broken skis, bent poles, odd gloves, and hats had lain sadly about, post-snowmelt. Upon the summit ridge rose deep snow mounds up at 11,942-feet. The ridge led northward. It'd felt fine to be alone. There was sunshine, easy terrain, and open views. All the others were ahead of me. I just knew. After four miles, I skirted around Bald Mountain's 12,856-foot summit and reached the edge of a cliff where I stood looking down over a miniscule glacial lake. I could make out Team Locust eating dinner below. I'd been the first into and the last out of Salida. Now I'd caught up. It was back to business.

Hope Pass.

June 22–25 found us blazing away, making great northward progress up National Geographic Maps 130, 129, and 127. The hiking was easy. We were nestled inside the mountains. We crossed open plains above tree line and climbed over a succession of passes, each one visible for miles before us. We'd approach, scale a pass, and then descend and head to the next one. It was the most scenic hiking that we'd had yet in Colorado. The San Isabel National Forest lay to the east and the Gunnison National Forest to the west, while mid-twelve-thousand-foot peaks jutted up all over the place. There were snow fields to cross. Our established pattern repeated itself, with Porno-Brett-Gabe taking longer breaks than Todd, Weekender, and myself. At the end of each day, my group would find a tent spot and then an hour later P-B-G would arrive. It was always the same with the jokes at night. One night it'd be South Park jokes. The next night, Chuck Norris jokes. Just random silliness. Always the same post-apocalyptic crap:

"Guns don't kill people, Chuck Norris kills people."

"When Chuck Norris took a vacation to France, the French surrendered, just to be on the safe side."

"Chuck Norris doesn't brush his teeth, he points his fist at his mouth and the plaque jumps out."

"Chuck Norris died ten years ago, but the Grim Reaper can't get up the courage to tell him."

"Behind Chuck Norris' beard isn't a chin; there's just another fist."

"When Chuck Norris is finished having sex, he doesn't ask the woman to leave, he punches her in the vagina."

It was hard to understand: crying, loving, healing, tenderness, compassion, patience, respect, support. Somehow there's a trend to detach and show that you're tough by taking everything that's good and right and decent in the world and turning it upside down. Make fun of everything. It's fine to shake up the system—expose hypocrisy, confront tyranny, battle censorship, deflate self-righteousness. But irreverence must have a limit. I'm diabolically liberal. Unsure. Sad. Concerned. Neurotic to a fault. And yet I don't agree that nothing is sacred. That dark mocking humor seems to shun tender emotions and serves to disallow the world to swallow one up. It's angry self-preservation. But where will callousness lead us? Team Locust loved to tell jokes about each other's mothers. The crudest jokes imaginable, detailing deviant, sordid sexual things that each other's mothers do. Weekender took no part. Neither did Brett nor I. Todd would occasionally get dragged into the fray. It was mostly just Porno and his lapdog Gabe who couldn't get enough. Gabe would've followed Porno anywhere.

On our fourth night past Salida—Saturday, June 25—Todd, Weekender, and I got far out ahead, as usual. We stopped to tent at a campsite by South Fork Clear Creek Road amidst car campers and fishermen who were scattered about in designated campsites. We built a fire, but then it started to rain so we abandoned it and retired to our individual tents. The others never showed.

We awoke on Sunday, June 26, within striking distance of our next trail town, Leadville. To get there, we merely had to scale monstrous 12,620-foot Hope Pass. Two early morning miles north up dirt Clear Creek Road brought us to an abandoned ghost town called Winfield. It had a dozen abandoned small wooden homes that were clean and perfectly preserved. Nobody lived there anymore; it'd been abandoned for decades. Commemorative plaques told how the town had once had saloons, stores, two hotels, a boarding house, a church, and a school. All in that small area. We rested and spread out our things to dry in the sun, after the rain from that previous night. Two additional miles up "improved" dirt Clear Creek Road 390 brought us to the base of Hope Pass. We stood at nine thousand feet and stared upward. A 3,620-foot climb beckoned us. The route was up and over. There on an otherwise deserted dirt road at the access trail that began the climb sat a young man alone beneath a portable circus tent. We said hello and inquired as nicely as we possibly could, just exactly what the hell he was doing there.

"We're having a training run today," he said.

"For what?"

"It's a fifty-mile training run, to prepare for the Leadville-100 in August."

I'd heard of it. It was a one-hundred-mile foot race—an ultramarathon—and one of the premier events of its kind in the country. It's actually incredible to see how very many people take part in ultramarathon runs around the country. I knew a little about them. Unlike the standard 26.2-mile distance of a marathon, there is no standard distance for ultras. It's whatever each independent race director wants it to be. The most common ultra-race distances are one hundred miles, fifty miles or fifty kilometers (about thirty-five miles). The most popular ultra run in America is the Badwater, which is a 135-mile race in California from Death Valley to Mt. Whitney—from the lowest point to the highest in the continental USA. The Badwater finishes at eighty-five hundred feet on the side of Mt. Whitney at the Whitney Portal, but the racers always go on past the finish line and climb up to Whitney's summit. Just because. Most of the ultra races are out west, but there are two prominent ones held east of the Mississippi. One is the Vermont 100-Mile, and the other is a race down in Virginia. I'd run one ultra, but that was only a fifty-mile race. It was actually easier than any of the three marathons that I'd run, for a variety of reasons. The first was that you make sure to train well for an ultra, because you're so intimidated by the distance you're going to have to cover—so you show up at the starting line in great shape. What matters most, though, is that ultras are held on trails, so you get to run on soft ground. It's more forgiving than running on hot asphalt. My race had been through the woods, under the shade of the trees. Also, unless you're one of the elite entrants, there's no pressure to run the entire way during an ultra. If you come to a hill in the woods you just walk up it. Both ultramarathons and standard marathons have a great feeling of camaraderie among the runners. That really endeared me to them. Squash tournaments are much the same way, with everyone happy. Tennis tournaments aren't like that at all. Tennis tournaments basically suck. They're way too cutthroat, and everyone's busy swaggering around. I'd crossed the finish line in all four of my distance runs, and I felt proud about that. I'd finished both distance trails that I'd tackled, too. But I wasn't feeling so sure about this one. My looming deadline spelled trouble.

"The training run comes over Hope Pass?"

"Yep. They're coming this way. They'll be coming southward, so you'll run right into them."

At least that'd be exciting. Climbing up a trail through thin woods began our ascent. The first third of the climb was up steep slopes under tree cover. It's hard to climb under the cover of trees, because you don't get the emotionally beneficial uplift of seeing your progress. Weekender went first and quickly disappeared out of sight. I'd been nursing a cough for several days: I'd felt something in Creede, and it'd grown worse in Salida. Coughing fits started hitting me every time that I took a deep breath. I coughed myself all the way up Hope Pass.

Todd fell out of sight behind me. That was unusual for him. He was a stronger hiker than I was, yet occasionally I'd have moments of getting ahead of him. I pushed forward in my middle spot. I felt exhausted a third of the way up. When I popped out of the trees, however, my heart soared, for the remainder of the climb was visible switchbacks up the vertical rocky side of that high mountain ridge. The climb was steep and we felt like mountain goats. I looked up and saw not only Weekender but several other climbers, as well. I could make out two solo climbers and a large group of kids—perhaps camp kids or Boy Scouts—who were spread out all over various sections of the exposed switchbacks above me. The Boy Scouts barely seemed to move at all.

Coughing my lungs out, I pressed forward, climbing. It was a hard push. I tried to catch Weekender, but I couldn't. I kept waiting for Todd to overtake me, but he didn't. I reached the camp kids and found them dressed for Mt. Everest glacial conditions, wearing thick jackets, pants, hats, and gloves. No wonder they'd only been able to inch along. They were young. I could feel their pain. They were dressed so thickly and were so tired that they could only take what Todd called, "mountaineering steps." It takes years of experience for an athlete to understand pain and push through it. The first week out is hard for everyone, no matter what. Those kids would all eventually reach the top where their fatigue would fade and leave them with the thrill of the view and their major accomplishment. I smiled as I passed, but I didn't say anything to them except, "Hey!" Anything more than that, to someone who's struggling, is patronizing and annoying.

The ultramarathon-training lead runners came into view as they crested the pass just as Weekender reached it. They crossed paths and then down several of them came southward toward me wearing very little clothing—just nylon shorts, mesh sleeveless shirts, mesh baseball-style running caps and micro-gloves with handheld water bottles strapped on. The first ten of them were impressive, but the rest of them after that seemed human.

I gained the pass and sat with Weekender on a snowy bluff at 12,620 feet, sandwiched between 13,933-foot Mt. Hope and 13,461-foot Quail Mountain. We looked northward down the pass and could see more racers climbing slowly toward us. We looked southward down the switchbacks at Todd, watching as he passed the camp kids and made his way climbing toward us. The top of the pass was busy with ultramarathon runners by the time Todd arrived. Black clouds came and obscured the sun. Another typical storm threatened; however, our hard work was over. Twin Lakes, our destination, was within sight just a few miles to the north, far beneath us. We raced steeply downhill, hurriedly, running, laughing, glissading through snow, descending to low elevation out of the snow, and then trotting down the path.

Typically, came the deluge. We'd gotten to within one mile of the Twin Lakes Highway before the heavens opened dropping swimming pools of rain, rain that was so heavy we couldn't help but laugh. It was like some jokester upstairs was overturning buckets. We couldn't see more than a few feet in front of us. We lost track of Todd. Weekender and I found a couple of different pathways leading to the Twin Lakes Highway. We chose a route in the deluge and reached the pavement, where we stood in the rain and pathetically stuck out our thumbs. It was a winding road, not good for hitchhiking. And certainly not during a downpour. Miraculously, we very soon got a ride five miles eastward to the T-intersection of Route 24 which led twenty miles farther eastward to the trail town of Leadville. Todd stood at the T-intersection. Somehow, he'd gotten a ride there, too. Things always seem to work out on the trail. The rain subsided to an imperceptible drizzle. The three of us hitch-hiked together, landing a twenty-mile ride from a young woman in a compact car. In town, we treated her to pizza and we mercilessly gave her an earful of useless information about CDT through-hiking.

Highest Town.

Leadville was the highest town in America. That had nothing to do with weed. It was the highest incorporated town in the continental United States, sitting at 10,152 feet. Cities at high elevation around the world included 8,675-foot Bogota, Columbia; 9,249-foot Quito, Ecuador; 11,152-foot Cuzco, Peru; 11,910-foot La Paz, Bolivia; and 12,002-foot Lhasa, Tibet. The highest town in the world was Wenzhuan, Tibet, at 16,730 feet. Leadville had three thousand people (an EEP town) and was sparse and wholly uncongested save for the spandex-clad bicyclists who were just now arriving in droves as part of yet another cross-state cycling tour. Famous people who'd visited Leadville included Susan B. Anthony, Doc Holliday, Oscar Wilde, Daniel Guggenheim, and Andrew Carnegie. Contemporary celebrities wandered through, as well, like Robert De Niro and Mick Jagger. That was what they told us in the pizza shop, anyway.

The cyclists created a colorful tent city on the high school track. They also took every hotel room in town. We passed the Leadville, Colorado & Southern RR, which gave three-hour scenic daytime train rides twenty-three miles out through the mountains and back and climbed six blocks eastward up East 7th Street to the Leadville Hostel: "The highest hostel in America." Again, that had nothing to do with pot. Its front lawn provided a westward view over the tops of the buildings in town, and beyond, out over the snowy Sawatch Mountain Range from which we'd emerged. The Sawatch holds Colorado's highest concentration of Fourteeners, including the first, second, third, and fifth highest peaks in the state: Mt. Elbert, Mt. Massive, Mt. Harvard, and La Plata. There are fifteen Fourteeners in the Sawatch Range including The Collegiate Peaks of Mt. Harvard (third-highest of America's Rocky Mountains), Mt. Princeton, Mt. Yale, Mt. Columbia, and Mt. Oxford. Who'd named them, nobody could tell me. It didn't seem to be public knowledge. For some strange reason it was rarified air.

"No vacancy," Wild Bill said, spitting over the porch.

Wild Bill was the hostel caretaker. We didn't rush off, though. We stood staring at him on his front porch.

"Capacity is forty people," he elaborated, "and we already have fifty crammed in here."

"Can we sleep in the yard?"

"Hold on a second," he said.

He wasn't about to turn us away. He went to consult with his wife. We entered and poked around. The hostel has dorm-style rooms, semiprivate and private rooms. Its spacious basement had a pool table, movie screen, sofas, and fireplace. The ground floor had two living rooms and a dining room with a long table. It was clean and cozy—clearly an expertly run hostel. Inside were some ultramarathon-runner trainees and a gaggle of the touring cyclists. We knew that we wouldn't find a vacancy anywhere in town. At least it was a Sunday and the weekend people would soon leave. We could sleep in the yard for one night in the meantime, if we had to. Wild Bill reappeared and took us out back.

"We'll make do," he said.

Wild Bill knew us. He knew about CDT through-hiking—that we'd come from Mexico, that we were hiking to Canada. The few annual CDT through-hikers always hike in to his hostel every year. He'd seen us before. He wanted to help. He wanted our money, too. He took us out back behind the hostel to a double garage and an apartment that he rented to his resident carpenter. The carpenter was gone for the night, so Wild Bill unlocked the guy's apartment and said that we could sleep on his floor.

Todd and Weekender walked down to a restaurant they'd heard of that served only steaks and martinis. My older brother would've loved the place. Throw golf into the mix, and maybe a little surgery, and he'd have thought that he'd gone to heaven. I remained in Cave Dweller mode, staying behind to organize my things and mingle with some of the guests. During a communal dinner, I listened to cycling and ultramarathon stories. A forty-year-old runner from Florida said that he came here for three weeks every summer to train at high elevation. Another runner was a school teacher from Boston. Leadville was a hub for ultramarathoners. Held here every year since 1983, the Leadville 100-Mile footrace now annually draws over five hundred entrants. It's called The Race Across the Sky, and the slogan is: "Gold, Silver & Guts." Giant leadville-100 posters lined the hostel's basement walls.

I sat chatting in the kitchen with the others after dinner. Drank one or two beers. At midnight, Wild Bill came and gruffly turned out the lights on us, leaving us in the dark as he then assumed a Jaws-Quint-like persona while launching into a crazy story about a group of high school kids who'd come here on a trip a few years earlier and had gotten caught in the mountains in a major freak spring snow storm. The kids had been dressed in blue jeans when the storm trapped them. They'd panicked and split up, getting separated in the mountains in a dangerous comedy of errors. Amazingly, there'd been no fatalities. All the kids and their teachers ultimately got rescued, but severe frostbite had necessitated a few finger and toe amputations. When he'd finished the story, we all sat with our jaws dropped, laughing nervously to ourselves. I walked out back with the hostel's guest masseuse. She had a temporary work space in the garage. We kissed for a while and ended up sleeping in each other's arms on her mattress on the floor. It was very discreet, as she didn't want to get a reputation at Wild Bill's. Her home was in Vail, but she'd travel to Leadville on Event Weekends to supplement her income by giving massages during bicycle tours and road races. She spent most of the night detailing how awful was her luck in life. I just listened. I was lonely.

The morning newspaper reported on Monday, June 27, that lightning had killed five Boy Scouts who were huddled inside an open-faced lean-to on the east coast. The bolt'd just entered and struck them, bouncing from one to the other and killing them all. With good reason it terrified me. Again with the lightning. Always with the lightning out here — fifty-thousand-degrees Fahrenheit; bolts can be twenty miles long. All summer, lightning had plagued us.

We took a zero day in Leadville. The hostel emptied, its crowd dwindling from fifty down to six guests. Todd, Weekender, and I upgraded from the carpenter's apartment out back into the hostel's basement bunk room. Jason-Brett-Gabe weren't due in. Their plan had been to stay back at Twin Lakes in a bunkhouse. My masseuse friend took our Team Locust threesome sightseeing by driving us in her truck eastward into the mine-filled mountains behind town. That gave us an even better view westward over town and over the Sawatch Range. Then she departed for Vail. I hoped that her luck would get better. Todd insisted that we rent Bottlerocket, the original Wes Anderson movie with Luke and Owen Wilson. We drank beer and lit a fire. Weekender could only stomach half of that maniacal movie; then he left to sleep. I watched its entirety. All the while Todd pointed at the screen, hitting me and laughing and telling me exactly when it was funny. It was his favorite movie. He had the film memorized and could recite long passages of it. Then Bottlerocket jokes followed us for the rest of the summer. It'd been a great two nights in Leadville. We prepared to set out again that next morning.

14,433-Foot Elbert.

Wild Bill kindly drove us back to Twin Lakes where we'd left off. By "kindly," I mean that he charged us a little, not a lot. It was Tuesday, June 28. He left us at a CDT trailhead at almost ten thousand feet. Porno-Brett-Gabe were a day ahead of us. They'd skipped Leadville in order to quickly reach the next trail town, Silverthorne, off Interstate 70. They were trying to speed there to get picked up by a friend and taken eastward into Denver for two days of lounging in front of a television set eating chips and watching Lance Armstrong race his final Tour de France. They were cycling fanatics. I was fine with the split. I didn't require a huge group to hike with. We'd see them again soon enough.

We were onto National Geographic map 127, which included Mt. Elbert, the highest mountain in Colorado. At 14,433 feet, Elbert rises beside the

CDT up a short side trail. It's the highest of America's Rocky Mountains as well as the second-highest mountain in the contiguous United States behind California's 14,505-foot Mt. Whitney. Elbert is only seventy-two feet lower than Whitney, and just twenty-three feet higher than Washington's Mt. Rainier. Todd and Weekender both wished to climb it. Normally, I don't detour much, but I agreed to it this time because Elbert was too close, too momentous, and too easy a climb to pass up.

Elbert's summit rose 2.5 miles west off the CDT. It was the highest Fourteener, but it wasn't by any means the hardest. The side trail was labeled on National Geographic map 127 as Best route to Mount Elbert. We had the choice of hiding our packs in the woods and climbing up and down Elbert's south trail to retrieve our packs and continue the CDT from where we'd left off, or, we could carry full packs up Elbert's south trail and then proceed onward down its north trail, which looped back to the CDT farther ahead. We took the latter option because it'd save a few miles, so up we went, climbing in full packs. We got stared at. All the day hikers climbing Elbert looked at us as if we were dumb. They gave pitying, questioning looks, like, "Why are you carrying packs up this mountain?"

It was an easy climb, but I practically coughed my lungs out. My continuing cough had become a major annoyance that just wasn't going away. Switchbacks led up the entire climb. It took less than two hours. Scaling Elbert wasn't something to brag about. There was snow on its very small summit. We took photographs. We were on top of the world. We had a panoramic view over all of Colorado. We could see mountains stretching into the distance in every direction. We could see the island of Japan far the west, and the island of England far to the east. A mere five miles north of Mt. Elbert stood 14,421-foot Mt. Massive, which looked huge. If Massive could've been just thirteen feet higher, then it'd be the highest of the Rockies and we'd have climbed it instead. It'd sound more impressive to say that you've climbed Mt. Massive as opposed to saying you've climbed Elbert.

"You climbed Albert?"

"No, *EL*-bert!"

"Elbert—who's that?"

We swiftly descended the North Mount Elbert trail. Marmots stood on their hind legs whistling at us from the rocks, unafraid. We weren't terribly taxed. Climbing Elbert felt easier than climbing Maine's Mt. Katahdin. The Hunt Trail up Katahdin is straight up rocks from near sea level to 5,267 feet, while Elbert is graded switchbacks from 9,000 to 14,433 feet. We dropped down into the trees and rejoined the CDT, pushing northward through the forest. It began to rain at dinnertime, so we stopped and tented for the night near the Mt. Massive side trail. In the morning, June 29, Todd and Weekender wanted to detour and climb Mt. Massive, but I was able to dissuade them. We needed to keep to the task at hand: reaching Canada. I had a job waiting for

131

me, after all. We pushed on, exiting the Mt. Massive Wilderness and entering the Holy Cross Wilderness. That's how we do it: press on from one wilderness to another. Day by day, week by week.

Visible to our east throughout that day were roads and even occasional views of distant Leadville. It was crappy, uninteresting trail on a level grade. There was no sensation of being in the mountains at all. It wasn't a wilderness experience. We were practically sliding sideways off the eastern foothills on this section while heading northward. We found ourselves wishing time away. Todd and Weekender wore their iPods, tuning life out, escaping, listening to their music. It left me with no one to talk to.

After twenty featureless miles on the day, we did a strange, unplanned thing upon reaching Tennessee Pass and paved Highway 24. A glance at our maps showed that the road dropped southward to Leadville. We'd previously entered Leadville from the west three days earlier. Since then, we'd been looping northeastward around it, so the town now lay to our south, and we had the chance to take a second stop there. It was dinnertime. We looked at each other. Without a word, out went our thumbs. We headed for Leadville—Round II—back to America's Highest Hostel. Wild Bill's face looked puzzled when he saw us on his porch steps again, but then he realized what we'd done, how this time we'd come down from Tennessee Pass. It was a Thursday and he had plenty of room. There was no bicycle tour to compete with. We ate, slept, and in the morning Wild Bill kindly helped again (charging us a little, again) by driving us northward to Tennessee Pass.

Man Down.

Congestion loomed ahead. We were twenty miles shy of Interstate 70 and the Copper Mountain Ski Resort. If this had been back on the PCT in northern California with my old friend Zoomsteen, it would've meant arriving at noon at the ski resort, eating, and then blazing onward for an additional dozen miles more. It's probably what long-since-departed, twenty-two-year-old Pony Express had done here. For my Team Locust, though, twenty miles would take a full day and mean arriving at the ski resort at dinnertime.

A few miles past Tennessee Pass, we hiked eastward across an open expanse of abandoned military-looking cement bunkers. It was the remnants of Camp Hale, the birthplace of the U.S. Army Tenth Mountain Division. Built during World War II, the base had trained soldiers for winter mountain combat. It was highly experimental, because American soldiers had never previously trained that way. Olympic skiers joined the military and came to train here for three years, hiking up thirteen-thousand-foot peaks with ninety-pound backpacks in blizzard conditions, in temperatures to thirty below zero. Things like that. Just to get tough.

After handling a minute skirmish versus the Japanese in Kiska, Alaska, in

1943—the only modern foreign invasion of American soil (Hawaii wasn't yet a state in 1941 when attacked at Pearl Harbor) —the Tenth Mountain Division went to Europe to fight the Germans in the mountains of northern Italy. They were incredibly successful. Their first encounter was the launch of a surprise attack on February 18, 1944, when seven hundred soldiers from the Tenth Mountain scaled an unguarded two-thousand-foot cliff up Riva Ridge Mountain in the middle of the night and at daybreak found the Germans agape, sitting eating breakfast. The Germans hadn't been guarding the cliff because they hadn't thought anyone could climb it in the daytime let alone the night. They hadn't known what Colorado training could do. And what great, handpicked athletes were those soldiers. All that subsequent spring, the Tenth Mountain pushed northward and fought the Germans back through the Alps all the way back into Germany. The American soldiers joked that if their winter Colorado training hadn't killed them, then nothing would.

It was a hot day. We left East Fork dirt road and climbed northeastward up into the mountains over 12,022-foot Kokomo Pass. We kept on high ground for the rest of the day and reached Copper Mountain Ski Resort from the south. We stood looking down its off-season slopes at the resort village and Interstate 70 in its front yard below. We looked down over the resort's high-rise hotels and its backyard of courtyards, mini-golf course, amphitheatre, and outdoor cafés. We could see tiny ants walking about, eating, playing catch with Frisbees and playing Frisbee-golf. How could ants do those things? Descending lower, we could see the shapes of humans coming into relief and dogs in bandanas running around with families with children who shrieked and chased each other. It was late afternoon on a beautiful sunny day. We descended through lingering patches of snow into the small crowd.

We sat at an outdoor café. My feeling toward that smorgasbord of motion and music was one of aversion. I desired simply to move past the people, the traffic and the noise of Greater I-70 as quickly as possible. Partly, it was the getting-stared-at. Another part was the sense of detachment, of not really feeling part of this world. It felt wonderful, however, to have toilets, bottled water, food, and drinks once again. To have trash cans, mirrors, and warm-water faucets. To have waitresses. Waitresses to look at and speak with and set food before us. We realized that we'd quite oddly slept three of those previous four nights in the Leadville Hostel, and now here we were at a restaurant again. Quite the wilderness trail. Northeast of here up Interstate 70 was the Dillon Reservoir, which was surrounded by the tri-town community of Silverthorne-Dillon-Frisco. Beyond that on I-70 lay Denver.

My cough hadn't subsided. I'd used throat lozenges in both Salida and Leadville, but they hadn't helped. I'd been coughing uncontrollably for almost two weeks, and finally I'd had enough. I couldn't take it any longer. I needed to find a doctor in Silverthorne. I needed medication. Todd and Weekender would be taking the Ley route northward across I-70 and along the scenic Gore

Range Trail through the Eagle's Nest Wilderness to hike northeastward into Silverthorne, but I wouldn't go with them. The "official" CDT route made no sense (shocking) in that from the ski resort it took an insanely crazy eastward jog and passed by Silverthorne-Dillon-Frisco to the east. I wouldn't take that way, either. I had a different plan. Instead, I'd ride the ski resort shuttle bus into Silverthorne to take a zero day and find a doctor. That was my plan.

It's strange, how you never see it coming. You never know what's going to trigger a decision. Eighties rock music played over the loudspeakers across the café while we sat in the sun at the base of the Copper Mountain ski slopes. And that ended Weekender's hike. You could see that Weekender was suddenly changed, just while sitting at that outdoor café. He grew tense. He went rigid. It gripped his aspect and wrenched his posture. The music had suddenly just done him in. Weekender wasn't the type to get annoyed over anything, but just suddenly he was beside himself. For the music reminded him of work. He started telling us about his job—about working industrial carpentry in New Jersey and New York on large projects alongside teams of contractors. How the others would daily play this same, big-hair, eighties anthem rock music, and it'd drive him crazy. He hated it. The music transported him back to his carpentry job alongside crews of electricians and framers. He'd left that universe behind. But now it slithered into his head and lodged there, sucking like a leech. I would've thought that since he hated the memory of it, that it would've caused him to want to stay on the trail even more, but instead it had the opposite effect of beckoning him home. We ordered food and sat eating, but Weekender couldn't relax. He couldn't get over it. He kept commenting on the music, kept expressing his annoyance over it. Kept asking us if we minded either eating someplace else or his requesting the manager to turn the fucking thing off!

I walked to the bus stop in front of the ski resort and rode into Silverthorne. Silverthorne-Dillon-Frisco had six thousand people, combined. Ski chalets dotted the hills around Dillon Reservoir. Those weren't the mansions of Aspen, which lay west of Mt. Elbert, nor even of Vail, west down I-70, but there was hustle and bustle and a dozen hotels. Beside Silverthorne central bus terminal on Blue River Parkway (no river in sight) stood the ultracheap First Inn Hotel. There was a diner in front of it. Clearly that'd be home. I slept well for once. In the morning, July 1, I rode the free public transportation bus to the Frisco Medical Center and filled out forms and coughed while being prodded and dolloped by fingers and a stethoscope. Dr. James Bachman game me a prescription to fill for Guaifenesin, having diagnosed me with having Pharyngitis—what doctors colloquially call "having a sore throat."

My zero day in Silverthorne was day number sixty for me—my two-month anniversary on the trail. I was eight weeks in. I felt that I should've been farther. We should've reached the Wyoming border by now, but we were far from it. We still had to pass through two more Colorado trail towns. I tried not to panic. I washed my laundry. Bought food. Showered and shaved. Silverthorne had an excellent hiking store, inside which I bought the National Geographic maps for the remainder of Colorado. I retired to my room and traced in red marker the CDT route for the rest of the state, hopping from map to map, to prepare myself for what lay ahead. That'd make my maps easier to read once I got out there—once I got out "In the Shit," or "In the Suck," as Jason and Gabe liked to say, pretending to speak like marines. Soon I'd be out there reading the maps in the rain, wind, dark, cold, lightning.

I heard voices coming from the hallway outside my room that evening, so I poked out my head and found that it was Todd and Weekender who by chance were in the adjacent room. They'd left their door open, as through-hikers do. Incredibly, that's how it works on the trail. We hadn't planned any meeting spot, yet I'd never doubted that I'd bump into them somewhere. They'd randomly come to that very hotel, as I had. Perhaps through-hikers' brains all begin to work the same way after a while. We develop the same instincts. We reach a town and we know what we need. We survey the landscape the same way. Then the hotel manager had simply placed those dirty hikers next to dirty me. I guess it made sense. Now they were into a heavy discussion.

Weekender had just informed Todd that he was quitting and going home. He was leaving the trail immediately, from here, first thing in the morning. It'd happened just like that. He'd planned on hiking New Mexico and Colorado that summer—but now he'd prematurely had enough. He had to return to his job. It made sense to leave from here, from I-70, with its easy access to the Denver Airport. That next morning, Saturday, July 2, in the diner at breakfast, Weekender said a tremendously brief good-bye. He rose from the table, gave us a handshake, and then he was gone. I'd never see him again. The eighties rock music at Copper Mountain Ski Resort had fried his brain.

12
Finishing Colorado

We who go mountain-scrambling have constantly set before us the superiority of fixed purpose or perseverance to brute force. We know that each height, each step, must be gained by patient, laborious toil, and that wishing cannot take the place of working.

— Edward Whymper, *Ascent of the Matterhorn*

Dignan.

These hikes are expensive, and I didn't limit myself. I needed a tent — I bought a tent. I needed snowshoes and maps — I bought snowshoes and maps. I needed a hotel room — I bought a hotel room. I bought food. Anything. Everything. I was fully committed. The farther you get, the more your thoughts narrow in focus. Things come into sharp relief. We were far from all the distractions that accompany starting a trail. We knew what we were doing now. We were pushing to Canada.

Smelling salts under his nose couldn't possibly have more greatly affected Weekender than had the eighties anthem rock music at the Copper Mountain Ski Resort outdoor café. Weekender was gone for good, so Todd was sad and quiet. He missed his friend. It was his first time all trip without him. He kept his head down and barely spoke a word. We'd be hiking just the two of us for five days to the trail town of Grand Lakes where we'd reunite with Porno-

Brett-Gabe to become a fivesome. P-B-G had skipped Leadville in order to take time off in Denver to watch the Tour de France, so now they were behind us. We'd be reaching Grand Lakes before them and would wait for them there. That was our plan.

Todd led us northward out of town (from behind a supermarket, actually), climbing two thousand feet up the Ptarmigan Trail to a high plateau. We were in northern Colorado, north of Interstate 70. I felt overjoyed to leave all the craziness, cars, and trucks behind. Dark clouds built overhead as they did every afternoon in the Rockies. We set up our tents between clumps of shrubs. We had a view thousands of feet back down over the lights of Silverthorne-Dillon-Frisco. In two days it'd be the Fourth of July. If this'd been two days later, then we could've gazed down upon fireworks over the reservoir.

Todd pulled out his cell phone and spoke with his parents for an hour. I think that was because he was lonely, missing Weekender. He thanked his parents for having mailed him "homemade elk jerky." Todd's father had killed an elk in Oregon and had prepared the meat and stuck some in the U.S. mail to Todd in Silverthorne, care of General Delivery. Todd had begun to have stomach pain. "It's the elk jerky," I said. But no, he insisted it was purely coincidental and had nothing to do with his new menu item. Todd had a wonderful, relaxed rapport with his parents. They spoke comfortably, as friends. Just talking. It's how I've never been with my parents. It's how I am with my players. It's how I hope I'll be with my own kids one day. In the meantime, it's more like a business meeting when I speak with my mother, and she's the chairman of the board. She's had three children and has survived cancer, hip, shoulder and knee replacements. There aren't many original parts. She's the toughest person I know. She's basically indestructible, and I do admire that about her.

July 3, we walked northeastward, early morning, working our way over onto National Geographic map 104. Todd picked up a faint trail on the western-side downslope of a massive and complex ridge. The trail was slim; the going was slow. We intermittently postholed through spans of soft deep snow and then accelerated upon hitting dry ground. We lost the trail several times. We circumnavigated steep slopes, encountering cliffs and fallen trees. Few people had come this way. I suddenly understood why Todd missed Weekender so much. It wasn't merely for friendship, but for route finding, too. Weekender could've helped Todd navigate and more easily find our way back to the CDT. I gave my opinion whenever I could, and we slowly pushed forward. Plato claimed that you can discover more about a person in an hour of play than in a year of conversation. This was play. All of it just play. Todd had proven all along to be spirited and capable. He reminded me for some reason of a goofy Gilligan, marooned on Gilligan's Island—except this Gilligan could hike unaided through any vast wilderness and return to the huts and get Ginger and Mary Anne.

Todd was lagging, due to his stomach pain. I threw out quotes from Bottle-

137

rocket to try to keep his spirit up. That was the crazy movie that he'd made me watch and memorize back in Leadville. We'd laugh and a quote would stay with us for hundreds of yards until the next quote would pop into our heads and we'd kick that new one around. In the movie, Owen Wilson played a quasi-psychotic named Dignan who led a dysfunctional three-person gang in attempting three lame robberies of the questionable targets of a relative's home, a bookstore, and their pièce de résistance, the Hinkley Cold Storage Unit.

"I'm sorry but I'm under a lot of pressure right now, and I just don't think this team is gelling."

That kept us going for a quarter mile.

"If he doesn't have the enthusiasm, who needs him?"

Another quarter mile.

"We know it backwards and we know it forwards because we've done the legwork and we've done the research."

Another quarter mile.

"Here are just a few of the key ingredients: dynamite, pole vaulting, laughing gas, choppers—can you see how incredible this is going to be? —hang gliding, come on!"

We laughed and just kept repeating the quotes over and over like we couldn't help ourselves. I'm a coach, that's what I do: I find a way to keep people going, whatever it takes. We followed the South Fork Trail northeastward from map 104 to 103, to the Bobtail Mine. We waded across a wide, shallow stream; then we dropped our heads and silently, bullishly, tackled a two-thousand-foot ascent up endless switchbacks on a dirt road. Halfway up, dark clouds swept in and thunder boomed, so we stepped off the dirt road and wedged ourselves underneath a fir tree. We waited lying under the tree for twenty minutes, but neither lightning nor the deluge came, so we rose and continued, finally rejoining the CDT upon 12,451-foot Jones Pass.

We were glad to be back on the CDT. Here, it was the Mt. Nystrom Trail, easy to follow. We remained high and topped out at 12,666 feet while hiking eastward and traversing around the southern-side downslopes of 12,947-foot Vasquez Peak. We slept beside the trail in unspectacular forest. We were quiet. Uninspired. We'd exhausted the Bottlerocket movie quotes. Todd was still missing his friend Weekender. A deep gorge thousands of feet below to our south held a mine. We could hear its noise all night long. It was awful.

F ourth of July.

July 4—Independence Day—would find us climbing five thirteen-thousand-foot mountains in a single day. It was glorious. We began modestly by traversing around the eastern side of the mountain that we'd slept on; then we crossed a stream before climbing a gorgeous rocky trail to just beneath Stanley Mountain's 12,521-foot summit in the Arapaho National Forest. We felt relaxed and took photographs of each other lying in deep snow next to stones that we placed to spell "July 4." Tremendous snowpack remains in the Rockies in the summertime. Usually it was so densely packed that we could walk right over it.

After several eastward miles on high ground, we descended to 11,315-foot Berthound Pass with its Highway 40 mountain crossing. It was a major road. A dozen cars were pulled off in a parking lot on the pass where there was a Port-O-Let and some construction going on. People in street clothes ambled about, stretching their legs and posing for photographs in front of an enormous elevation sign, for kind of a "This-Car-Climbed-Berthound-Pass" type of thing. It didn't feel high to us. It was simply the ground we were walking on. Rising above the Berthound Pass parking lot on its eastern side was the Berthound Pass Ski Area. Our task, as always, was to climb. There was no marked trail. Our maps showed that we were to get to the top of the ski mountain and then hike northward along a high ridge. A dirt road switchbacked up the mountain, but we ignored that and climbed straight up the grassy slopes, sucking wind as we went, our hearts pounding and threatening to leap from our chests.

My cough medicine was working, as my cough had disappeared. We climbed eighteen hundred feet to the Berthound Mountain summit and found ourselves high above tree line, up in the clouds and thin air of the Rocky Mountains. We climbed one mile northward up a gradual ridge along a trail—the CDT—to the 13,132-foot Mt. Flora summit. On the summit was an abandoned weather station. Fierce wind blew cold air so we huddled behind the building and ate a quick lunch. So far, so good. It was to be an epic day.

The "official" CDT sadly dropped eastward from Flora's summit to far down off the ridge where it then looped eight miles northwestward before climbing back to rejoin the high ridge again on top of James Peak. It was a low, safe route. But a shortcut existed here: a shorter, more dangerous and far more thrilling route to stay high and follow a four-mile knife's edge ridge walk from Flora directly to 13,294-foot James, while along the way bumping up and over 13,130-foot Mount Eva, 13,391-foot Parry Peak and 13,250-foot Mount Bancroft. That was the Ley recommended route (the "Ley Alternate"). For some reason Todd felt that he'd have to convince me to take the dangerous way, but he didn't know me well enough. He hadn't seen me in the South San Juans. Of course I'd take the knife's edge. I relish the mountain-goat routine. I wouldn't have traded it for anything. I wished that the entire trail was that way.

We walked the high ridge like two kids in a candy store, with smiles on our faces despite the cold and the blasts of gale-force wind. We popped up and down, scaling the peaks one by one. It was our most intense rocky cliff-scrambling of the summer. It felt like walking the Dragon's Back in the Goat Rocks Wilderness in Washington on the PCT. We lost hundreds of feet between the peaks, always having to immediately gain it back again. From each summit on the ridge, the next peak would appear far away with daunting cliffs to negotiate in between. A few spots had hundred-foot vertical scrambles, which caused adrenaline surges inside us as we picked our way hands over feet up steep rocky faces. We were actually bouldering—nothing technical, but terrifically satisfying nonetheless. We took the peaks one at a time, without hurry or panic. We looked out over all of Colorado. There was nobody else on the ridge. The cold air kept us hopping and hollering. It felt adequately intense.

We slept in a boulder field at 11,671-feet beside the dirt road crossing of Rollins Pass. We'd climbed five Thirteener-mountains in a single day. It'd been a long Independence Day. We watched two random cars drive up and park on the pass. A few people emerged and climbed eastward, scaling an unnamed hillside. We could only guess that they were trying to gain a vantage point eastward, to see Fourth of July fireworks over distant Denver.

Just thirty-five miles remained for us to reach the town of Grand Lakes, and no major obstacles stood in our way. Our hard work was over. Left was a long descent ending at a series of lakes. We'd cruise right in. If this'd been on the PCT, then it would've meant one day and then sleeping in a hotel in town. But out here on the CDT, thirty-five-mile days just weren't in our repertoire.

A short morning climb westward on July 5, over snowpack, took us across to the western side of the Continental Divide. Todd found our trail and led us northward for three miles, on a route that led us all the while parallel to, and just below, the snowpack and high ridge. The earth dropped steeply away to our west and we looked out over dozens of miles of Switzerland-like valleys far below. Todd named the flowers on the hillsides: Columbine, Shooting Star, Paintbrush, Yarrow, Lupine. Me, I just saw white, red, red, white, and purple flowers. We looked down and saw elk and deer running below us. Ahead on some cliffs we saw two white mountain goats. We finally climbed to meet the ridge and the Continental Divide at landmark Devil's Thumb Pass.

Everything took the name Devil here because the cliffs were so steep and devilish. The map showed things named Devil-this and Devil-that. A huge rock stuck out like a thumb: Devil's Thumb. A pond was visible two thousand feet below a cliff, seen only by peering death-defyingly over the edge: Devil's Thumb Lake. The Divide continued northward from there, but the CDT had us turn ninety degrees westward descending into a sopping wet everything-melting valley. We slipped through wet snow, postholing into streams, sliding through mud while trying to follow our barely visible trail. The shape of the valley funneled us down, so the exact route didn't matter. It was just like the valleys that funnel you down the north sides of the passes in the High Sierras on the Pacific Crest Trail. We dropped two thousand feet out of the snow and back down into the trees.

National Geographic map 102 showed that our next stretch would follow the High Lonesome Trail arrow-straight northward bumping easily along at between ninety-five hundred to ten thousand feet. It sounded fine, but unfortunately it didn't feel high but only lonesome, as it led us through the trees,

140

through uninteresting forest. Todd had been dragging all day, like he'd had a two-hundred-pound backpack. His elk-jerky food-poisoning stomach-pain had subsided that previous day, but now it'd returned with a vengeance. He lay down on the ground in the middle of the forest, with a fever and profuse sweating. He took out his sleeping bag and lay upon it, drifting in and out of sleep. I had nothing to do but sit beside him. Todd wasn't one to ask for help. He was a strong and indestructible guy. At some point he'd just rise and continue hiking. I knew that he'd be okay, but I stuck with him just to make certain.

Mosquitoes bit fiercely, so I took out my sleeping bag and took a nap myself. We both arose two hours later, disoriented. We were far from the town of Grand Lakes. It was going to be a low-mileage day. Nothing about the final thirty-five miles into Grand Lakes was supposed to have been hard, yet we were struggling mightily. Todd felt dizzy and couldn't see straight, so leadership fell to me. He struggled to his feet and followed. Of course, as always, that led to disaster.

Vomit.

In rapid succession, we were to leapfrog northward and hit Monarch Lake, Lake Granby, Shadow Mountain Lake, and finally Grand Lake. At the end of the final lake was our town. It was midafternoon by the time we descended the Arapaho Pass Trail northward and walked along a perfectly groomed path on the western bank of pint-sized Monarch Lake. We had one lake down and three to go. We rested for a few minutes at some picnic tables on the northern shore. Then came a road and civilization. We walked two miles up asphalt Roaring Fork Road past fishing shacks, mobile homes, barking dogs, and scampering children to giant Lake Granby's southeastern tip. We gazed across its expanse. At least I gazed and Todd squinted (probably not seeing anything).

Here, I made a mistake. Instead of turning eastward and climbing the inland Knight Ridge Trail to the top of a bluff and the northward-leading ridge parallel to the lake, I noticed what looked on the map to be a lakeside trail that'd be longer but would keep us at level elevation at the water's edge (no climbing!). On paper, walking Lake Granby's eastern shoreline appeared to be an easy, lakeside reward. Had Todd been lucid instead of zombified by homemade elk jerky, he'd have seen the error of this and would've led us more smartly. But he was far gone. I'm certain that he didn't even know what day it was. It was like the old candy bar commercial where a football player gets whacked unconscious and when the trainers rush out to revive him they ask him, "What day it is?" And he answers, *"I'm Batman!"* I'm pretty sure that if I asked Todd which way to proceed that he'd get a faraway look and say something irrelevant like: "I have paper clips in my pocket."

We actually needed to reach the town of Grand Lakes quickly to get Todd to a doctor. Despite my map's showing the existence of the lakeside path, in reality there was none. The contour of the shoreline led us in and out of tiresome inlets and peninsulas. We walked over small, round treacherous stones. Hours dragged and we seemed to be getting nowhere. It was a nightmare. I kept looking back at Todd. He didn't know what was happening.

Dusk fell and we stopped for the night, lakeside, where conservatively the mosquitoes numbered in the billions. It hadn't been a good day. Todd found the energy to set up his tent. A short while later he called out and asked me for water. It was like how Pony Express had called out for help in the middle of the night in the blizzard in the South San Juans. I dressed and prepared to leave my tent and brave the mosquitoes to pass Todd some water, when suddenly I heard him unzip his tent and begin retching. Nice! The sound of projectile vomiting is unmistakable. A couple minutes of that and Todd said, "Never mind." He collapsed back in his tent.

July 6, we awoke excited to get to Grand Lake Village. Todd felt better. His cramps and fever were gone. He was dehydrated and weak, but lucid. We walked two hundred yards along the small, uneven lakeshore making terrifically slow progress, when suddenly Todd stopped, peeved, and looked at me with a kind of a *"What-the-hell-is-this?"* surprised realization. He hadn't known we'd been doing this the night before. He couldn't let it pass. That way was futile. It was utterly too slow. He knew what needed to be done. Even in weak shape, Todd took control. He checked his map and insisted that we turn ninety degrees eastward and climb seven hundred feet inland cross-country up the cliffs to find the high Knight Ridge Trail on the bluff. The climbing was painstaking. We picked our way carefully. Todd was so weak that it took him forever. Finally we gained the high ridge and quite surprisingly (to me, anyway) we immediately stumbled upon the clear path of the CDT. I should never lead. I'd lost us some time. At least it was easy sailing from there.

Past Lake Granby, we descended northward to Grand Bay Inlet, then along a clear, well-maintained, practically manicured footpath farther northward along the eastern shore of Shadow Mountain Lake, its motorboats and water-skiers zooming along the water. We looked across at the homes with their docks on the lake's western shore. We were close and nothing could stop us now. Our final mile led over a bridge into Grand Lake Village. We walked ten blocks past dogs, children and homes to the main drag of town on Route 34, called Grand Avenue. Town was just a long roadside strip.

Grand Lake Village occupies the southwestern corner of the Rocky Mountain National Park. It was a pine tree town with pine smell in the air. It was the easternmost point of land that we'd stand on all summer. Here was a bend in the trail, a pivot point. We'd trend northwestward from here to Canada. The first hotel we could find was the Lone Eagle Lodge, a gas station ranch with a Jacuzzi in its parking lot. The owners were Polish. Across the street was a killer diner. We dumped our packs and stumbled over. Todd hadn't eaten in days. He was afraid that he might vomit whatever he ingested, still he attempted

142

to force himself to eat.

"Maybe it's the high elevation. You should try the oxygen," our waitress said, referring to the oxygen canisters they sell in all the town's convenience stores. Town was at eight thousand feet.

"It's not the altitude," Todd said, his skin yellow and head bent, unable to raise his eyes to look at her.

"Nope: it's the homemade elk jerky," I cheerfully chimed in, smiling and cramming my mouth with salad.

This was the lowest elevation that we'd had in weeks. I was famished and ate to my heart's content. Team Locust was to reform here, but there was no sign of the others. Todd and I shared a room and stayed up late watching the World Series of Poker on television. Televised poker was a new phenomenon. We'd been watching it from every hotel room all summer. It felt wonderful to shower, shave, wash with soap, and sleep in a bed. Todd threw up in the bathroom in the middle of the night. Projectile vomiting again.

We took a zero day in Grand Lake Village on July 7. We were expecting Porno-Brett-Gabe to arrive. It was a bright, beautiful, pine-tree-smell summer day in the Rockies. Perfect temperature, perfect sunlight. I felt lucky to have this rest. Todd didn't seek a doctor. He felt that he was on the road to recovery. He ate without throwing up, and he felt that he was getting better on his own. P-B-G indeed showed up in the afternoon. They found us at our hotel and took the room next door. It was nice to see them again. I was glad that they'd appeared so quickly. They'd been slowly gaining on us, due to Todd's having hiked sick for several days. They asked, "Where's Weekender?" We told them his story, about the brain-frying music back at the Copper Mountain Ski Resort.

Outside in the parking lot Jacuzzi that night, Team Locust sans Cave Dweller (and sans Weekender) sat soaking with a visitor that P-B-G had met, a guy named Nick from New Jersey who was a CDT through-hiking alumnus and was working for the summer as bartender at a resort in the mountains north of town. He was strong, loud, crass—he was Porno on steroids. Nick sat soaking with the others and told them stories about what the rest of the trail would be like. I lay in my room in bed watching Clint Eastwood and The Eiger Sanction on TV. I'd seen the movie a bunch. But this time I suddenly found myself identifying with the old bearded climber whose young wife flirts with the young climbers in the hotel before the expedition. The old guy was trying to remain vigorous and regain his youth by tackling the Eiger. I felt like that now. Weekender was gone, and so it was just me here at age forty-one surrounded on this trail by four twenty-six-year-olds whom I was always trying to match. Back at my job at the college, I was surrounded by twenty-year-old squash and tennis players whom I was still always trying to beat. It was such hubris to think that I still could. Me, in the Middle of my Life. In the Middle of the Country. The Man in the Middle. I couldn't help noticing that in the movie, the bearded climber is the first one to die. We spent a second night at the hotel, watching poker again.

Radler Trinken.

Reunited Team Locust set out, five together, from Grand Lake Village at noon that next day, walking northwestward along Route 34. It was July 8, trail day number sixty-six for me. We'd successfully hiked up through most of Colorado. Only one trail town remained: Steamboat Springs. That'd surely be a marquee trail town. It was a place that I'd heard of before, one of those vaguely familiar-sounding places in Colorado that we all think must be beautiful and, invariably, are. It was something to look forward to.

We made an impression walking down the road in a pack. Heads turned, staring out car windows. My four young compatriots all had similar slim, vertically aligned backpacks with vertically hanging mattress pads, making them all look svelte like tall pencils. Meanwhile, my mattress pad attached horizontally to the back of my pack, which made me look like a pear. Some kind of evolution had occurred since my last hike. Their way was more optically pleasing, like how vertical lines on pants and shirts make one appear tall and lean. The others walked a few yards ahead of me. They were an impressive group. Three of them were identically clad Fidel Castro look-alikes, while Todd looked nothing like the others. Todd with his muscular calves sticking out below his nylon parachute shorts. If this'd been the start of my first distance hike, then I might've made modifications, but this was the second half of my third hike and it made no sense to change things now. My system was serving me well. I just resembled a pear amidst pencils.

Vintage Team Locust: we didn't even make it out of town before stopping. A go-cart course at the west end of town past a health food co-op and a horse-riding business proved too great a temptation. We had the course to ourselves. The manager asked us not to smash the go-carts, but we were aggressive. I hopped into a car in the front line and I held off Brett for twenty laps to win the race. The others got silly and fell out of contention early on, bumping into each other and laughing. But Brett remained inches behind me for twenty laps, searching in vain for a way to pass. I kept up my concentration and held him off. I had to constantly check over my shoulders on the straightaways, angling in front to block him whenever he tried to edge by. It was passive-aggressive behavior. I was angry because of all our long breaks and pauses. Here, in northern Colorado on a gorgeous sunny day, I was mad at my deadline, mad at these others for not having a deadline, and mad that we still had quite far to go. Mad, Mad, Mad. I guess I'd just wanted that one tiny victory—a go-cart victory—in order to take out my anger on the world.

I simply can't enjoy anything. I'm crazy. I know.

Departing the go-carts, I didn't have a clue of our current route. I knew only that we were taking some kind of gigantic cutoff, like the Creede Cutoff. I hadn't known in advance about that one, and I'd no idea about this one, either. The "official" CDT looped eastward into the Rocky Mountain National Park, but Todd's Ley Route had us bisecting that by walking northward out of town. With this group, I'd usually position myself in the number two spot whenever we were strung out along a path, by now I took the caboose. I followed the wise guys up some roads into the wooded hills carrying my pear-shaped backpack. Drinking came next.

Two miles north of Grand Lake Village, go-cart residue still fresh on our hands, we reached the Grand Lake Lodge resort where worked Team Locust's new friend Nick, the bartender and former CDT through-hiker from New Jersey. He'd invited us. That was news to me. The place had a really cool swimming pool and acres of rustic wooden porch. Suddenly I found myself bellied up to the resort's bar at noon with the others, Nick pouring us drinks. Nick went psychotically on about how much he loved the CDT, repeating: "There are no fucking rules out here! You make the trail any fucking way you want!" But on hikes, I didn't like sitting in bars. I tried to be okay with it. I tried to remain calm and not freak out and panic. I was just trying to survive. I had a choice. I could skip it. I could skip the South Park jokes and the farting and sleeping-with-each-other's-mothers jokes. I could go off alone, make my thirty-mile days and be lonely. I could ditch Team Locust and go off alone and get lost in the Great Divide Basin. Get lost in the Wind River Range. Get lost in Yellowstone. Lost in Montana. Hike alone and get eaten by grizzlies. If this'd been the Appalachian Trail where white blazes marked the route, then I could've left this group and not need to worry about the consequences. There'd actually be other people out here, if the trail was marked. But it wasn't marked. And there was just us. I had to stick with them.

I ordered a Radler—twenty-four ounces—half beer, half lemonade. It's a drink from Germany that we used to pound down on the terrace after tennis matches in the hot sun on the red clay courts at Tennis Club Ubersee. It was passive-aggressive behavior again. The others couldn't have known it but that drink separated me and took me away to another place. Away from Team Locust. I'm not sure how it'd occurred to me to order it, but it'd just suddenly popped into mind. It was a sublime memory of someplace far away. Someplace else. Anywhere else. I needed that to treat myself. To trick myself. To transport me away to some other place to ease the pain.

They weren't bad guys. I liked these guys. That was the thing. But they were prepared to reach Canada late in September, and that wouldn't do for me. So I hated them as much as I loved them. They were my curse. They also happened to be my saving grace. For who knew where I'd have been without them? It was their group, their hike, their plan. They'd arranged all this. I was just some random straggler tagging along, some cranky old dude who was a semi-strong hiker. Who had high motivation. Who made occasional jokes, offered occasional wisdom. Their hike was going to include impromptu go-carting in towns. And drinking at bars in resorts in the woods. It didn't matter to them if I didn't like it. It was okay, though—I was off just then in my own little world, on the red clay courts in Germany with my Radler. Proust understood that—the little triggers can take you away.

We were onto map 115, heading westward. The rest of the way to Steamboat Springs was all westward. We'd shaved off miles by taking the Rocky Mountain Cutoff, but then we'd used it up at the go-carts and bar. Just slightly and pleasantly buzzed, we hiked westward up North Supply Jeep Road and climbed the Blue Ridge Trail where we rejoined the CDT. We followed a westward ridge into the Never Summer Wilderness. At the end of the day we descended off-trail through deep snow into the small crater of a valley, to sleep beside circular and perfectly picturesque tiny Bowen Lake.

Calm Down.

We climbed over 11,800-foot Bowen Pass and later 9,300-foot Willow Creek Pass that next day, July 9. A dozen dirt-bike motorcyclists had zoomed past us, chewing up the trail, polluting our eardrums and annoying all the animals. Upon Willow Creek Pass was a paved road crossing Highway 125, and when we emerged from the woods out onto that desolate road, we noticed that Gabe wasn't with us. He always brought up Team Locust's rear. He was the weakest hiker in our group. This time, neither Porno nor Brett had lagged behind to wait for him, and we waited by the roadside for forty-five minutes. Finally, Brett stood up and prepared to go search for him.

"Calm down, calm down," Porno said.

It was something he always said. Like at the base of a big climb, someone would remark about it, express hopelessness over it, and Porno would say, "Calm down, calm down." It was him mimicking some obscure movie, but we never asked which one. It didn't matter. It was funny, and soon the rest of us had all starting saying it, too, at random moments over inconsequential things: "Calm down, calm down..." Gabe finally came out of the woods onto the road wearing his iPod and walking slowly, defiantly. He was angry. He said that he'd taken a wrong turn, but then he'd figured it out. I wasn't the only one who could get lost.

With Gabe back in the fold, we found the trail north of Highway 125 and directly ahead lay a climb that the others had been dreading and talking about all day—a three-thousand-foot climb up 12,296-foot Parkview Mountain. We climbed two tough miles up a dirt road through forest and emerged in a logged clearing beneath the mountain's summit. There was no path, so we made our own route, climbing up loose gravel. We spread out across the cliff face and practically raced one another. This was a scree climb, with loose gravel giving way underfoot like we were walking through quicksand or running on a sandy beach. Our legs grew numb. It was a treacherous, lungs-heaving climb. The mountainside was entirely exposed so we kept track of each other easily. Strong Porno was first (even with his heaviest backpack); then Brett and I had a parallel course. Todd was still sick and weak and was taking his time a little behind us. Gabe was last, but he did an excellent job keeping up.

On top, we sat on deep snowpack and got chilled by a fierce, cold wind. A tiny weather hut on top could only hold one person and was filled with rat droppings, so we stayed out of it. We boiled noodles and ate dinner and candy bars, but it was so cold that we couldn't linger long. The sun set as we descended a glorious ridge above tree line down the western spine of the mountain. It was beautiful and relaxing for thirty minutes, but then darkness fell exactly when our descent turned steep and we dropped off-trail down through a forest of dense trees. We stopped to put on our headlamp flashlights; then we continued cross-country in the darkness. It was a small shortcut. We were looking to soon pop out onto dirt road 730. I tried not to fall behind. We were just five beams of light working over and under blowdowns and debris. We stuck close together, fighting forward. No one got hurt, and we soon found the road, as expected. We set up our tents on the shoulder.

We were onto map 200 now. Todd took us off-trail again, July 10, steeply down to little swiftly flowing Arapaho Middle Fork Creek, which was in a gully that we had to climb northward up out of, cross-country, off-trail, through dense undergrowth and millions of fallen trees. We were supposed to find Arapaho Divide Road 104 on a ridge on top of this climb. We felt as if we were climbing into the clouds, so it was difficult to imagine that we would suddenly come to a dirt road high on top. We stopped several times to consult with each other and check our maps to get our bearings. It was tricky business. We grew unnerved and a bit testy, even with the five of us sticking together and pooling our opinions. We knew that we were on course, yet the climb seemed overly long. It was steep, and we had to fight off-trail through thick scrub. We gained a high open boulder field where the trio of Fidel Castro communists elected to climb vertically up one final steep cliff, just to make absolutely sure that they'd reach the highest point of land and gain the ridge and the dirt road. Todd and I curved eastward around the side of the cliff. We worked our way around boulders and rocks and then veered back to the ridge where we discovered the dirt road, reaching it thirty minutes ahead of the others. We waited for them.

From then on, it was road walks all the rest of the way into Steamboat Springs. Again with the road walks! Westward six miles on dirt Arapaho Divide Road 104 through the forest was iPod walking for the others—no great views and nothing to see, just heads down, teeth clenched, jaws set, walking and swatting mosquitoes. We spaced out to take a break from each other and to clear our minds. At the end of the dirt road, we stepped into the open once again, meeting gravel country road 103. The sun beat down. My feet hurt and we were out of water. We found a stream which came down from between rolling hills, but then we noticed hundreds of cows roaming the hillsides around the stream, so the water was certainly contaminated. Porno-Brett-Gabe carried a water-purifying kit, and they let me borrow it to pump water. It was lukewarm and putrid tasting, but I had to drink it. We tented in a cow pasture off the road beside a barbed wire fence.

On the morning of July 11, we hiked eight dirt road miles northward and reached paved Highway 14 by midmorning. A nine-mile Highway 14 hot pavement walk to a place called Muddy Pass would take us to the end of the section, for we'd exit at Muddy Pass and hitchhike twenty miles off the CDT down to resupply in Steamboat Springs. I cheated, though. My heart just felt so low. It was pure despondency. I just didn't want to have to face the nine mile, foot-burning pavement walk. The others set out westward, single file, spaced out dozens of yards apart along the hot asphalt highway. I couldn't bear the thought of it. I stood my ground and stuck out my thumb. A construction crew was working the road near a bridge, and very few cars passed. A car would pass only about once every five minutes. I sat and waited. I sat for thirty minutes thinking that I might never be able to get a ride from here, when finally a truck stopped.

If I live to be one hundred and hitchhike every minute of every day from now until then, I'll never again have a ride as perfect as this one (given that I'll never get a ride from a Living Garden model, like Todd seemed to land at will). It was the best ride that I'd ever had. It was three Hispanic men in the front cab of a flatbed truck. The wooden flatbed out back was a platform possessing no side railing nor anything upon it whatsoever. Not a speck. The flat surface was the size of a queen bed, and I lay down on my back spread-eagled, facing the sky with my pack under my head like a pillow. I didn't know the physics of it: would the wind blow me off? Would I roll off on the turns? There was nothing to hold on to and nothing holding me down except gravity—and I'd been hiking for sixty-nine days so I didn't weigh much. The truck was heading all the way into Steamboat Springs, so I'd hit the jackpot. I peeked down between my legs as we sped off, and in a short while saw my fellow hikers one at a time as I rode past them. To each one I'd raise an arm clutching my hiking stick and wave it briefly. They were decent about it—about my cheating. Each one of them, in turn, laughed and waved. Normally, I would've felt bad or guilty. But something had come over me. I was happy. I was overjoyed to be done with the section and riding all the way in.

Steamboat Springs.

My flatbed ride passed Muddy Pass and adjacent Rabbit Ears Pass (near its highly visible rock formation that looked like a rabbit's ears) and took us on a winding descent into Steamboat Springs, depositing me in the parking lot of the Rabbit Ears Motel. Out in front, a ten-foot-tall hotel sign topped with pink ceramic rabbit ears. It was a cheap hotel, but that was all we ever needed. The post office lay across the street, next to the town's recreation center, which was home to natural geothermal hot springs and two outdoor swimming pools. The others were due to meet me at the Rabbit Ears, and by the time I'd shaved, showered, and organized my pack, they'd arrived. They'd walked the nine hot highway miles to Muddy Pass; then they'd hitchhiked in.

It was day sixty-nine for me, a Monday. Here, we were roughly halfway. If the second half of the hike also took me sixty-nine days, it'd put me at the Canadian border on September 20, twenty days late to work. Twenty days past what I'd promised. Worse was that, Team Locust would probably slow down near the end instead of speeding up. That played on my mind. I felt great psychic pain. Something was going to have to give. It was nothing new; I'd known that for quite some time, had known it with certainty ever since No-Bathtub Salida. Yet it hurt nonetheless. I needed space so I took a single room and stuck Todd next door with the others. No problem for them—they enjoyed having four in one room because it meant more clutter on the floor and more jokes about each other's mothers.

I felt such a mixture of things: fear of getting older, doubt, and dread. Cristina was still in Spain and couldn't help. I had her number, but calling her in Aryns de Munt and speaking the few Spanish words I knew to her parents, my former in-laws, would've been just too awkward. As emergencies went, I felt that I could survive this one. Just questions weighed heavily. What was I giving up in order to have these hikes? Would I ever get my life together? What in the name of hell was I doing, and where was this taking me? I think that I've occasionally hurt people. I'd never meant to. I wished that I could sit them all down and apologize. I've been hurt by people, too—have been crushed by them. It's such a strange struggle that's life. "Don't struggle," Cristina would tell me if she could. I'd once had a squash player from Hong Kong, a fantastic player, who would see me get upset and uptight and frustrated, and he'd put his hand on my shoulder and smile and wink and say: "Don't push the river—let the river flow."

I walked alone up the street to experience the town's cafés, tourist shops, and ice cream stores. The Yumpa River leads behind a long row of stores in the town of nine thousand people. I could hear the sounds of children laughing and squealing, wafting up through the alleyways from swimming holes on the river back behind the buildings. I could hear dogs barking at kayakers and rafters. I bought a T-shirt that said: Got Oxygen? I bought a second one and mailed it to Weekender back in New Jersey. I ate dinner alone in a Chinese restaurant. I went and watched a movie alone, Steven Spielberg's remake of Orson Wells' War of the Worlds. Surely, instead of crunching us up, individually, one by

149

one, all over Earth, any aliens keen and for some unknown reason bent on the destruction of little insignificant us, would just send us a germ. I stayed awake until one thirty in the morning, tracing red lines over the one hundred pages of photocopies that I'd made of Todd's Ley maps for Wyoming. The comfort of carrying National Geographic maps would end after Colorado and so I wanted to have at least some version of the Ley maps.

I checked out of my Steamboat Springs room that next morning, on Tuesday, July 12. There'd be no zero day here. The others had all gone off down the street, taking care of their various chores and errands, like laundry and shopping. Typical to a place like this, there was a killer health food store. I could've picked up a million things, but I bought only some vegetarian beef jerky. It'd give me good memories of all the vegetarian beef jerky I'd eaten back on the Appalachian Trail twelve years earlier. Just the smell of it took me back there, in proud Proustian fashion. Triggered memories flooding back. We ate lunch all together at an outdoor café at noon. Todd and Brett had more chores to take care of, so Porno, Gabe, and I walked to the town's recreation center, on the eastern side of town, across the street from our Rabbit Ears Hotel.

We bought day passes at the Health and Public Recreation Center, and we walked out back to find that it had three hot geothermal mineral pools, an Olympic-sized lap pool and also a smaller pool with a three-hundred-foot waterslide. The place was teeming with teenyboppers, along with mothers and their young and infant children. A fleet of lifeguards kept watch over the circus, over all the splashing. The lifeguards were teenaged girls in matching red one-piece bathing suits. Blonde hair in ponytails. Chapstick liberally applied. Relentlessly smacking chewing gum. Sunglasses and deep summer tans.

I soaked in a thermal pool, then lay on a deck chair for two hours and got sunburned. I couldn't figure out if I was in a hurry to leave town, or not. It's horrible, not to be able to even assess your own needs and emotions. I always just want to be somewhere else. That's the curse. Porno and Gabe were happy here. They tubed down the waterslide and laughed and splashed, roughhousing with all the squealing kids. The lifeguards had to whistle at them twice. Our backpacks stood lined up adjacently behind a row of chairs on the deck. It was late afternoon by the time Todd and Brett showed up. Then off we went, Team Locust, to the road to hitchhike back up to Rabbit Ears Pass, Muddy Pass, and Dumont Lake. I could see this clearly on my National Geographic map 118, the final map for the state of Colorado.

Ichobod Crane.

The next two days, July 13 and 14, found us hopping northward from lake to leach-infested lake—Fishhook Lake, Lake Elmo—over 10,300-foot Buffalo Pass and into the Zirkel Wilderness where we walked through precipitation that turned from rain to hail to snow and back to rain, all in the space of one hour as beams of sunshine and a rainbow were visible all the while. We sogged through a bog of ice water up to our shins, our feet growing numb. We surprised a herd of elk that was so large it took five minutes for them all to gallop past. In their wake, we found potato-sack-sized circles matted down in the grass into beds at the edges of the field where mothers had lain to nurse their babies. I touched the grass and felt its warmth.

"Lots of PUDS back there," a guy said to us, walking southward down the trail straight toward us.

"What's that?" we said.

"Pointless Ups and Downs," he said, and he looked at us as if we were crazy and ignorant hikers.

He was a solo southbound section-hiker who went on to tell us that the terrain ahead of us in the Zirkel Wilderness was virtually impassible because of all the snow. We didn't have a chance of getting through it, according to him. We'd probably die. He'd been out on the trail for less than a week, so he wasn't yet acclimated. He knew that he was getting hammered by everything, but just because he was getting hammered didn't mean that we would—we'd been out so much longer and were used to this by now. So we took his words with a grain of salt. We thanked him for the information; then we walked through the snow.

"He goddamn tried to *Zirkel* us!" Porno said.

It was a new term that we decided to give to anyone who'd warn us over the treachery and impossibilities of what lay ahead. It was amazing how common it was for people to do that. It must be in the human DNA. The term Zirkel also became gibberish that we started using in place of conversation. Just due to boredom.

"Zirkel?" one of us would ask, apropos of nothing, looking at another.

"Zirkel," came the answer.

Later, one of us would point at a distant hillside and say, "Zirkel."

Another would nod wisely, and knowingly confirm, "Zirkel."

Soon, we just walked along hour by hour, one or another of us saying: "Zirkel, Zirkel, Zirkel—Zirkel? Zirkel?"

Todd lit himself on fire at lunch. It was July 14, our last day in Colorado. His stove had leaked fuel onto this foot and it caught. He was barefoot at the time. That was how long our lunch breaks lasted; you had time to take off your shoes and socks while you ate. Those were real kick-back-and-take-off-your-shoes-and-stay-awhile length breaks. We were under the only tree that we'd found that could offer us shade. Todd's foot flamed and he screamed and leapt up and hit his head on a tree branch. He was okay. We kind of mostly just laughed. Porno found ointment for him to rub onto his foot.

"Motherfucking Zirkel!" Todd screamed.

"Calm down, calm down."

We hiked twenty-two miles on the day, over a brutal roller-coaster section of trail that was easy to follow yet dug deep and destroyed by motorcycle riders who rumbled by. Todd and I hiked far out in front of the others. Todd had by now regained full strength once again after his food-poisoning fiasco. It was eight o'clock at night when he and I looked ahead and spied a clearing and, nailed to a tree, a small wooden sign for Wyoming. We both started to run for it, to be the first one to reach Wyoming. Todd got out ahead of me, but I was close enough behind so that just as he was about to cross the line of the sign on the tree, I threw my hiking stick out ahead of him like the headless horseback throwing his pumpkin-head at Icabod Crane so that it sailed out ahead of Todd and reached the state before he did.

"My hiking stick reached Wyoming before you did!"

We tented at the border. Waited for the others. Colorado was done. Todd pulled out a cigarette and started smoking again.

13
Great Divide Basin

But what then when something is in the way when you go between places, no? Plow ahead: go: collide: kabong. *Where is their straight shortest then, yes? And how many two places are there without there is something in the way between them, if you go?*

—David Foster Wallace, *Infinite Jest*

Enter Wyoming.

I can remember exact shots hit by exact people at exact moments in time down through sixteen years of coaching. I can remember exact moments as if they'd all happened yesterday. The years have begun to whiz by like the yellow dashes on the highway which blur into a straight line. It's the absurd things that I've enjoyed most. One summer day, a skinny kid with a baby face stepped off the bus in Lewiston, Maine, having traveled up to visit from El Salvador to see if he liked our school. He was someone that I was eagerly waiting for. A single squash racquet stuck up in amateur fashion from a book bag that he wore around his shoulders. This young man had beaten a strapping Canadian named Matt Serediak, 3–1 in games, at a Pan-American event one month earlier, yet you'd never have believed it by looking at him. Serediak was a four-time all-American at Cornell, and this pip-squeak had demolished him. You can't judge a book by its cover.

His name was Walter Weisskopf, and if I keep coaching the rest of my life, I'll never have a player as good. He's the best to have ever played squash in Maine. It was three years ago, when he stepped off the bus. He's played for me three years now and has one year to go. Clubs fly him down and host him to play tournaments in Virginia and New York. Summers, he plays tournaments in places like Jamaica, Ecuador, Columbia, and Rio de Janeiro. He hadn't wanted an Ivy League university, but he'd wanted to find a small college, instead. He'd written to me and a few other coaches. When I'd learned that he was a high school student at the German School in El Salvador, I'd started writing to him in German, in what little German I'd picked up while playing tennis there. Next thing, he visited and loved Bates. He's not much to look at in street clothes, but see him wearing shorts and see him move on the court and everything becomes clear. He'd studied chemistry, physics, and biology all in German at his high school. English was his third language.

Everyone calls him Che, for "Buddy." In his three years at Bates, he's earned the highest grade point average on either of my teams. He doesn't drink; he has no vices. He plays squash, and he stays up late at night studying. His parents tell me that they've never understood where his discipline comes from, but that he's always had it. He'd played squash in the early mornings before school back home, then trained for hours every day after school, and then studied all night. He's a borderline insomniac. He majors in economics and takes upper level math courses. He's never missed a practice or a match. Over three years, his record is 67–6 playing in the number one position for Bates, including his having defeated the number one players from Stanford, Yale, Dartmouth, Cornell, Brown, Williams, Amherst, Navy, Rochester, Franklin & Marshall, Bowdoin, and more. He's a freak of nature. I've never known quite what to say to him. I support him as best I can. But I watch him play and my jaw drops.

You get one player of that level on your team, and the level of the whole program rises. I try not to show favoritism, but my players tell me that every sentence out of my mouth is "Che-this," and "Che-that." I myself had once played number one for my college tennis team for two years, until my junior year, when in came a big, tall, freshman from Germany to take my spot. Joachim Hammer (his real name) was a computer science major who did nothing but play tennis, eat, study, and sleep. He was perfect. A machine. My coach loved the guy. He wasn't like me. I was the degenerate who'd joined a fraternity and would show up hungover for weekend practice or matches. I got in a fistfight and missed a semester of play. Even quit the team my senior year. I was a mess. I try to tone things down with Che. I want to support him and acknowledge him and reward him for his accomplishments, but I have to be careful and treat everyone the same.

At round-robins, players from other schools find out on what court Che is playing, and they sit and watch. One day a young man from India who played number one for his out-of-conference school came to watch Che, having heard about him but having never before seen him play. This was a quality player from India. He'd wanted to assess Che's level himself. I don't mean disrespect or cultural insensitivity, but this is how the story was related to me: he sat down behind the three-glass-walled court that Che was playing on at Yale and watched a mere one point before turning to my assistant coach and saying, *"Oh he's good."* He watched a second point, turned to my assistant again and with a smile said, *"He's berry good! He's a berry good player!"*

His opponents will occasionally do things like if they win a single point against him in competition, they'll stop play and turn and face the audience behind the glass and raise their arms and self-mockingly say: "I won a point!" Che is fast on his feet, fast with his hands, intensely well-conditioned, preternaturally calm, and uniquely creative as a player. I cannot grasp how he imagines some of the shot combinations that he puts together. He's a person of few words. He never exaggerates or repeats himself. I have seen him lose. And on those occasions he makes no excuses. He's nothing but class.

Once he graduates, I'll have to go into the future without him. I've gotten used to winning. Actually, my teams have won before Che, and they'll win after Che. But with him here now, it all becomes just so easy. So easy for me to sit back and let the show run itself. Success breeds success, and in having Che, top players hear about our school and apply to come. My players all say that I recruit well. So they always have good teammates and they always have good practice partners. Does that make me a good coach? I have one final season with Che. He'll earn his fourth all-American award and will win the Intercollegiate Squash Skillman Award for the outstanding senior male player-sportsman in the nation. I've been like a kid in a candy store. Me, with a player like this, at my little school in Maine.

Success is addictive. But if I'm going to coach for twenty more years, then I'll have to find a way to regulate the competitive addiction. If I don't find a way to temper it, then I'll be miserable. And I won't last. I don't believe in my heart that winning and striving to succeed are what matters. Coaches are supposed to teach sportsmanship, ethics, perspective. I try to, but these college kids arrive fully formed. They learn right from wrong as toddlers. There are limited modifications one can make at this point. The coach sets a standard of what behavior is allowed, and some players get booted and cannot meet the standard and cannot play on the team. These kids are also taught at a young age to care about winning. They're taught by their youth soccer coaches, baseball coaches, swim team coaches that they must try to win. It's horrible. It's already so deeply ingrained in their systems by the time they reach us that they don't want to hear their college coach telling them that winning doesn't matter. They don't want their college coach preaching to them in praise of mediocrity. My players like me because I speak with them truthfully about everything. I want them to know what I think about life. For my philosophy, many of them care while others don't. I tell them all anyway. I coach with sarcasm and irony. Some of my players like me as a generalist, while others just wish that I was the world's leading technical instructor. I'm the former, but I can't be the latter. They're glad to be on my winning teams, but they know that doesn't mean I'm an expert coach.

It's just been a lesson, to witness Che—to witness someone so good at what he does. It's all about vision. He's practiced so much that he operates automatically. His stroke mechanics and shots are ingrained deeply inside his system. His racquet preparation is so early it's stunning. He sees things like they're happening in slow motion. It's freakish. Tom Brady at quarterback, Roger Federer playing tennis, Tim Duncan playing basketball—they seem to have all the time in the world to get done anything that they need. I feel that way during noontime squash, when I play against my friends who are community members and hackers. I park myself on the T, which is the middle of the squash court. From there, I keep the rallies going and move them around. I'm in such control against them that it feels like slow motion to such a degree that I can see into the future. Then I start to fool myself into believing that I'm a very good player. But if I step onto the court with Che, everything suddenly becomes a blur. Things happen too quickly for me to make sense of. I'm always retrieving. I never have time to make sense of his shots and strategy. I never have time to prepare my racquet, feet, and body in time for my shots.

The college pace is slow to Che. Even at the top college pace, he sees into the future. He can see things before they happen. A science show on TV about the DARPA Challenge described the attempt by scientists to build autonomous robotic vehicles to cover a 132-mile course through the Mojave Desert. All vehicles but one were built to use sonar to bounce sound waves out against objects and read the return information to determine the next course of action. Most of the vehicles floundered. The scientists likened these robots' efforts to driving in the fog. The opposite of that is how Che plays, with such vision and clarity. We take vision for granted, but it's an amazing thing. I suppose that I was starting to get a little homesick for my players and my job. They're never far from my thoughts. Soon enough, I'll return to see them.

Awakening at the Wyoming border on our fourth day past Steamboat Springs, July 15, day number seventy-three, we were just twenty-two miles shy of Battle Pass and our exit to the town of Encampment. We'd reach it this day. And buy soft drinks. In the first half mile of our new state, Wyoming, we crossed a dirt road and encountered a huge flock of sheep which we had to wade through like Moses parting the Red Sea. We were midway through the chaos and deafening noise of the bleating sheep, our arms raised like wading into a cold ocean, when Gabe got silly and began flapping his arms and making squawking noises. Just then, up rode two shepherds on horseback wearing rifles and cowboy hats. Caught in the middle of their sheep, we sheepishly waved—rich kids in our backpacks. They scowled. We surmised that we were in a cowboy state now. Wyoming is the Cowboy State. The New Yorker Magazine recently had a satirical three-page piece about two guys who buy the state of Wyoming with the intention of remodeling it, which started like this:

My partner, Scott, and I recently purchased Wyoming, which we are in the process of having renovated, and, yes, I do know the square footage (something like two trillion seven hundred and thirty billion square feet, give or take). But that's just not a very practical type of measurement when you're dealing with all the plumbers and contractors and security staff and reporters and other non-wealthy service personnel we have to give instructions to. Nowadays, everybody involved in redoing substantial properties like ours uses Global Transverse Mercator Units (GTMUs), which you get off a satellite feed. GTMUs, we've found, are much more accurate for detail work like wainscoting, and are able to deal with vast alkali flats and so on, too. Basically, we are looking at this purchase as a tear-down. There's really not a lot here you'd want to keep, except one or two of the Wind River Mountains and some old nineteen-twenties Park Service structures in Yellowstone. Scott and I bought for location—it's convenient to anywhere, really, if you think about it—and for the simplicity of line. We wanted someplace rectangular, a much easier configuration from a design point of view, and we won't have to fuss with panhandles and changeable riverine property lines where we're going to get into disputes with the landowner next door. Spare us the headaches, please!

Our elevation for the past few days had been generally at around nine thousand feet. We pushed for town. The day lacked difficult climbs so we made quick time. We stepped out of the woods into a dirt parking lot off Route 70 by early afternoon. It was the spot for our eleven-mile hitchhike northeastward down out of the mountains to the low-lying town of Encampment on the plains. Parked there in that otherwise empty lot sat a woman inside her sports utility vehicle. She must've pulled off the road for a quick rest. Unthinkingly, Brett walked straight toward her intending to ask for a ride into town. The woman was clearly startled. The sight of us all suddenly materializing hairy-faced from the woods had unnerved her. She fumbled to roll up her windows and lock her doors. She pulled away with Brett still talking, waving, motioning, and walking after her. Even after she'd gone, Brett pretended to keep on asking her for a ride, a rare bit of improvisational comedy from serious Brett. It made us all laugh.

"Nice job, Brett."

"God, you really blew that one."

"That was our only chance."

"Great, now we'll never get a ride."

157

"Well done."

"Why don't you go stand by the road and scare someone else?"

Harry Potter.

Only three cars passed in the ninety minutes that we sat by desolate Route 70 on 9,915-foot Battle Pass. That mountain road that'd take us down to Encampment was closed in the wintertime from November until April. We finally piled into the bed of a pickup truck. Encampment was home to 443 people, and lies down at 7,300 feet, an old mining town at the base of the Sierra Madres. As if on cue, tumbleweed actually blew by on the street as we jumped out of the truck bed of the tattooed old ex-military man who'd saved us. The old guy had pointed out distant mountains to us on the way down, including the one on which his wife was buried and where he'd one day be buried beside her. Town had an overly wide main street and a half-dozen buildings. We took rooms at the ranch-style Bighorn Lodge conveniently located next door to the Split Rail Restaurant and Bar. The post office and Laundromat stood two doors down. That's just about all there was of town. It'd do nicely. Anyone there who needed a city fix could drive south to Steamboat Springs.

Encampment was founded in 1898. A copper mine up in the Sierra Madres above town once ran a sixteen-mile-long tramway down to a foundry. Remnants of the tram stand near a neighboring mining village that's famous for having once had a two-story outhouse, the top level of which was used only when the snow lay so deep that it covered the bottom level. People weren't allowed in the top level otherwise, due to the obvious complications that would create. Learning this, Porno cried: "Look out below!"

Cristina was home from Spain, according to my calendar. I needed to speak with her, but I had no phone in my room and I couldn't call her from this town. I needed a real conversation, not a distracted chat from whatever miserable payphone I could scrape up. I'd wait for the next town. In the meantime, here I'd recharge my batteries. Our hotel rooms cost under forty dollars. We entered the Split Rail Restaurant, whose hand-painted sign commanded: "experience the wide open wonders of wyoming." A few local families were inside eating. They stared. We were an oddity: two wearing Star Trek dry-fit uniforms and three tan-clothed communists in full beards impersonating Fidel Castro, and all of us covered with dirt. We sat in a large, round, padded booth, and we tested the limits of its all-you-can-eat salad bar. We made our waitress laugh. She put up with us. The others ate barbecue.

In Team Locust, I was the only vegetarian. I'm used to that. Happens wherever I go. It's frustrating and makes me sad. I just feel that it's so important to the planet, and I wish that there were more. I wish it was everyone, and one day eventually I know that it will be—but I'll be long gone by then. Not that my actions are perfect. Far from it. I'd occasionally spoken with Brett about it, trying to influence him, because he was the thoughtful one in our group and was the most outspokenly environmentally conscious one among us — and lots of people go veggie purely for environmental reasons. He'd listen to me and agree that I made sense. But then he'd sit and eat a burger right in front of me mere seconds later as if I'd never mentioned anything at all. I'd once had a player like that. It was infuriating. It was back in my earliest years as a coach, back when I was young and more radical and had a bumper sticker on my car which read, Eating Meat Is Obsolete. People would notice that bumper sticker. Late one night I'd passed through the men's basketball locker room when I'd noticed a Top-10 Things To Do This Weekend list that someone had written on a chalkboard. It was a bunch of stuff about drinking and going to parties, but the top item listed was: Eat Meat. Because it isn't obsolete!

On weekend trips with my squash teams, in restaurants, I lay out the ethical arguments against factory farming to all who sit near me — how it demonstrated our greed and cruelty as a species. I'm loads of fun! I'd had a few of my women's players convert to vegetarianism based on our conversations, but I'd never had a man convert because of my words. There was a guy named Scott McCarley who really seemed to listen, the way philosophical Brett was the only one in Team Locust who seemed to listen. Porno couldn't have cared less, but would've replied to my words with something like: "Mmm, I love this burger!" Todd was unwilling to hear and would've changed the subject to say how "fon-tostic" was some pointy peak in the Sister's Wilderness. And Gabe had his hands full trying to find himself. Like Brett now, back then McCarley would listen to me and nod, but then when the waitress would approach he'd order a pepperoni and sausage pizza as if I hadn't spoken a word. It went on like that, until I finally gave up on the guy. In some ways it was more frustrating to face that than to face an oblivious person. Then, quite amazingly, two years after McCarley graduated, I one day got an unexpected random note from him in the mail telling me that he thought I might like to know that he'd become vegetarian. So it'd taken effect after all. Just a delayed reaction. I wondered if that'd be the case with Brett. He certainly wasn't showing any sign of eliminating animals from his dinner plate, but I held out hope.

After dinner, we shuffled over to the bar. It shared a front porch with the restaurant. Uncharacteristically, I lingered, drank, and played foosball and pool. Frat boy Porno won both those games, defeating the rest of us. His type was familiar to me: the highly competitive, medium-height athletic frat boy who'd played high school sports yet who didn't play a varsity sport in college but excelled in all kinds of intramurals — basketball, floor-hockey, soccer — and then back in his frat house basement at night played and grew expert at darts, pool, foosball, Quarters, Beirut, and all manner of things. In Encampment, his training paid off. He rocketed foosballs with gunshot-popping sounds into the back of my opposing goal with calm, practiced jet-quick flicks of his wrist. He was a gamer like that.

159

It was hotel checkout that next morning of Saturday, July 16; then for breakfast in the restaurant next door we ate obscene amounts of food. An hour later, in Aunt Martha's This 'n That Crafts and Convenience Store across the street, we ate ice cream and rummaged through her gifts and antiques. Her sign read: The usual and the unusual. We'd had ice cream there that previous afternoon, too, while washing our laundry, so we were in tight with Aunt Martha. She'd taken to us, adopting us, asking us about the trail, where we were from, and how we were doing. Brett suddenly shocked us all by asking her for a ride out of town, back up into the mountains. He wasn't Yogiing. Brett was too direct to stoop to that. He was the classiest one of us all. Instead, it was a polite request. Brett had accidentally scared the bejeezus out of that SUV woman in the parking lot back on Battle Pass that previous day, but this was different. Aunt Martha explained that afternoon plans precluded her from driving us, but she said we could take her car and drive ourselves back up to the trail. She said we should leave her car and the keys at Battle Pass, and that she'd ride up with a friend that following day to retrieve her car. She handed Brett the car keys. Our eyes popped open. It was amazingly trustful generosity. We thanked her profusely and bought more ice cream.

Suave Brett's landing us of the car keys was enough to solidify his status in our group as the politically gifted and professionally competent one. The rest of us had all fallen into recognizable niches within Team Locust, as well: Todd as the goofy mountain man; Porno as the spirited leader of the communist trio; me as the Yogiing Coyote trickster; and bobble-headed Gabe as my nemesis, put on earth to annoy me and get under my skin.

We'd our very own SUV now! It was tempting to hop in and drive all the way to Canada. We loaded our packs in the SUV and drove a short distance down to the town's Grandview Park to the third annual Grand Encampment Cowboy Gathering of Carbon County. No, we weren't rushing from town just yet. There was live music and a cowboy poetry reading. There was a very small crowd. It was nice to see families and children. People are the same everywhere you go—they really are. In the fields out behind the park was a replica frontier town erected to show what life had been like long ago in the west with home, church, school, blacksmith's shop, and fur trading stand. There were open-aired tents stocked with goods for sale like old knives, arrows, and hatchets. We wandered about, examining drums, antlers, and skins. I finally grew tired and returned to the park to lie in the grass near our SUV. Gabe came over and napped beside me. A high school–aged girl sat under a tree nearby reading the sixth Harry Potter book. I asked if she liked it. She did. She was proud to say that the book had only been released nationwide that previous night when the clock had struck twelve, and that she'd driven down to Steamboat Springs to cue up to buy it alongside a large crowd of others who'd all dressed in Harry Potter costumes for the midnight sales bash. In just one sleep-deprived day, she was already on page four hundred. She wasn't going to stop until she'd finished. Simply to avoid being Mr. Creepy-Guy, I stopped pestering the girl and I napped next to Gabe while waiting for the others.

Dead Crow.

The trail slants northwestward across Wyoming. During it's run up the state, it holds three distinct aspects: the first third of the trail in Wyoming was the desertlike Great Divide Basin, then the middle third was the Wind River Mountain Range, and lastly the trail cut through Yellowstone National Park. All trip, Todd had been speaking about of the glories of the Wind River Mountains. He'd never been there, but he'd heard from numerous sources that it was the highlight of the CDT. But first we had to walk through the Great Divide Basin, and that'd be difficult because inside it lies in The Red Desert. That'd be rough because I knew it was going to hurt my feet again.

We exited Encampment and drove ourselves westward up to Battle Pass in our very own SUV. We left Aunt Martha's truck at the pass and got immediately inundated by bloodthirsty mosquitoes. We picked up the CDT trailhead and walked northward. We had only one small ridge to cross before we'd descend to the outskirts of the low Great Divide Basin. We climbed leisurely up above tree line. It was evening and we were only looking for a place to set up our tents. We eased our way up a grassy hillside amidst patches of snow and we found a cement structure atop a pile of rocks. We climbed and sat on the cement flattop, taking photographs and surveying the surrounding land. Then we continued northward thirty minutes longer, gaining the open, gentle, grassy ridge. We tented high amidst some bushes, surrounded by fields of snow. Our nighttime view looked eastward down over the lights of Encampment as well as the neighboring hamlet of Saratogo, lying low on the plain.

On the morning of July 17, Gabe rose and farted relentlessly, as he was prone to do. They were loud and deliberate noises, to show off for Porno. For once I couldn't take it. I'd let it go before, but I'd enough. I said, "You know something—it's not always funny!" He disagreed: "Yes, actually it is always funny." We argued back and forth for an hour while walking along, over whether or not excessive farting at some point loses its charm. The others just listened and couldn't believe that we were debating this. Sometimes the bickering between Gabe and me was like that of two pack dogs, each trying not to hold lowest-in-pack status. Todd and Porno were both needed for their route finding and leadership, while Brett was needed as Porno's old college friend. But Gabe and I were dispensable Team Locust members, so it fell on us to be needed, and we'd end up bumping heads over things. The others would've handled that farting bit differently. If called out on it, Porno would've farted even louder and then laughed so loud that you'd have to laugh, too; Brett never would've farted that way to begin with, as he was too classy; and Todd would've said: "Dude, whatever!" and wouldn't have said another word about

161

it. But Gabe wasn't one to back down from an argument and neither was I. I stated my case. Gabe and I argued, and it created tension. But Gabe didn't fart audibly again for a week.

I followed Todd. Always a wise strategy. We were to veer northeastward down off the high ridge, but we left it too soon and spent two hours off the trail, descending, bushwacking cross-country around a high ridge. It caused us to have to climb steeply again up cliffsides to regain the ridge and get back on track. Even when Todd got lost things turned out okay. Late afternoon, we crested a final hill and walked down out of the trees to barren, waterless low ground.

The Great Divide Basin's desert wouldn't begin until we exited the north side of our upcoming trail town Rawlins, but here was a taste. We wouldn't have any more trees for the next one hundred miles. We tented under a nearly full harvest moon on a wide rolling mountaintop with a 360-degree view and a sky filled with stars so bright that we didn't even consider setting up our tents. The air was still. No chance of rain. We lay on the ground in our sleeping bags. It was utterly glorious.

The morning of July 18, found us facing a waterless thirty-six-mile dirt road walk northward into Rollins. My feet began overheating immediately. We passed wild horses, deer, and pronghorn sheep. We stopped to watch the horses arc, curve, and veer away upon spying us. There wasn't a single car on the dirt road. We could've been on Mars. The going was tedious. It was iPod time for the others, all of them cocooned away, plugged into their earphones.

Our water ran out. The sun beat down, and there was no escaping the oppressive sun. Porno-Brett-Gabe shuffled off the dirt road to eat their communist lunches in a field one hundred yards away, scrunching down under the hanging planks of a dilapidated shed for shade. Todd and I kept the flow and continued without them. We were shooting to reach a water source called Muddy Creek. We found it beside the dirt road, just a stagnant puddle at the base of a deep sinkhole amongst weeds. Todd bent down and filtered the lukewarm water when suddenly he screamed and jumped backward, for inside the water floated a large dead crow. Fantastic!

We were two miles ahead of the others and we just kept going. The dusty, dirty desert road undulated, twisted and turned. Our footsteps kicked dust into the air. We were parched. Our lips chapped and cracked. The warm dead-crow water wasn't tasting good. Our skin turned scaly. Except for my foot pain, I felt numb to the world. I wore a bandana under the back of my baseball hat to protect my neck from the sun. I ground my hiking stick into the dirt as I walked, to lessen the strain on my burning feet. The others never caught up. In was early evening when we saw our first car of the day. It was a midsixties couple from Rawlins, out on a leisurely pickup truck drive south of town. They stopped when we flagged them down. Sometimes people should be more wary than they are. Blind trust is wonderful, but who can smartly apply it every time? Each of us has only one life, after all. Todd let me do the talking. He knew the routine. It was quite important now that I use my skills. Brett was direct, but he missed all the coyote trickster fun of good Yogiing.

"Hi!" I said, waving, smiling.

"Hi," they answered, taking a good look at pitiful us.

"Thank you SO MUCH for stopping," I said. "This is crazy out here."

"That's all right," the man said. "How are you doing?"

"Oh, we're totally okay," I said, and paused. "Absolutely. We're on our way into Rawlins. We're hiking the Continental Divide Trail."

"Where'd you start?"

"We all started down in Mexico," I said. "About three months ago. There're five of us. The others are back behind us, but they're coming along. You'll probably see them in about an hour. We're all hiking to Canada. It feels like we started a year ago."

The couple was interested and clearly very nice. They would've offered us water on their own, but to plant the seed in their heads—the real fun of Yogiing—and shake them out of their reverie concerning all the questions they suddenly had about through-hiking, I repeated myself a bit: "Yeah, the others'll be coming along at some point. You'll see them. They stopped awhile back, but we had to keep going because we ran out of water."

"You need some water?"

Bingo! Jackpot.

"Oh my god, that would be great. That would be amazing. Thank you so much. We didn't know if maybe you had some."

It never was my intention to be cynical or unpleasant to anyone, let alone people who were trying to help us. It wasn't that type of a thing. Truth was we were thrilled to have someone to converse with. It was always fun to meet and joke back and forth with others in this way. Sometimes it was fun when people teased us and gave us the business ("You really are crazy now, aren't you?"). It was also fun to elicit horror, sympathy, and wonder. And we really needed the water. A person could surely die out here. The guy and his wife started rummaging around.

"This really is amazing," I said. "You're pretty much saving our lives. We ran out of water about three hours ago. It's been so hot all day and there's just no shade. The only water that we found had a dead crow lying inside it and we had to drink that."

Todd loved my improvisational addition of the dead crow story, which I'd thrown into the mix for good measure. He'd later claim that it was inspired. In Todd's retelling of the story to the communists later, my having mentioned the dead-crow-in-the-water portion of our plight had viscerally caused the couple to nearly wretch, and then they'd practically begun catapulting cold water bottles out of their truck at us.

Regular, Respectable People.

Rejuvenated, Todd and I kept going well after dark. It'd been a long while since either of us had recorded a thirty-mile day, and here was our chance. We walked until ten thirty at night, shuffling northward in the moonlight. We knew that we were getting painfully close to the unmarked paved road that led ten miles westward into Rawlins. We reached the road and collapsed, having made it what we calculated to have been a thirty-six-mile hiking day. At last!

The first car that we saw that next morning of Tuesday, July 19, stopped and gave us a ride into Rawlins. We could've walked it in, but instead we took the ride. My feet hurt so much that I could barely stand. It was a minivan cluttered with rocks of every imaginable shape and size. The driver was an amateur geologist from Texas, who was on a break from work, out with his dog collecting rocks. He told us that he and the dog slept in his truck at night. It was easy to smell that that was true.

Rawlins had 9,380 people. Todd and I took a room at the Jade Hotel, which had owners from India and smelled like curry. It was a parking-lot ranch hotel with cars stationed inches away from the hotel room doors. At forty-two dollars for a double room, we could hear TV noise coming through the walls around us. We left our door open to the world, as hikers do, and spread out our things and aired out. We had the whole day free. We walked the streets, washed laundry. Bought soda, water, and juice to hydrate ourselves. Main Street in Rawlins had signs in many of its storefront windows advertising imminent closings. I found a barbershop and paid for a buzz cut. Someone mentioned that Rawlins was a hotbed for Methamphetamine labs. The town hadn't died yet, but it seemed on its way.

Newspapers were all filled with news of a bombing in England in the London subway, The Tube, which'd killed hundreds. It was sad to read. Shit happens everywhere. Bates College recently had a music professor who was sent to federal penitentiary for twenty years for cooking crack cocaine in her oven and selling it. Also, the captain of the Bates men's lacrosse team had gotten stabbed by a knife and killed at three o'clock in the morning a couple years back in an off-campus altercation with local teenagers while walking home from a party. Lacrosse teammates who testified in court admitted under oath to having each drunk as many as twenty beers apiece that night along with smoking pot and snorting cocaine. They were in-season at the time; an odd but predictable detail. Colby College recently had a young women, a student from Maine, get raped and killed while walking to her car in the parking lot outside her dormitory at seven o'clock on a Sunday morning. The man who confessed to the crime had a history of mental instability and was on the run, up from Florida, already wanted by the police. Bowdoin College had a visiting student fall off a roof and die during a party at one of their social houses a few years back. It's an unsafe world. Tragedies can happen anywhere, anytime. Sometimes it's your fault, sometimes it's not. Sometimes you're on the wrong roof or in the wrong subway at the wrong time. Sometimes you cook crack cocaine in your oven, sometimes you don't. We're in control, until we're not.

Famished, we discovered a world-class diner in the middle of the action off Main Street: Square Shooters Eating House. It was the busiest store on the street by far. A bumper sticker on a truck parked outside read: Gun control means using both hands. We sat in a booth. The menus had an illustration on the covers of a cowboy swinging a lasso under the slogan: square shooters, for regular respectable people. It was a bright, clean, sprawling place, like the pancake mega-restaurant in Snoqualmie Pass off Interstate 90 on the PCT in Washington, except without the dividers, and instead of anonymous interstate travelers, in here everyone seemed to know each other. People were talking across the aisles and calling the staff by name. Rawlins was a center for sheep ranching. The menu had a section offering bag lunches for cattle workers to take out into the fields. A flyer on our table propped up beside the ketchup jar listed the house rules. It was intended as a joke—sort of—but the rules suddenly started to give me a creeped-out feeling:

Do not shine your Boots with the Tablecloth.
Dudes and stuffed shirts will be admitted at their
*   own risk.*
Customers will refrain from Whistling or Shouting
*   for Service.*
If you've had a "Hard Day" on the Trail, don't take it
*   out on the waitress.*
Unless you own a "Parcel" of land in the State of
*   Wyoming, you ain't got no Rights.*
Cowhands and sheepherders must shake the Dust
*   from their Britches before being seated.*
You get Hanged for Rustling in Wyoming...no
*   pilfering our Horses, Sheep-Dogs or Women.*

I didn't know what it meant to be a Stuffed Shirt. And for that matter, nor did I know what it meant to be a regular, respectable person. Were we regular, Todd and I? If not, were we allowed in? What if we limped? Or had lisps? I've a close friend who's in a wheelchair. He just played a tennis tournament in Flushing Meadows in New York City and beat a world-ranked wheelchair tennis player who'd flown in for the event from France. Was he regular? And who were they trying to protect, anyway? Or was it them just policing their own?

The counter sold postcards of generic nature photographs—grizzly bear, buffalo, and bighorn sheep. Charismatic Mega-Fauna. We ordered eggs, pancakes, home fries, and toast. I ordered extra potatoes and loaded them with salt. I can never seem to get enough salt. We drank Cokes, water, orange juice, and coffee, still struggling to hydrate (and yes, of course we knew that Coke and caffeinated coffee were diuretics). We got a couple odd looks, but we were accepted. The restaurant was going out of business we learned, after operating for sixty years. Maybe they'd run out of regular people who could eat there.

We reached Porno-Brett-Gabe on Todd's cell phone. Todd had a cell phone, but he almost never used it. P-B-G'd taken a room at a different hotel. We all met for dinner at a Thai restaurant called Anong's Cuisine, which was new to town and had a chef who'd just arrived from California. At the next table sat a bicyclist in spandex writing notes on paper. Outside was his bike and a tow-cart stacked with gear. We invited him over to eat with us. He was a Korean journalist named Euntaek Hong who was riding lengthwise across America and was sending essays to his hometown newspaper. He interviewed us and took a group photograph, promising to write us up in an article, how he'd met a crazy group who were out hiking the Continental Divide mountain chain. We'd soon be celebrities in Korea!

Euntaik gave us his hotel room number in town, and that night we kidnapped him by Carbon County Cab and took him with us to a movie theatre to watch the Johnny Depp remake of Willy Wonka and the Chocolate Factory. The volume was so loud that during the songs I thought my eardrums would burst. The others didn't seem to mind. I think it was possibly due to their having been listening to their iPods all summer. I slept well in Rawlins. I was mentally exhausted. My feet ached. I made helpful telephone calls to my family and friends, to catch up. Cristina was back. She told me what I knew she'd say: "Don't torture yourself." The Red Desert began north of town. I kept trying to prepare myself for it.

Red Desert Crossing.

The Red Desert is what's inside Wyoming's Great Divide Basin. The CDTA's map of the Continental Divide Trail shows the trail splitting in southern Wyoming and leading on two sides around the Red Desert and then rejoining, thus creating an oval. It's the only spot like it on any of the three triple crown trails. For whatever weird reason, the CDTA's marked both ways around it as the CDT route, but if a hiker takes one way and neglects the other, then they're really not technically hiking every inch of the CDT. The red desert is barren and waterless. It was going to feel as if we were back in New Mexico.

Awakening late in Rawlins on Wednesday, July 20, we returned to Anong's Thai restaurant for lunch. We had Srirasha noodles and red and green curry. The chef sent us out a complimentary cake as we'd made friends with him the night before—he and the communists all talking about California. We lounged in the town library through the afternoon, and made mini-excursions to buy groceries. We met a homeless man in an alley who led us into an abandoned building to show us a series of enormous, complex murals that someone had painted on the walls. He wouldn't tell us who'd painted them. It might've been him. He denied it, but he had paint on his jacket.

We set out at dusk to post some cool night miles. We walked northward out of town on flat, straight, paved Highway 287. We walked single file up the road's wide shoulder. Darkness fell and the stars and moon shone. My backpack was far too heavy. It was the heaviest it'd weighed all trip. Through fear of the desert, I'd loaded it with dry food and had overdone it with nuts and also with having packed six liter-sized water jugs. Gabe screamed and we all shuffled over and saw that he'd almost stepped on a rattlesnake. We put on our headlamps and shone them down on the ground. The snake was alive but didn't move. It'd been warming itself on the shoulder of the road at night, on asphalt that'd retained the heat from the sun. It was small. It was the first rattlesnake that I'd seen all trip. No, rattlesnakes weren't an issue out here. We pushed it off the road with a stick and watched it grudgingly uncoil and slither away. We walked with our headlamps on after that, training light on the pavement before us.

It was after midnight by the time we'd finished the twelve miles it took to reach our goal, the abandoned paved road into the desert. We set up our tents; then we each pulled out a can of lukewarm Budweiser beer. We'd each brought just one. In town, we'd talked about Weekender's tradition, and we'd decided to adopt it thereafter. I liked the tradition. We savored our lukewarm beers, eyes closed, sipping them slowly in the darkness. Except for Porno, who drank his straight down. We all looked over at him and he just looked back and belched and said: "I don't sip shit."

Four Days in the Red Desert, inside the Great Divide Basin, awaited. July 21, we exited northward-leading Highway 287 and walked northwestward up a cracked, abandoned asphalt road. The sun blazed down. Its strength was unnerving—made us want to curl up into a ball and die. There wasn't so much as a single bush for a dozen miles in any direction. Nothing out here was large enough to offer us shade. Midmorning, spread out, heads down and each of us deep in our individual reverie on the abandoned Mad-Max, Road-Warrior, cracked-to-hell asphalt road, a cyclist came up behind us offering us a break from the monotony. The man got off his bike and we greeted him. He was cycling from Mexico to Canada, following the Divide at moments like this, whenever he could. His gear was high-tech, including a banana hat that protected his face as well as the back of his neck from the sun. Expensive sunglasses. We all walked together, talking. He'd identified us as through-hikers and he volunteered that he'd through-hiked the Appalachian Trail.

"What year?" I asked.

"Nineteen ninety-three."

"That's my year! What was your trail name?" I asked.

"Eddie-B."

"Get out!" I said. "Get the hell out! I know you! I met you! Your name is Ed Burgess. You're from Maryland and you work in computers."

He was flabbergasted, stunned that I knew all this.

"I met you just one day," I said. "We only talked for like ten minutes."

Everyone stared at me as if to say that if it'd only been ten minutes, how had I remembered it?

"Everyone knew Eddie-B!" I clarified. I said to him: "You used to run ultramarathons. You told me about it. You were thirty-five years old back then. You must be forty-seven now."

"That's exactly right."

I was excited. I said to the others: "This is Eddie-B! This guy was the fastest hiker in '93. He hiked the AT in two months."

"Sixty-eight days," he corrected.

"He blew by us all, and everyone told jokes about him for the rest of the summer."

"What was your trail name?" he asked.

"Sneakers," I said.

It wasn't ringing a bell for him, but that was okay. I hadn't expected it to. I said, "I met you at the Walasi-yi Center in Neels Gap. It was my fourth day hiking. I was with a few other people and we'd all limped in there exhausted. Then you waltzed in with a day pack. Everyone had heard that you'd made it those forty miles from Springer Mountain to Neels Gap in one day, so I sat and talked with you for about ten minutes and pumped you full of questions because I was a total novice. Then you took off and none of us ever saw you again. But then we heard stories and read things about you in the journals in the shelters all summer. We all had Eddie-B jokes. It was really funny to us at the time, out there in the cold, drizzly Georgia mountains."

I couldn't believe that this guy was now standing before me. It'd be the equivalent of twelve years from now running into Todd or Porno on a trail somewhere, like on the summit of some random peak in the Adirondacks. In the twelve years since, he'd made a few short hikes and had continued his passion of ultramarathon running, he said. Then his knees had given out, so now he just biked. He got back on his bike and rode on. He was always passing me, that pesky guy. Probably I'll see him again in an old folks home one day, and he in his walker or in his wheelchair will box me out and reach the salad bar before me.

We hiked thirty-one miles that day, in trying to reach a Ley map reservoir so we could end the day with a swim, but we came up three miles short. It was a Team Locust record push. Angels appeared from out of the clouds and sung songs to us. The road had changed from pavement to dirt. The day's effort ruined my feet. My feet had been fine when on ice walking through Colorado's snow in my running shoes, but the Red Desert found them superheating again. They'd grown so tender to the touch that my heels hurt in making the initial foot-plant at the start of each footstep. After that came even greater pain on the balls of my feet as I'd flatten each step and push forward. Without the push, I couldn't have kept the pace—but the push was excruciatingly painful. Inching along would've hurt less, but then I'd have gotten left behind to die a thousand deaths in the desert of dehydration, starvation, loneliness, sunburn, rattlesnake bite, spider bite, grizzly bear bite, gunshot, earthquake, poison frog, pestilence, broken limbs, Lyme disease, scurvy, scabies, rickets (well, maybe not rickets), Giardia, Rocky Mountain spotted fever and Dead-Crow-In-Water disease.

It wasn't much fun. Yet somewhere deep inside I realized that I liked this. I loved it. Maybe I enjoy pain. Maybe that's why I hike. It certainly explains why I love squash. The others had ailments, too: Gabe had sunburn, Todd had backpack rash, Porno had his testicles chaffing, which he shared abundant details about. We were all dehydrated. Brett said that dehydration makes all the little aches and pains worse. We sipped our water to conserve it. We lay down to sleep on a bare hilltop, no greenery within eyesight in any direction, just the shapes of mountains rising on all the distant horizons, surrounding us. We were in the desert. In the basin. We had yet another sky filled with stars overhead. We went to sleep knowing that we could go swimming that next morning.

Todd had been aware of the location of the reservoir all along, and it'd factored prominently into our thoughts, functioning as incentive in the form of salvation. We rose early on July 22, and in three miles found the reservoir directly beside our dirt road, as Todd had said it would be. I had my photocopies of Todd's Ley maps, which I'd made back in Steamboat Springs by staying up late at the night tracing the trail's route in red marker—but out here it all looked the same. I couldn't make sense of the very far apart contour lines.

The reservoir was a man-made pond in the dirt in the middle of nowhere. A smidgeon of foliage grew around the shoreline, and a fence led around the perimeter to keep cows out. Strangely, there were cows out here in the Red Desert, along with the deer and elk. These, as well as all the cows that we'd seen that summer had plastic tags on their ears, even the babies. Something about that made me feel awful. Imagine the most beautiful thing in the world: a mother giving birth. And then someone comes along and staples a colored plastic tag on the calf's ear. The baby looks at its mother and sees the plastic tag on her ear, too. It must make them sad to see that in each other, to know that they can't protect each other any better.

Those cows with the plastic ear tags were parched in the desert. They were thirsty as shit. They were all owned and marked for inevitable slaughter. All would be rounded up and pushed into trucks and pushed out of trucks, and pushed into lines to keep a date with a sledgehammer. They'll wind up in your burger. They see this pond and approach it: "Hey, great, water." But the fence keeps them out. So they walk around to the western side and lie in the tiny trickle of muddy runoff. Beggars can't be choosers. I wished I could help the cows. We spent one hour swimming and eating at the reservoir. It was wonderful to have water, but we still lacked shade.

Around two o'clock that afternoon, heading westward, we came upon dirt Ore Road crossroad which led eleven miles northward to the hamlet of Jeffrey City, population twelve. Todd'd heard that there was a bar. So of course we decided to hitchhike in. The shadelessness had worn us down and was killing us. A bar would mean a much-needed roof to sit under. We desperately needed a break from the sun. Our plan was to reach the bar to hydrate and escape the sun for a few hours, then return to this spot and resume our hike in the evening to make some night miles. But no cars came. The longer we waited, the more we wanted to reach that twelve-person town. While waiting, we invented a rock-throwing game. Brett placed one of his empty water bottles fifteen yards away and we all picked up small stones and tried to hit it. Surprisingly, Todd hit the most. He said that he'd played on his high school baseball team. Every time that he struck with a shot, he'd scream out his last name like it was a sports commentator worshipping him on some highlight reel:

"Bradley!"

"Oh! Bradley!"

"Yes, Bradley!"

A pickup truck finally came. We'd almost given up. You can't control cause and effect's trillions and trillions of iterations, like all those back since fish first crawled out of the sea, which had led this driver here. It was the first vehicle in an hour, and the guy stopped and gave us a ride. The restaurant-bar in Jeffrey City was empty and cold—perfect! The couple local residents inside were uninterested in our appearance. We drank water, soda, beer. We ate salads, sandwiches, french fries, ice cream, pie. We were thrilled that they had all this food and these drinks. We lingered for three glorious hours. The others watched television and didn't stop eating. Gabe and I moved into the darkness of an adjacent room and we lay on the tiled floor on our mattress pads and sleeping bags and slept. I can't pass up the opportunity for a nap. Napping is the greatest luxury in the history of the world.

An oil company engineer gave us a ride southward down dirt Ore Road, back to the CDT. We thanked him profusely, stepping out of his truck at six o'clock in the evening, and continued westward. That break in Jeffrey City with its water and the nap had been wonderful. It'd saved us. Jeffrey City itself was on Highway 287, so we could've road-walked there from Rawlins. Not only that, but Highway 287 then led onward around the desert and passed through the subsequent trail towns of Lander, Dubois, and even West Yellowstone in Montana. The whole way could've been a highway walk. I was surprised that the CDTA didn't have that be the case. You can trace little back-way Highway 287 from Beaumont, Texas, at the Gulf of Mexico, all the way up through Dallas, Amarillo, Denver, Fort Collins, Laramie, Rawlins, Jeffrey City, Lander, Dubois, Yellowstone National Park, West Yellowstone, and on up to Helena, Montana, where it ends shortly afterward in the small town of Choteau. The CDT took us constantly southwestward of that road, and so we'd always exit northward and eastward to the little trail towns.

We hiked briskly. I didn't enjoy it. It was as if we felt bad or guilty over having taken an afternoon break and were now compensating by ridiculous surge-hiking at a "Four-Plus" rate of speed. Up a series of hills, we discovered an uncharacteristic green oasis of trees and undergrowth inside a fenced enclosure the size of a tennis court. It was an aberration, the first trailside greenery that we'd seen in days. The perimeter fence kept out livestock. We knew we'd find water inside. We weren't desperate, having just come from town, but on the other hand one doesn't pass up water. We hopped the fence and found a trickle. Todd disappeared to forage around. We heard him cry his name, *"Bradley!"* He reappeared carrying a deer antler. It was bone-white and tremendously heavy. We passed it around taking turns examining it. The weight of it spoke to the impressive neck muscles that the deer must've had in order to carry such antlers around. The liberating feeling that deer get when shedding antlers every winter must be similar to what a hiker feels upon arriving in town and dropping their backpack to suddenly walk around packless. Soldiers say that the greatest thing about being a soldier is taking off your pack.

Strangely, I fell in love with that antler. As a vegetarian, I've never been a huge Antlers-On-the-Wall kind of guy—but just something about that one struck me. I made a deal with Todd, that I'd pay for our next two hotel rooms if he'd not only give me the antler but carry it out to town. I just didn't think I could carry it. My feet hurt too much and I couldn't shoulder the extra weight. Todd wavered until I told him that I'd throw in a pizza, too. I just couldn't get over the chance that I had to mail the antlers to my young nephew and niece in New York with a note explaining that it'd come "From the Red Desert of Wyoming." We petered out at midnight and flopped down on an exposed hillside. We slept under the stars for a second straight night of unsurpassed views.

On July 23, third day in the Red Desert, I experienced my most painful hiking day of the summer. My feet hurt so badly that I fell far behind in the morning. All I could do was shuffle forward. The others disappeared ahead out of sight. Only when they stopped for their daily midmorning break did I inch up and catch them. But I didn't sit down. I had momentum and didn't want to lose it. The trail led over a rocky hillside. So to keep in motion I continued without pause—to get ahead in order to not fall behind. On top of the hill, I grew confused at a fork in the trail, so I stopped to wait for Team Locust to rise from its break and catch up. But they didn't materialize. I waited a long time, until I suddenly grew concerned that something had gone wrong. A twinge of panic overcame me. I started swiftly backtracking southward, adrenaline surging through me, thinking that perhaps I'd missed something and had come the wrong way. After a hundred yards, though, here came the others climbing up the rocky path toward me. Nothing was wrong, I just hadn't waited long enough. My feet hurt so much and I felt so angry. Emotions were exaggerated for me. Perhaps it was due to my lacking Prozac. I spun around to the north with both fists clenched. I threw my hiking stick as far as I could. Angry, angry, angry.

My feet hurt so badly that I wanted to cry, yet my pride wasn't about to allow me to ask Team Locust to slow down and wait. I strengthened my resolve. My intense anger—at what, at my feet, at the trail, at the others?—charged my day. I felt foot pain throughout the day, but I pushed it away and hiked at the pace of Team Locust without falling behind again. I used my anger as fuel to keep up. I was mostly silent the whole day. Walking took such will that I had to stay buried deep within myself. I hadn't imagined that I'd be able to do it, yet on I went throughout the day, pushing, pushing. Suddenly, without my realizing it, the hours had passed.

Our day had been spent walking exposed dirt roads, hour after hour under the blazing sun. We found our first water source at dinnertime. Following his Ley maps, Todd found a spring tucked off the trail, behind large boulders in an acre-sized grassy enclosure where clean water rested in a small covered well. We lifted its iron lid and hung our bodies down into the well in order to reach the water in the basin below. Clouds rolled swiftly in and the temperature dropped like an anchor, to the point that it was actually chilly. We'd been practically dying of heat, and now we had to bundle up. There were only extremes out there. We sat for an hour, eating, covering ourselves under our tarps from a brief trickle of cold rain. I'd already taken ten Motrin this day, to ease my foot pain. Just like I'd done on the PCT, I was taking handfuls of Motrin every day. I sat and ate with my shoes and socks off, to chill my feet.

Sweetwater River.

Our day's goal was to reach the Sweetwater River near the end of the Red Desert. It'd make our dehydration problems disappear. We left the well and hiked six more miles until dusk. The day's end found us crossing a dried-out marsh and then descending down a wedge through large boulders. We weren't yet within sight of the river, but we could tell that we were getting close. We stopped after sunset in a sloped clearing which contained a herd of sleeping cows. The startled cows leapt up, cried out, and scurried away over and around the boulders. They didn't have time to organize. Some ran down toward the river, while others scrambled up around the boulders to escape us. We'd accidentally split their group for the night. I worried that we might've split mother from child in the chaos. I felt sad for the cows. Gabe laughed about it. It was the end of my most painful hiking day on the entire trail and everything was making me angry. All summer we'd seen how amazing cows

172

are with mother-and-child bonding. I actually got into a fight with Gabe over it, over the splitting up of the cows at night. Porno and Todd couldn't have cared less. Diplomatic Brett, who picked his spots and picked his battles, wouldn't enter into it.

"How can you not care?" I hissed.

Even Gabe was surprised by my vitriol and backed away and let this one alone. My words, sadness, and anger probably scared all of them. Nobody likes to argue with an unstable person. It made me feel lonely. I knew that I had to get home. Home to Maine, and home to my life. My time out here was counting down, was slowly but surely grinding to an end. Cow patties lay everywhere. Through the weeks and months, we'd grown inured to them, and we slept amongst them without a second thought.

No through-hiker could ask for anything more than to awaken to face an easy downhill to a river, especially in light of having just crossed a desert. Our descent to the Sweetwater River on the morning of July 24 felt like a reward for all our hard work of the past few days. We were saved. The river was wide, shallow, and slow. Rocks stuck up out of the water everywhere. The branches of fluffy willow trees overhung the banks. Beyond the riverbanks were high bluffs, like in New Mexico's Gila River Valley, except that these bluffs weren't as high, nor as close, nor as steep. These bluffs sloped away, so there wasn't nearly the same level of claustrophobia here. The river snaked back and forth. The trail was a narrow sliver that constantly disappeared, because in many places it'd been washed away. We had to ford back and forth through the river dozens of times while constantly searching for the trail. The fords served to cool my feet.

We fell into the rhythm of the bends, the fords and the searching for the trail. We followed the river for hours, trying to keep to the path. It became a competition, to see which of us could find the trail first. There were some cows in the river valley. They marched down, up and away from us, just like the ducks had done in the Gila. There were birds in the trees. The animals didn't know quite what to make of us. This was going to be a town day. That was the best part of all. We followed the river for twelve miles—which is a very long way. Just when we thought our river walk might never end, we came to a bridge and road crossing, as Todd's Ley maps had shown we would. We left the river and began an overland, off-trail, cross-country trek through chaparral, aiming to reach our gateway out, Route 28.

Mormons.

Everywhere were small, tough bushes, the same landscape as that near Mexico. They lay irregularly situated, so we couldn't get a smooth gait but had to zigzag through them. It was easy to chart our course. It required simply gazing northward across the desert floor toward the hills on the horizon, for our destination was Route 28, just beyond the hills. It was midafternoon when we found a dirt road that'd take us our final few miles. That was when lightning stopped us in our tracks. Pitch-black clouds rolled swiftly in from the west. That was how it always began. We hadn't reached the hills and the trees yet, but were still standing exposed on the desert floor. We'd nowhere to hide and the storm was heading straight toward us. Nothing could stop it. We were five miles shy of the hills. Brett'd been walking far out ahead, and we could see him, a tiny figure, pushing for the trees. The rest of us had no chance to race there but we had to hunker down. We could see lightning bolts strike the earth as it approached. It was a low storm with low clouds and admirably strong, healthy lightning. This was bad.

Just before the storm reached us, a pickup truck came southward. It was nice to see humans, but they were headed in our opposite direction. I rose in my unofficial capacity as our group's designated Yogier, for Team Locust had long-since agreed that I was the best bull-shitter, fibber, and used-car salesman in the group. The others wanted to see if I could use the Dead-Cow story. There wasn't any real Yogiing objective this time because we were okay on water. No, stopping the truck was more out of habit than anything else—just to make a friend, just to connect. It was a young couple: guy was nice, an ex–University of Wyoming football player. I mentioned our hike and they handed us one beer apiece. They left and we sat sipping our beer, except Porno, who guzzled. We played our rock-throwing game ("Oh, Bradley!"), and waited for death ("Calm down, calm down"). Lightning was about to kill us. We all knew it. We were scared shitless, yet we remained outwardly cheerful and resigned to our fate. We'd been walking innocently along and now here we were through no fault of our own about to be burnt to cinders by huge bolts from the sky. We didn't feel good about it.

Three cars in a caravan came southward on the dirt road, heading into the desert. Again: wrong direction. I rose to Yogi us more beer. Or something. Anything. Whatever. I flagged down the lead car and it reluctantly stopped. You could tell that there'd been some internal discussion about whether to stop. Strangers don't always realize that we're just a ragtag bunch of dehydrated hikers begging for morsels. They can't be expected to know that, and we never blame people for not stopping. Life is simply too crazy. For us, every time a through-hiker hitchhikes you put your life into their hands—for you never know who's going to pick you up. Likewise, the drivers don't know us. Stopping this caravan was just silly. We were about to die anyway, so what did it matter? I stood in the road trying to look harmless. I approached the lead car and spoke through the passenger window, which they'd rolled down only six inches. I was punchy. I tried to be friendly. I smiled and said:

"Hi! Thanks for stopping. How are you? Hey, you wouldn't happen to know what we're supposed to do to avoid getting struck by lightning, would you?"

That was a joke. Just a joke. For they had to have been aware of the impending storm. Even from their cars, it must have petrified them. But they didn't get it. They shook their heads: they didn't know. They rolled up the window and pulled away. The picture suddenly became clear to me. Each of the three cars was filled with people in gray-colored suits with puzzled looks on their faces. They stared at us strange wilderness men with our backpacks. They were Mormons. Out in the desert nearby there was a Mormon landmark called the Willy Pushcart Monument. In the 1800s, thousands of Mormons had walked to Utah across this very ground while pushing carts filled with their belongings. The monument celebrates them and also commemorates a tragedy in which two hundred Mormon push-carters had died after getting pinned down in a snowstorm here in 1856. It was the worst disaster in the history of western overland travel—more deadly than what had befallen the Donner Party in California ten years beforehand. I walked back to the others who'd all burst out laughing at my failed Yogi attempt. "Nice job!" It was my worst Yogi of the summer. But then, I'd had a tough audience.

Peals of thunder and ferocious lightning bolts arrived. Our time was at hand. We screamed and laughed insanely at each bright, healthy strike. It was the most impressive thing we'd ever seen. We'd discussed kneeling on one foot each on our foam mattress pads, like the traditional Russian dancers on their one-legged deep knee bends. That, so that we wouldn't be grounded; but instead we each lay elongated lengthwise in a foot-deep trough that lined the gravel road. It was too scary to watch, so we lay with our heads down and eyes closed, hoping, hoping, hoping, and hoping that we'd live through that next half-hour and survive. Some rain came with the storm, but that didn't bother us. The sound and the fury of the storm made the minutes pass slowly. We didn't speak to each other but just hysterically shrieked a little at each particularly loud, crisp crack. We wondered if Brett had made it all the way to the trees in time, but we guessed that he hadn't.

The brunt of the lightning passed and we picked ourselves up, hoisted our packs, and hustled on up the road toward the trees and the rise into the hills. There were still occasional rumbles of thunder. The storm wasn't entirely over, yet it wasn't overhead. We reached the hills and the trees at six o'clock and started to climb. There was no sign of Brett. A second wave of black clouds passed with a temporary flurry of lightning, and we lay down again and sur- vived that, too. We crested the ridge of hills and while descending its northern side came to a sign at a fork in the road. Southwestward three miles lay South Pass City, population zero (just a ghost town preserved as an historic site), while northward two miles lay Atlantic City, with a much larger population of forty-three. We could see Brett's rain-splattered footprints in the dirt at the road sign. He'd walked westward, so Porno-Gabe went that way for a com- munist reunion. Todd and I chose the north fork, because two miles sounded better than three. Both ways led to Route 28, where a thirty-five-mile hitchhike northward led to Highway 287 and into the trail town of Lander.

Todd and I reached the pint-sized hovel of Atlantic City at dusk. Light came from a cluster of homes that were nestled so far down in a scrunched-up, twisting valley that it seemed like the set of a horror movie. Just then a pickup truck pulled over. We climbed inside and got a ride up to Route 28 and on down Highway 287, downhill into Lander. Team Locust was shell-shocked, split up, discombobulated. It was a fitting end to our crossing of the Great Divide Basin.

14

Parasite

A flagellated protozoan parasite that infects the gastrointestinal tract of humans. Infection causes giardiasis, which manifests itself with severe diarrhea and abdominal cramps. Other symptoms can include fatigue, nausea and weight loss.

—dictionary definition: *Giardia lamblia*

NOLS.

    I dreamt during our first night in Lander that I was hiking the Appalachian Trail. There was a trail, but we weren't on it. We were off on some kind of a vague, parallel alternate route chosen by someone I was hiking with. They kept assuring that it'd be all right. I was with four guys, but only tangentially, as I didn't really know them but instead had just sort of found myself with them. Each town we came to would end up being some kind of outdoor store with a food court and racks of clothing for sale. I kept arriving at these oases with nothing, and each time we reached the little pit stops I'd end up having to buy a hiking stick and a backpack, because I always seemed to keep needing them. There were occasional short, steep climbs in the dream where I couldn't move my legs and couldn't actually get anywhere. Also, a couple times at the little outdoor shopping towns I was climbing over dinner tables and being inappropriate in public. I only remembered the dream because Todd had woken me up out of it in the middle of the night with his screaming. It was something he occasionally did—start screaming in his sleep. He screamed for a couple seconds; then he mumbled incoherently and went right on sleeping. It didn't even wake him up. I'd heard it a few times already that summer.

Dreams are the mind struggling to create a narrative out of the fragments and snippets of thoughts that are flashing and buzzing around in our brains while we close our eyes and turn off to sleep. Back when I was a kid with a paper route, I used to have a recurring dream where I'd find myself walking through people's backyards, from one to the next without end. When I was a diver on the swim team in high school, I'd dreamt of leaping off very high objects into dark water far below—dark water that might contain sharp metal objects just beneath the surface. After college, I'd taught tennis in the Hamptons out on Long Island for two summers, and after one stretch of teaching lessons for forty-five consecutive days, I suddenly had the identical dream for three nights in a row that I was standing on a tennis court feeding tennis balls out of a ball hopper to strangers. Ever since college, I've occasionally had an awful, uncomfortable dream that I have a math class to pass before I can graduate, and I find myself at the end of a semester having never gone to class and with a final test placed before me covering material that I've never seen before and couldn't possibly be expected to understand.

Sometimes I dream that I'm trying to coach a large number of young men and women and I'm yelling at them and they aren't listening to a single thing that I'm saying. The scene descends into chaos. I have no control over it. Everyone's okay and everyone's all right with it, but they're just not listening to me. There's also a dream I've occasionally had in which I'm playing a game that's kind of a combination of tennis and squash. I'm in a room that has a net in the middle and objects are lying all over, like furniture, pipes, lumber, and wires. So anyone hitting a ball to me would surely get a wildly fortuitous bounce off some part of all the dense crap on my side so that I couldn't possibly return it. I can't move through all the junk to get to the ball, and the ball is going to take an impossible bounce anyway. In my dream, it matters that I'm playing, and it matters to me, the situation. It isn't life or death, but it's my turn to retrieve the ball, and it'll be astronomically hard for me to do this. Still, I have to try. None of those dreams ever wake me up screaming, though, so I guess things could've been worse. Todd never remembered his dreams, so there was no telling what demons he was battling.

Lander was a great trail town—neither too big nor too small, and with a sufficient number of restaurants. We were excited to learn that the National Outdoor Leadership School had its international headquarters just down the road from our hotel. NOLS programs sent kids not only out into the Wind River Mountains north of town in their backyard, but also all over the world—backpacking in Mongolia, canoeing in the Yukon, ocean sailing off Baja, and hiking around India and the Amazon. Eighty-one thousand people have graduated from its programs. The NOLS reputation is so strong that four hundred universities award college credit for their courses. The kids get tested and learn expert hiking skills. So much so that when the topic of through-hiking

178

a triple crown trail arises, NOLS kids invariably say that if they ever decide to do it, they'll start with the CDT. They believe that the Appalachian Trail would feel too easy for them.

Todd and I awoke on Monday, July 25, and took a zero day in Lander. We walked from our south-side hotel, the Holiday Lodge National 9 Hotel, down a little hill into town and over to the NOLS building at 284 Lincoln Street. Outside on the sidewalk were three young staffers. They were recent college graduates who'd come here to get certified as trip leaders. They gazed at Todd's calves and then looked up at us inquisitively. The size and definition of Todd's calve muscles always left us with the duty of explaining things. We said that we'd started at the Mexican border eighty-three days ago and were hiking the CDT to Canada. One of the girls wore a Bowdoin College women's ice hockey jersey. Bowdoin, in Maine, is just twenty-five miles from Bates. She said that her younger brother had graduated from Colby College—also in Maine—and had been on the rowing team. I knew the Colby rowing coach, I told her. She said that one of their coworkers had just graduated from Williams College, in Massachusetts. That's where my younger brother had gone. It's a small world. NOLS has tons of New England Small College Athletic Conference kids on its staff. And the kids in its programs go on to later matriculate at the eleven NESCAC schools in bunches.

I wasn't sad over having yet another break from Porno-Brett-Gabe. It tired me to be in a group and to have to keep track of everything that was going on. Our hotel was up on a little ledge on the south side of town. Up there with us was a McDonald's, a convenience store, and the Lander post office. Early afternoon, I limped to the PO with my deer antler in hand. I carefully wrapped it in bubble wrap and felt overjoyed to mail it away to my nephew and niece in New York. They'd open the box and say: "Crazy Uncle Johnny..." It gave me pleasure to think of that.

We ordered pizza and watched the World Series of Poker tournament on television in our hotel room all evening. We were hooked on it. I had a long talk with Cristina, and it calmed my nerves. She listened when I told her that my numbers weren't going to add up. It made her sad, she said, because she knew that I already knew how she felt about this, and yet I'd ask her anyway. She believed that through-hiking was okay for some people, but not for me because it was tortured and forced. I couldn't totally disagree with that. I always valued her opinion.

I was behind my one-state-per-month timeline. We had four days left until August, and we weren't close to reaching Montana. I couldn't bear to crunch the numbers exactly, for it'd throw me into despondency. Fatalistically, I'd long since realized that, concerning my September 1 deadline, we weren't going to make it. I mailed my motorcycle key and Las Cruces Pacaccio Storage key to Jessie Gibbins in Silver City. She'd volunteered to store my motorcycle in her garage. It'd have to stay there awhile, I told her. There was no way that I could both finish the trail and then fly down to New Mexico and collect the bike and ride it eight days back to Maine.

Gestation.

South Pass City was an old mining town outside Lander at the north end of the Red Desert. Its population was zero, but it's been preserved as an historic site, with day vendors who come in to work a few stores that sell maps and books detailing the history of the area. Brett had reconnected with Porno-Gabe there that night of our lightning scare. They'd slept on a porch outside one of the preserved buildings. Then they'd hitchhiked to Lander that next morning. The following morning after that, Tuesday, July 26, they picked up Todd and me with a ride they'd arranged, so Team Locust rode back to the trail, to South Pass City.

South Pass City, on South Pass City Road—a mile off Route 28—had five shops restored and open to tourists. It'd once been a hub for western migration. All the overland western routes through the massive, impenetrable Rocky Mountains had crossed through the only break in the chain—the Great Divide Basin. It wasn't just Mormons who'd traveled westward through this break in the Rockies, but masses of people had come through here. The trails that led through here were the following: The Oregon Trail, The California Trail, The Pacific Trail, The Mormon Pioneer Trail, The Pony Express National Trail.

It made sense, for migrating people to come through here—to come through this break in the mountains. None of us'd had a strong enough appreciation for the significance of the Great Divide Basin at the time. It wasn't until arriving in South Pass City and reading the maps and books on the shelves in the preserved ghost town stores that we appreciated it. On through-hikes, it always seemed to happen that way. Now, it lay behind us. We were due to start climbing again. What purportedly was the most scenic piece of the whole trail began here—the Wind River Range.

We walked two miles northwestward cross-country through chaparral to Route 28, but then we couldn't find our point of entry northward into the mountains. We spent one hour searching for it, walking up and down the open road, covering the same ground over and over, trying to find the route that'd take us to the exact spot we'd need to climb into the foothills. The view from the road offered the dichotomy of looking southward over the barren Red Desert, while five miles north of the road rise the foothills and then mountains of the Wind River Range. It was clear that we were about to ascend high into mountains and encounter fresh rivers and snowfields once again. We just couldn't get started. We were stymied.

Salvation came in the form of an old cowboy who drove up on an all-terrain vehicle. He hopped off his ATV and smoothed out a spot in the dirt with his hand; then he took a stick and drew a map to show us where we needed to go.

It took me back to sandlot football when the quarterback or anyone else who had a play would draw it in the sand. We thanked him warmly, and off he rode. We walked a few hundred yards but grew confused. It was rolling topography with multiple intersecting dirt roads. We chose a dirt road and set off northward. We seemed to be on the right track. At dusk, we stopped and tented in a grassy clearing filled with cow patties. Cows mooed from across a fence as we set up our tents. It was a cold night. We'd reached the beginning of the trees. In the morning, we'd climb. We'd broken the gravity of the town of Lander. We were past the Great Divide Basin, and now we had mountains again!

It was a whole new ballgame. Awakening on July 27, we climbed into the woods. We picked up the clear groove of our unmarked trail. We felt fine. The groove utterly disappeared two miles later, however, and we fanned out and picked our way over blow-downs and dense undergrowth until we found the trail again, reassembled, and walked onward. Like a finely tuned machine. We hiked and climbed all day under a canopy of trees. It felt wonderful to be up out of the desert and have shelter from the sun. The climbing was easy. My feet felt fine. I was shortly going to be able to ice them in snow. They wouldn't bother me again for the rest of the summer.

We crossed streams and traversed roller-coaster wooded mountains. We climbed across a magnificent boulder field which had rocks the size of buildings. We laughed and smiled in awe. What forces could have piled those boulders there in such a way? At four thirty in the afternoon, we sat for dinner at the edge of an unsavory warm-water pond. There, I made a fateful mistake. I'd frequently drunk untreated water. Up in the mountains again, I'd stopped treating my water with iodine pills. Todd drank all his mountain water untreated as well. He'd used his water purifying pump in the Red Desert, but he'd ceased using it and was now just drinking straight from the streams we'd crossed. The thing was that we could all see that this pond-water was bad. The amebas and protozoa inside it were so large that I could scoop up water and see them circling and swimming around in my jar. One of them actually waved and winked, taunting me while swimming the backstroke. Cocky little bastard. That was probably the one that got me. Some were large enough to require a leash.

My stove was a Jet-Boil, made in New Hampshire. It was so powerful that it sounded like a jet engine. It boiled water in thirty seconds. The others were jealous of it. I scooped water from the pond, boiled it, and added Lipton noodles. I should've boiled the water longer. That was all I'd needed to do. I'd known that the microorganisms were in there, but I guess I'd just assumed that boiling water would instantly kill them. I was impatient and hadn't boiled it long enough. I almost kind of knew that this water was going to make me sick, but I didn't stop myself from making my dinner with it. The repercussions would come later. Instantly began the gestation.

We ended the day with a dramatic climb onto 11,500-foot Temple Pass.

We were back in the high stuff, back into snow above tree line. From atop the snowy pass, we looked northward over high peaks. At sunset, we spread out and descended the north side of the snowy pass, glissading, slipping, sliding, laughing, falling a half mile down through soft snow to long, narrow and iceberg-filled Temple Lake. Snow surrounded it, but we found a dry patch and set up our tents on a ledge above the water. I felt nervous without knowing why. That little hint of intuition: something was wrong.

Cirque De Towers.

We awoke on July 28 and slowly descended alongside a trickling waterfall down a gorge in the Bridger National Forest, down to 9,690 feet at small Big Sandy Lake. We hiked the marshy eastern shoreline to the lake's north end where a sign pointed the way for the Big Sandy Trail. Team Locust split once again there, as planned. The communists left to meet Brett's aunt at the Big Sandy Lodge four miles down a side trail, while Todd had a different resupply arrangement. I stuck with Todd. We'd hike two more days and then hitch out to resupply in the trail town of Pinedale. Then we'd all reconvene in a few days at a trailside lake. Todd and Porno were the captains of their respective teams, and they had it all worked out. The rest of us went along.

Straight from the lake, Todd and I climbed two steep miles up rocky ledges to twelve thousand feet and the top of Jackass Pass. The effort exhausted me more than usual. I was worried because Gabe wasn't on hand to bring up the rear and keep our pace down. Todd hiked out in front, racing ahead, and I struggled to keep up. Jackass Pass holds the southern end of the Cirque de Towers. The Cirque was what Todd called the best of the best of the entire trail. The official CDT route lay a dozen miles west of the Cirque, once again missing that which shouldn't be missed. We were off again on one of Todd's Ley Alternate Routes, which here happened to be the actual Continental Divide. Far as I could tell, the CDTA's strategy seemed to be to follow the Divide in the places where it didn't make sense, like going around the gorgeous Gila Wilderness and to avoid the Divide in gorgeous places like this, where it made sense to follow it.

From up above tree line, we stared across at the fourteen Cirque peaks that curve westward in a half circle. The Cirque de Towers looked like high, jagged needles. They're what get depicted on all the Wyoming Rocky Mountain postcards. The fourteen individual pointy peaks that stuck up along its way were Warbonnet, Warrior, Warrior II, Pylon, Watch Tower, South Watch Tower, Wisconsin Couloir, Block Tower, Symmetry Tower, Sharks Nose, Overhanging Tower, Wolf's Head, Bollinger, and lastly, the most famous, Pingora Peak. The spires stuck into the sky like sharpened pencils. The Cirque cliffs were so vertical that contour lines of it appear as solid blotches of ink. Instead of our remaining high and hiking the semicircular ridge—which would've probably taken a month—our plan was to move northward as the crow flies, and descend off the ridge to Lonesome North Lake, and then climb northward back up to the rim's far edge. If you traced our route and also the curved shape of the Cirque, it would make a half-moon.

We descended down to 10,166-feet, where we stood beneath the Cirque looking straight up at its tall organ pipes, feeling as if we were inside it and the only two people alive on Earth. We crawled across boulders making our way around little Lonesome North Lake; then we climbed northward back up to the ridge, up a steep mountain wall of loose rock, to the top of eleven-thousand-foot Texas Pass. Todd spotted rock climbers who were halfway up the sheer eastern face of Pingora Peak over our left shoulders. They were so high on the cliff that they looked like specks. Stopping and pretending to watch their progress was a great way to rest on our climb and still save face: "We're not resting, we're watching the rock climbers." We didn't linger on Texas Pass. We took a last look behind us, then dropped northward down out of the heavens to Texas Lake. We'd passed the Cirque de Towers, just like that. They hadn't disappointed. Then came an awful thing, suddenly: diarrhea.

Burbling.

Leaving the Cirque De Towers behind, we worked our way northwestward. I could see everything clearly on my maps. I'd bought two special maps that National Geographic makes for the Wind River Range: one for the southern and the other for the northern half. Our route followed a series of lakes—from the deep snow around Texas Lake to Barren Lake to Shadow Lake. All corresponded perfectly to my map. The Shadow Lake Trail and then the Freemont Trail took us to rejoin the CDT on the Highline Trail. It was high rolling plains dotted with small trees and the occasional pond. There was plentiful water, but none of it was fast-moving or cold. I was thirsty for delicious cold mountain water, but that wasn't what lay here.

The Cirque de Tower peaks receded behind us. We were past the difficult stuff and everything would've been easy if not for the diarrhea. We could've posted a big mileage day here, but instead I felt weak all day. My stomach felt queasy. Something was wrong. Something was burbling inside. I thought back and realized that I'd felt weak the latter part of that previous day, too. Somehow I knew that I had a parasite. I knew that it must've been Giardia. I even knew that I'd contacted it just the day before back at the lake where all of us had eaten dinner, when I'd cooked using the water with the rodent-sized microorganisms inside. Quite amazingly, the effect of the parasite had hit me almost instantaneously. I'd thought that having Giardia meant experiencing violent stomach cramps that made you writhe on the ground in agony, but I only had tremendous weakness, no energy in my step. And the diarrhea. You can't forget the diarrhea.

The hiking couldn't have been easier, but I plodded along slowly. Every half mile, I'd have to pull off into whatever woods I could find to get behind a tree. Todd kept waiting patiently for me. The diarrhea was scandalous. I quickly ran out of toilet paper. It made the experience worse. If that was possible. To the uninitiated, know that it's bad to run out of toilet paper during such times. Todd carried handy-wipes and gave me a couple of those. They lasted five minutes. After that, all I had left for toilet paper were the photocopies that I'd made of Todd's Jonathon Ley maps for the state of Wyoming. I'd so carefully and meticulously photocopied them back in Steamboat Springs and had stayed up late into the night tracing the trail's route in red marker and highlighting significant spots. I hadn't used them a single time. But now I was finally putting them to use. The Jonathon Ley maps turned out to be a very big help!

We tented eighteen miles shy of our exit to Pinedale. Back on the Pacific Crest Trail during the days when I'd hiked swiftly with Zoomsteen, then eighteen miles out would've meant that we'd have risen early and would've reached town by breakfast. But the next day, July 29, ended up being my weakest hiking day of the summer. It was like when I'd gotten stricken with Lyme disease back on the Appalachian Trail years earlier—like that one day when I'd only been able to hike two miles before collapsing in the trail. The tiniest bumps up and around the small hills and ponds exhausted me. Todd was ready to fly, but I could only move at a snail's pace. He was patient. I had to stop frequently to rest. The weakness and the diarrhea continued. I couldn't eat a thing. I ran out of my Ley-map toilet paper. Don't make me paint that picture. It's best not to go there. I crashed at the end of the day, after making it only a mere sixteen miles. It was a poor showing, yet even that left me exhausted. We were only two miles shy of our exit, but I hadn't been able to squeeze out that last little bit. We set up our tents by the trail as light rain fell. I would've done anything to have made it to town for a roof overhead, a bed, and a bathroom, but I hadn't had the strength. I'd reached the unfamiliar point where I couldn't take a single step more. A small-scale lightning storm passed over us at night. I was so achy and miserably that I couldn't sleep.

It was history not repeating itself, but rhyming. One type of breakdown or another had hit me on all three trails. It'd been Lyme disease on the Appalachian Trail, forcing me off the trail for a week before I'd resumed my hike, and it'd been personal issues on the Pacific Crest Trail which had forced me to take ten days off to see Cristina before I'd resumed. I'd never had Giardia before. It was serving to wipe me out very nicely.

Faler's Thriftway General Store in Pinedale on the western side of Wyoming's Rocky Mountains found Todd and me roaming its aisles midmorning on Saturday, July 30. We'd walked the two miles to the side trail, and then walked a few miles down the side trail past horses and day hikers to a parking lot trailhead and a hitchhike westward into town. I searched Faler's aisles for something, anything, appealing to eat. I bought canned pineapple and also a

184

salted warm pretzel. But I found that I couldn't even eat those. All my strength was gone. I felt tremendously sick. I could feel my stomach gurgling, twisting, and turning. We crossed East Pine Street and took a room at the ranch-style Sun Dance Motel next to the Mountain Man Museum (closed: shit!). Todd had two bags of groceries. His plan was to spend one night here and in the morning head back to the trail to meet the others. That evening, I lay in bed sweating with a fever while Todd arranged his gear and prepared to depart.

I woke up late on the morning of July 31, at first only vaguely aware that Todd was already gone. He'd raced away to meet the communists at the prearranged rendezvous lake. Pinedale had just 1,181 people. I remained there for a zero day because I couldn't continue. Strangely, I never went to see a doctor. It was proof that I wasn't thinking clearly. My thoughts were stuck on the panic of separating with Team Locust, missing a stretch, and having to reunite with them later. I'd have to meet them ahead at the next trail town. I guess I'd supposed that my sickness would pass and that after a few days of rest I'd start eating again and my symptoms would disappear. I just hadn't known what I was dealing with.

Awakening a second morning in Pinedale, on August 1, I was this time at least able to get myself out of bed. I bought jeans from the Cowboy Shop and Stitchin' Post, just to have a change of clothes handy. Then I hitchhiked out of town. From Pinedale west of the mountains, I had to reach Dubois on Highway 287 east of the mountains. No east-west over-mountain roads existed. My choice was to go up, around and back down or down, around and back up. Either way. The northern route led through Jackson Hole, Wyoming, but I didn't feel like having rich people stare at me, so I chose the southern route. It'd take me back over to ever-present Highway 287 and through Lander again, which I knew so well. That'd feel familiar.

My first ride, down Route 191, dropped me at the desolate crossroad of Farson, Wyoming. Wyoming was the least-populated state in America and Farson seemed perfectly willing to stand up and symbolize that reality. The locals called it "Four Corners," but it's not to be confused with the real Four Corners, which is the only spot in America where four states converge at a single point (Arizona-Utah-Colorado-New Mexico). I somehow landed a ride from there northwestward up Highway 287 into Lander. My previous Lander stop, pre-Giardia, had seemed like an earlier lifetime. I took a room at the same hotel. Watched professional poker on TV again. I ordered pizza, but I couldn't eat it.

On the morning of August 2, I ambled to the north end of Lander and stood ready to hitchhike farther northward to Dubois when dark clouds blew eastward over the mountains and dumped rain. I found shelter by lying for two hours on the floor in the entryway of a Veteran's Club; then I rose and hitchhiked by gaining a ride from a gentleman with New Hampshire license plates on his burgundy SAAB, who said he was out west lining up clients to sell his pottery. I tried to be good company, but my energy was low, and I had to just give up and close my eyes and rest my head against the window. The grave of Sacajawea lay off the road fifteen miles north of Lander. She'd helped Lewis and Clark walk across the country while carrying her infant son. A little known fact was that she'd lived to an old age, and her son had lived a full life, too. She lay there now, revered, in a Native American burial site. Now she was a hiker!

Bear Spray.

Inauspiciously starting August, I took a room at the Stagecoach Motor Inn on Dubois' main drag on Ramshorn Street. Tiny Dubois had a population of 850 people. They pronounced it "dew-boys," they told me, for some reason as an act of defiance against its French origin (if you say "do-bwa" they throw cow-patties at you). The Stagecoach had a swimming pool out front and a sculpture that was a massive pile of deer antlers, stacked and forming an arch. Town had four restaurants, two bars, a bookstore, a post office, a small library, a couple of small grocery stores, some homes and a hiking store that was so new it had only half-stocked shelves. The town sidewalks were wood-planked, to charm tourists.

I slept three nights in Dubois and mostly remained in bed. Neither my AT nor PCT prolonged breaks had caused me to miss an inch of trail. But out here I was missing trail. This wasn't like the AT or the PCT where you could separate from a group or a hiking partner and just go on alone and meet someone else. If you have a group and you separate from it out here on the CDT, then you aren't going to suddenly meet another group to join. It wasn't just that I was off the trail, but it was where I was off the trail. And where I'd have to get back on it. I wasn't about to hike through grizzly bear territory alone. No, I had to stick with Team Locust. It was all I thought of while lying in bed. I waited for the others and hoped that they'd indeed eventually arrive.

The Cowboy Café, next to my hotel, was Mecca in Dubois. I developed a thing for my waitress, but she didn't give me the time of day. I couldn't help noticing, though, that every time a guy entered the café wearing jeans, cowboy hat, cowboy boots, and a long-sleeved plaid shirt it really seemed to perk up her interest. I just sat in my Star Trek uniform. The jeans helped at least a little. I tried to make her laugh. I showed her my magic trick of splitting a napkin in half and then reattaching its molecules to make it whole again. Amazing! Magic! She filled up my coffee cup and I asked her this question:

"A bus driver is heading down a street in New York City. He goes right past a stop sign without stopping, he turns left where there's a No Left Turn sign, and he goes the wrong way down a one-way street. Then he goes on the

186

left side of the road past a cop car. Still, he didn't break a single traffic law and he didn't get a ticket. Why not?"

She stared at me.

"It's because he's walking!" I said.

More magic! She forced a smile, then walked away to help a cowboy table.

I gave considerable thought to grizzlies. It was time to face that reality. Grizzly bear territory begins at Togwotee Pass just outside town. Dubois was where I'd chosen in advance to receive a mail drop containing both a canister of Bear Spray and a Bear Vault storage barrel. The bear vault was an airtight, scent-proof, clear plastic food container that was just small enough to fit inside a backpack, but then there was barely room for anything else. But what could be more important than not attracting a grizzly bear? Word on the street had it that we weren't supposed to carry heavily scented foods like tuna fish or peanut butter into grizzly territory, nor were we to sleep where we cooked nor sleep wearing the clothes that we've cooked in. We weren't to sleep at night anywhere near our food. And we definitely weren't supposed to rub honey-salmon barbeque sauce mixed with raspberries all over our bodies in either the day or the night.

My Frontiersman Bear Attack Deterrent bear spray was good from twenty feet. It came in a canister and holster that attached to our backpack belt straps. Under duress, we were to simply pull the canister from its holster and spray away to theoretically stop an advancing or possibly even charging thousand-pound bear. No problem.

Three grizzly bear stories that I'd heard from my old Appalachian Trail friend Hydro twelve years earlier had stuck with me, having been etched in my mind. I couldn't speak to their validity. The first was a tourist bus driving through Yellowstone. Passengers looking out the windows saw a backpacker emerge from the woods and start walking across an open field. Then they saw a grizzly bear silently walk out of the woods behind the man, gaining on him. Horrified, they pounded on the bus windows and watched helplessly as the hiker suddenly turned around to face the grizzly. Thinking clearly, the hiker didn't run or panic but instead raised his hiking stick calmly over his head with both hands and waved it gently back and forth to make himself appear ten feet tall. The bear, confused, turned and walked away. The bus passengers couldn't believe it.

The second story was of a man who'd been mauled—killed—and partially devoured by a grizzly in the mountains. A group of twenty people stood gathered at the dead body a day later including police officers, park rangers, hunters, and people in a search party. All of them were standing around tackling postmortem and attack-assessment incidentals like measuring the bite marks and bear prints, when unbelievably the grizzly bear suddenly came charging over a hill straight at the huge crowd sending everyone screaming and scattering. The third story was of an elderly couple who got attacked. The grizzly was busily chomping on the old man who cried out to his wife: "Run! Get away!" But the old woman took binoculars from around her neck and swung them and bonked the grizzly on its nose and the bear ran away. The old man lived.

In Dubois' pizzeria, I read a magazine article of a local attack. Two men were mountain biking in the nearby woods while their dog ran beside them. One of the bikers had climbed a hill out of eyesight of the other. He'd paused to wait and was standing off his bike when a grizzly came out of the woods and confronted him, advancing toward him. The man held his bike up between himself and the bear to try to hold it back. That worked for a few seconds until the bear swatted the bike away and knocked the man to the ground. The man had been screaming and calling his friend all the while, and the exhausted friend was frantically pedaling up the hill, knowing that something was drastically wrong up on top. The straggler and his dog crested the hill to find the grizzly bear on top of their friend—and the bear, seeing that it was three against one now, pretty much lost interest in the encounter and sauntered away. The attacked man lived, but had lots of stitches all over his arms and legs.

The Discovery Channel once had a show I'll always remember, which featured a series on polar bear encounters. One was of a native Eskimo who had a polar bear rear up in front of him and prepare to take a bite. The man held his forearm up vertically in front of his face, and that confused the bear because apparently polar bears, unlike grizzlies and black bears, can't turn their heads horizontally to give an attacking bite. The man's forearm was longer than the bear's open jaw, so the bear froze while standing on its hind legs, thinking things over; and the man took that opening to push forward with his hands into the bear's chest, which tumbled the bear backward. The bear then walked away. The man's wife had witnessed it, and when interviewed she described seeing her husband "pick up and throw" the polar bear.

Timothy Treadwell wasn't so lucky when he and his girlfriend were suicidally deliberately hanging out in the late fall in an area of Alaska that was densely populated with grizzlies. They were both eaten. You don't just prance around and play with top–of–the–food chain wild creatures. So many different outcomes are possible. And then there are the claws. You can't forget the claws. Grizzly claws can basically cut down a sapling.

But it would be okay.

Certainly I'd be fine.

After all, I had my little canister of bear spray.

"Don't worry, it'll all work out!"

The grizzly thing was real—but an even greater concern to me was food. I couldn't eat. I couldn't find anything that appealed to me. I couldn't force anything down. I was resting, but I wasn't taking medicine or eating and gaining back strength. It was ridiculous that I hadn't been able to think straightly enough to get myself to a doctor. It somehow just wasn't registering that the

Giardia would continue to affect me for a long time and that it wasn't going to go away without medication. I felt mentally ready to set out hiking again, but I needed to find something I could eat. I finally settled on the idea of making cheese-lettuce-tomato sandwiches. They'd end up being a disaster, though, because I made the mistake of fully preparing them before leaving, when instead I should've put the wet tomato slices in a separate ziplock bag. I should've known that everything would get smooshed in my pack. Again, I wasn't thinking clearly.

I left a note for Team Locust at the post office, and I inquired there everyday as to whether they'd arrived. Finally, at seven o'clock on the night of August 4, Gabe came knocking on my door. The others had all arrived in town and were down the street at a different hotel. They took a zero day on the fifth. Then we all ate breakfast together on Saturday, August 6, at the Cowboy Café. Brett's aunt was gone, but now his parents were here visiting from California. They were absolutely as nice as could be. They drove a boxy high-tech sports van that was decked out for road trips and carried all of us easily. Inside was a refrigerator, bed, stove, and all manner of things. Brett's parents were young, athletic, attractive. One of those "perfect couples" you sometimes see. I was far closer to their age than I was to Brett's. They'd met as undergraduates at USC and got married right out of college. His father was a defense attorney who handled workers' compensation cases for illegal aliens and others. They had money. They were perfectly generous with us. They drove us to the trail by Togwotee Pass. We were north of the Wind River Range and just one day shy of entering Yellowstone. We were about to walk into the national park. To walk in on our own ten Team Locust feet, into the home of buffalo, wolves, and grizzlies.

189

15
Old Faithful

By now you know,
It's not going to stop
Until you wise up.

—Aimee Mann

Eyes.

Wyoming was supposed to've been a breeze, but instead it was feeling like a slog. The Red Desert had taken its toll, as had my Giardia. At least we'd only Yellowstone left to negotiate. All summer we'd been hopping from modest town to modest town—but the dignity and quiet grace of our experience in the CDT's small trail towns was about to be interrupted in a major way here by the fanfare and carnival atmosphere that's Yellowstone National Park with its roads, tourists, and restaurants. Yellowstone is the oldest national park in the world. Its founders in 1871 knew that there was something here worthy of being protected. People have to come see it in order to learn to value protecting it, but when everyone flocks here it becomes less pristine. That Yellowstone would be an aberration from our quotidian calm and flow wasn't welcome. We were about to be thrust into the shit. Walking through the habitat of charismatic mega-fauna like wolves, bison, grizzlies, elk, deer, and pronghorn sheep was beside the point; it was the people in their campers and on their motorcycles, vacationing here from around the world, yelling at their kids, and eating ice cream, that would impact us most.

Togwotee Pass was the slightly arbitrary demarcation line north of which a grizzly bear could be sitting by the trail at any moment of any day. That possibility gave our hike a new tingly feeling. We had to be alert at all times. Prior to the hike, I'd had two thoughts about grizzly prevention (neither of which involved karate lessons): to carry an umbrella that I'd open upon an encounter to make myself seem large; and to hike with my sleeping bag highest up and partially protruding from my backpack, so that upon seeing a grizzly I could reach back with my hiking stick and hook and lift it—somehow find the nerve!—raising it out of my pack. Again, to make myself appear larger. I wasn't now practicing either trick, though, because sticking with Team Locust had alleviated my grizzly fear.

Preventive grizzly measures on which we'd all agreed included sticking close together and making noise, especially upon entering and exiting transitional areas like passing from forest to meadow, meadow to riverbed, or the reverse. These weren't black bears. I'd never been afraid of a black bear in my life. But grizzlies, on the other hand, are larger, vastly more powerful, more aggressive, and less predictable. Todd and I were carrying the same brand of clear plastic bear vault to keep our food inside, airtight. Porno-Brett-Gabe had rope and would hang their food from tree branches at night.

Off we went on August 6, pepper spray canisters ready at our hips. We walked along making noise, singing, clicking our hiking sticks and ski poles against rocks. Our rotating lead hiker periodically shouted out things like: *"Go away, grizzly!"* It made us punchy, and we laughed and laughed. Portions of the trail had been dug into deep, dusty troughs by a multitude of horse and horseback riders. I tried to hike smoothly and breathe evenly, as it was my first day back and I was weak from Giardia. I focused my energy on reading my body with the hope of smoothly restarting my hike and keeping up and being okay. When we stopped to eat, I opened my cheese-lettuce-tomato sandwiches. Having spent only a mere half day in my pack, they were already a disintegrated soggy mess. A total disaster. The others laughed, like: "What were you thinking?" I had to jettison the sandwiches. They started calling me Jet because they said that I was always jettisoning something.

Suddenly, we stumbled upon the greatest landmark of the entire trail. A small creek that we'd come upon led to a fork. We all had a simultaneous rush of enlightenment—lightbulbs flickering to bright in our dim through-hiker brains. We'd temporarily zoned out, so fixated were we by our grizzly-bear fear-induced distraction—but we all knew the significance of this spot. Here was the place where the waters divide. It was the symbol of the entire trail. Here was Two Ocean Creek, the one spot on the Continental Divide where a single small creek in the woods flows southward and splits so that its left branch leads eastward and theoretically ends up in the Atlantic Ocean, while its right branch leads westward and theoretically ends up in the Pacific. A sign hung on a tree at the fork and gave the mileage that each fork would have needed to take on its imagined ocean-bound course. We dropped our packs and took photographs of ourselves straddling the water and even lying in the water at the fork. Nothing ever remained sacred with Team Locust for long, though, as episodes usually devolved swiftly into silliness. I was okay with that, though, as it was my exact irreverent Don Quixote, Wacky Packages, Saturday Night Live sense of humor. What happened was that Gabe tossed a Cheese Doodle into the water upstream from the fork and theatrically said:

"Okay. Will this Cheese Doodle go to the Atlantic Ocean or the Pacific Ocean?"

We silently watched the Cheese Doodle float eight feet and get lodged against the riverbank under a stick.

"That was anticlimactic," Brett said.

We tented just into some trees on a forested hillside above a meadow. We ate dinner; then Todd and I sealed our food inside our plastic bear vaults and stashed them in some bushes thirty yards away from our tent spot. Porno hung his trio's food high off a tree limb deep in the woods. Then we retired, each of us into our individual tents to sleep. As darkness fell, I lay awake thinking of all the stories I'd heard through the years, whether true or not, of bears ripping hikers out of their tents. Between me and a thousand-pound grizzly was just a thin nylon membrane. If it happens, it happens. There was nothing I could do.

It was our first night in grizzly territory. I drifted to sleep, but hours later awoke with a start in the darkness to the sound of Todd yelling in his tent. It wasn't the screaming that he did when having nightmares. Instead, this was wide-awake yelling. There was commotion, conversations already in progress, headlamps shining into the woods, their beams crossing each other back and forth. Everyone was awake.

"What's happening?"

"Todd thinks he saw a grizzly bear and it's circling us!" Porno said, laughing.

"Shut up! Listen!" Todd said.

We heard branches breaking. Porno and Brett kept snickering, saying that it was only an elk. For the rest of the night, the elk kept circling us on the wooded hillside, crunching brush around us. It was what I'd experienced several times with deer back on the PCT, when they'd circle at night waiting for someone to walk outside and pee somewhere so that they could lick salt from the urine. I drifted to sleep again while Todd yelled to scare away whatever was out there. Still convinced that it was a grizzly, Todd cried: "See? There are its eyes!"

Team Huddle.

We found elk tracks near our tents that next morning. We all laughed at Todd's false grizzly sighting.

"It was a grizzly with elk hoofs!" Porno said.

"Go ahead and laugh," Todd said. "But I just saved your lives."

Condensation had drenched our tents overnight. Dew-wet tall grass lined the trail and we brushed against it soaking our legs when we set out to start the day, August 7. It was a cold morning. It felt like fall. Our breath came out in little clouds in the cold air before us. I wore shorts as I'd done every day of the hike, even all through the rain, storms, and snow. My low-cut socks were not even ankle high, so there wasn't any extra fabric to saturate. Mist rose from the earth. It wasn't until the first rays of sun came over the hills to strike us that we warmed up. We came to a wooden signpost which read: Welcome to Yellowstone. Our entrance was unceremonious, out in the middle of nowhere—clear evidence that few people entered the park by walking into it. Near the sign lay a ranger cabin, boarded up. We sat for forty minutes outside the cabin, eating snacks and spreading out our tents to dry.

Beneath Yellowstone National Park was volcanic lava waiting to burst. A perfectly gargantuan bubble of lava (a silicic magma reservoir) was pushing the ground upward so that the whole area is due to blow on an epic scale at some point in the next seven hundred thousand years. It apparently blows on an epic scale about once every six hundred thousand years, and its last major eruption was 620,000 years ago. It'll cause one of the largest explosions to ever happen on earth. It's blown twice before and is one of four Super Volcanoes on the planet. The others are Lake Toba in Indonesia; Lake Taupo in New Zealand; and Long Valley in eastern California, which I'd walked over on the PCT.

The Yellowstone explosion will be one thousand times more powerful than Krakatoa, and twenty-five hundred times more powerful than the 1980 Mt. St. Helens eruption. Everything east of it will be buried in ash, and the ash will blow into the atmosphere and cause a perpetual worldwide winter that'll last for several years. It'll cause devastation of the world's agriculture and cause mass starvation. And here we'd be walking right over it. If it started to go, we wouldn't be able to run away in time. Yellowstone gets about two thousand earthquakes a year (only a few of which are actually felt), and we wouldn't be able to run from those, either. It was such a scary concept that it made me want to move to the northwestern side of Yellowstone and abandon the east coast. What a crazy thing it is, to live in fear. Yet the west coast gets air pollution blowing over the Pacific Ocean from China. You can't win. Ignorance is bliss! Robert Frost: "Have I not walked without an upward look of caution under stars that very well might not have missed me when they shot and fell? It was a risk I had to take, and took."

We hiked all day and slept in a camp spot that Brett had reserved for us from back in Dubois. One isn't allowed to sleep just anywhere in Yellowstone. Our camp spot was down a side trail in a clearing beside a gentle river. No one came to check up on us. The next day inside Yellowstone, on August 8, we entered a river valley and walked around hillside after hillside that'd been scorched in a major fire in 1988. Miles of earth had been scorched and they still showed evidence of the fire. We stopped to tent that night in a field of fallen and burnt trees on a wide, flat plateau above and on the western side of the Snake River Gorge. That wasn't a reserved campsite, but dark clouds had rolled in and we wanted to set up in time to beat the rain.

Rain fell lightly at first, but soon came harder. The next thing I remembered was being woken up by a loud crash of thunder, followed instantly by a bright flash of lightning. The thunder and lightning cracked over and over. It was terrifying to be lying out underneath it. It was so loud that it sent chills down my spine. The strikes were so close that this time, even more than the others, I thought I might die. This time it really very likely might happen. The world brightened at each strike, and the strikes came in rapid succession.

Inside our nylon tents amidst the fallen trees, we were the tallest thing on the plateau. Forget the Super Volcano. Forget the wolves and grizzly bears. Forget the ruthless efficiency of microscopic Giardia lamblia that'd given me diarrhea and forced me off the trail. Fuck all of that. Instead, it was quite clearly lightning that was going to kill me. Adrenaline surged through my body. I couldn't have been more awake. Rain cascaded down, but I could hear commotion from the other tents. I could hear urgent tones of voices raised over the rain, and tent flaps zipping open. It was a telltale sound. I knew what was happening and I responded instantly. We all seemed to be on exactly the same page: we were scared out of our minds. I whipped on clothes and was outside my tent within sixty seconds, sneakers on my feet, clutching my nylon ground tarp after yanking it out from under my tent. I hadn't grabbed my head-lamp flashlight, but the others wore theirs. I moved into their light and in one frightened mass we huddled and crouched down and climbed over and under the fallen trees, inching our way to the riverbank. We scaled fifteen feet down the steep sandy edge of the riverbank and huddled there for twenty minutes in the deluge while waiting for the lightning to pass. It was the scariest lightning storm of the summer. We were cold. We ducked our heads and leaned together getting drenched. We waited for the storm to blow by. Finally, it passed. We'd lived through it. We'd dodged another bullet. We climbed back to the field and over the fallen trees back into our tents to collapse.

Boiling Pools.

We rose early on the morning of August 9 with our things wet, and we hiked silently through cold, wet morning grass again. We met a southbound through-hiker named Uncle Green Bean face-to-face. This was the guy that Todd and Weekender had met weeks earlier back in the parking lot on Monarch Pass in Colorado. They'd sat there together amidst thousands of bicyclists and had talked with this guy for two hours about the trail. Uncle Green Bean had at that moment been on his way to Canada and had been staking things out. He'd

194

made it this far, down from Canada. No, he hadn't seen any grizzly bears, he said. We all stood talking for thirty minutes. The whole time, I wanted to sit, but the ground was wet and I just leaned on my hiking stick and waited for all the talking to end. He said that he was doing fine and was finding the trail okay. He didn't try to Zirkel us by telling us that we'd never make it. We didn't try to Zirkel him, either, but we admitted that the Red Desert was tough.

We walked farther into Yellowstone. White smoke spires drifted up out of the trees in the landscape before us. They were thermal vents letting off steam, beautifully set to blue-sky backdrops. In the middle of nowhere we came to a hot, bubbling water pool about six feet in diameter. It was shimmering blue water, perfectly clear and boiling. We approached cautiously and peered straight down to its bottom, where the water rose up through a vent. It was inviting to jump in, but that'd be suicidal. Falling into a thermal vent and getting burned to death in a desolate, untrammeled corner of the park wasn't a high-mortality item in Yellowstone, but it has happened.

We passed several more burning blue water pits. They felt gloriously uplifting after our trying, scary night. We stopped at a sandy spot near a very large geothermal pool and we laid out our wet tents, clothes, and sleeping bags. We sunbathed for an hour, warming ourselves while internalizing this fantastic land. When Lewis and Clarke had passed westward through Montana in 1805, they'd met Nez Perce, Crow, and Shoshone Native Americans who'd all told them about this fantastical place, but they hadn't believed that the stories were true. Even after this place had been "discovered" by white men, it still took decades for people back east to realize through eye-witness accounts and drawings that this place with all its geothermal activity really was here. For quite a long while, people had thought that it was just a myth or a hoax. That it couldn't actually exist as fantastically as people were describing it.

I felt almost happy, if that was even possible for me. It didn't last long, though, for Gabe started spouting pornographic Haikus. He made them up as we walked along through this tremendous beauty. He kept trying to make them as foul as could be. I tweaked a bit. It wasn't as bad as that time years ago when I'd smashed a squash racquet into little bits in my office in anger one day — but I told him that Haikus follow a form and it's not only the number of syllables but also that giving a simple expression of nature makes it a Haiku. He said that he was reading Dharma Bums, and that Kerouac's character was making up drunken Haikus, so why couldn't he. I'd recommended the book to him, so I was glad that he was reading it. Still, it launched us into an argument about censorship and art and whether Gabe's Haikus about other people's mother's pussies were merely verbal diarrhea or were worth listening to. I told him that it was difficult being bombarded by them. Again, the others stayed out of it. It was just bobble-headed, nervous Gabe and me bickering again like an old married couple. It just burned me, though, because I knew where it was all headed, and I just didn't want to have to walk up to the Old Faithful Geyser while listening to Gabe's Haikus about mighty ejaculations.

RVs.

Several small public villages existed in Yellowstone National Park. Of course each was a tourist trap. The park felt like Isla Sorna in Jurassic Park, and we were the fossil hunter Jack Horner who gets caught out in the island with the two kids (maybe Gabe and I were the kids), and who has to run a gauntlet of dinosaurs to make his way back to the main lodge. The main center in Yellowstone was the Old Faithful Village, but there were five additional little fortresses, the villages of Grants, Canyon, Mammoth, Madison, and Fishing Bridge.

We reached our first road crossing in Yellowstone. We were a day's hike shy of our planned stop at Old Faithful Village, but our close call with lightning the night before had taken such a toll on us that we improvised and hitchhiked northward up the road to nearby Grant Village. It was a difficult hitchhike. Everyone was vacationing and nobody wanted to pick us up. It was all families in RV campers in bumper-to-bumper traffic. Those people had come from every state and from around the world to see these mountains and this wildlife. That was what they were here for, not to pick up strange hitchhikers who'd emerged from the woods with dirt all over their faces. It'd surely surprised them to see us on foot way out here in the first place. They must not've been expecting to see people with backpacks and hiking sticks out walking through the park. It wasn't a big deal to us — it was just what we did every single day.

Our ride dropped us at the Grant Village cafeteria and store. We needed a break. We needed a meal. We sat quietly at a back corner table in a cafeteria that was filled with tourists in street clothes. We were safe and dry, but dirty, unshaven, and wearing our dry-fit Star Trek uniforms and Fidel Castro uniforms. The food wasn't delicious. Still, it felt nice to give money for something already made. We felt disoriented. There were a large number of fantastically overweight people here. Day-by-day and month-by-month we'd all been growing increasingly skinnier, and here we were suddenly glimpsing overweight Americans. I know that weight gain is a difficult thing for some people to control, but it felt startling to see unfettered obesity. It's the same as when you fly back to America after spending many weeks abroad. Suddenly, out of nowhere, Todd emphatically yet discreetly uttered at our table:

"Are you absolutely fucking kidding me with the lightning?"

We just laughed. I still felt nervous over it, still had an odd feeling in my stomach. Or was that the parasite? We hadn't talked much about it, but now it came out, how scared we'd been. We lounged in the corner and read our maps. We drank soda, stretched, washed our faces in the bathrooms. We bought a newspaper. There was no news of the coma baby that I'd read about back in New Mexico, the one where they were keeping the mother alive, just long enough to deliver the baby. Then we hitchhiked back to the trailhead where we'd left off. We hiked through the remainder of the afternoon, following easy trail and making noise to ward off grizzly bears. We tented in a designated camping spot in a thicket of trees. Yet another lightning storm scared us, but this one was extraordinarily brief. This one didn't force us out of our tents to huddle together in the dark in the pouring rain down the side of a river embankment waiting to die. It was no fun sleeping under constant lightning storms.

August 10, was day number ninety-nine for me. We awoke in great spirits because Todd had been promising that he knew the location of a hidden thermal pool that was cool and nonlethal enough that we could soak in it like a hot tub. We set out up the western shore of Shoshone Lake, then across broad marshland. Cold and sore, we were longing for a hot soak. But Todd couldn't find the pool. We spent an hour searching for it off in the woods. We found a thermal pool that drained into a cold river, but we couldn't find our hot tub.

We resumed our hike and came to a treeless crusty hillside called Shoshone Geyser Basin. It was an entire mountainside teeming with thermal vents, with hot water leaking and dripping all over and running down the hill. It had the smell of sulfur, like rotten eggs. We dropped our packs and took out our cameras and spent an hour roaming and exploring. I couldn't tell if I was walking on thin crust or solid ground, so I tiptoed carefully and tried to be smart while exploring. We peeked into thermal vents, listening to the hissing. Some of the pools were open and exposed, while others were housed in protruding anthill-shaped formations from crusted-over minerals that'd bubbled up through the centuries. On the north side of the crusty hillside, the path widened and we met a few tourists. They were the first people that we'd seen on foot in the woods for weeks, excluding the old southbounder Uncle Green Bean. Those tourists had ventured about ten miles south from Old Faithful Village. They were geologists and naturalists. We knew because we met them and they told us so. Todd and Porno branched off and gave one final search for the lost hot tub, while Brett, Gabe, and I sat by the trail and waited.

I finally rose and decided not to wait any longer but to hike alone the final ten miles into Old Faithful Village. The trail was practically like a sidewalk here, so there wasn't any issue of getting lost. The others were planning to pause and watch the eruption of a geyser named Lone Star, which erupted twice daily and would serve as a warm-up for Old Faithful Geyser. I pushed northward over eight-thousand-foot Grant Pass, and then it was smooth sailing on a level, manicured path the rest of the way in. I made excellent time. It felt nice to walk alone and not to have to worry about others. The final mile was a descent down a rocky mountainside to the giant valley of Sand Basin, which contains Old Faithful Village and is ringed by mountains. The descent offered views out over Old Faithful's dozen village buildings. I crossed its traffic-filled access road, waiting for a break in the cars, and entered the village. My goal was to get a hotel room, drop my pack, shower, and lie in a bed. There were three hotel-room lodges in the village. Biggest was called Old Faithful Inn. Its parking lot was filled to capacity with a gazillion RVs, motorcycles, and SUVs.

Basketball.

The roof of the inn was under construction. It was an enormous, seven-story building. A chain-link fence and construction trailers lined the front entrance, and a narrow path funneled tourists inside through work piles. I walked inside under scaffolding wearing my backpack amidst hundreds of strollers. The inn is called, "The crown jewel of national park lodges." It's the central lodge in the central village in the premier park in America. The author of the New Yorker piece who'd satirically described buying the state of Wyoming as a tear-down project, had referred to this as one of the few items worthy of keeping: "There's really not a lot here you'd want to keep, except one or two of the Wind River Mountains and some old nineteen-twenties Park Service structures in Yellowstone."

The Old Faithful Inn had three hundred rooms and a seven-story atrium with four levels of balconies. Tourists on the upper balconies could look down at the bustle below. The inn, built in 1904, had almost burned down in the great Yellowstone fire of 1988. It was rustic and large-scale with little hallways leading to hotel rooms, restaurants, and gift shops. Out the back door was the village's central bus terminal which was bustling with people who were lined up to get carried off to distant spots in the park to see the wildlife. I waited in a long line at the front desk, but when I finally reached a receptionist, she told me that not a single hotel room was available in the entire Yellowstone National Park. I took that at face value. I'm a literalist. There were no vacancies at Old Faithful Inn, at the two smaller hotels in Old Faithful Village, nor in any of the other five villages. I asked if there was anything I could do, and she said that I could keep checking at the desk throughout the day to see whether they had any cancellations.

I sat in the lobby and read a brochure listing fun facts about the park. Seven presidents had visited Yellowstone while still in office (it was unclear whether the implication was that seven meant a lot or a little). The two most common causes of death in the park were car accidents and drowning. The fastest land animal in the park was the pronghorn sheep which could run sixty miles an hour. Shoshone Geyser Basin, the hillside that we'd walked across and explored, had over one hundred active thermal vents. There are ten thousand active vents in the park. I read brochures which detailed the park's bus trips. The one that sounded appealing to me was to see the buffalo herds in a place called Hayden Valley, to the northeast of massive Yellowstone Lake. I put down the brochures. I just wanted to get behind a closed door and drop. I just wanted to lie in a bed. Collapse into Cave Dweller mode. I didn't feel so hot, like maybe a sickness was coming on. Scores of people came and went. Everybody was clean.

Every hour, I inquired about rooms, but there were no cancellations. The lobby felt like the lodge in Jurassic Park—it was an oasis of safety from all the wild beasts lurking around outside it. It just had that feel to it, like a massive T. rex might come crashing through the doors into the seventy-foot-tall atrium any second to eat a few of us and send the rest of us scattering as velociraptors hunted us through the upstairs hallways to make us hide in metal kitchen cupboards. Even the buses leaving out back were like the carts in that movie, carrying tourists through the holding pens. Then Nedry will shut down the system ("Who could've planned for that?"), giving Malcolm the chance to talk about Chaos Theory, and meanwhile the monsters will run amok.

At four o'clock in the afternoon, the others arrived; Team Locust reassembled. We walked over to Snow Lodge, one of the two smaller buildings, and we ate together in a café. Again: not delicious. Then we split up for several hours to shop, eat, write letters, air out our sleeping bags, and sit outside the second-largest building, which is called the Old Faithful Lodge, from where you watch the Old Faithful Geyser erupt. There was a printed time sheet listing Old Faithful's daily eruption times, so crowds of people would swell outside onto its large semicircular wooden viewing deck to catch each eruption, and then the crowd would dissipate. Flowing in and flowing out. I'd love to have seen a fast-time-elapsed aerial shot sequence of the crowd's ebb and flow.

I felt invisible, walking around the lodges alone. Back at the inn, a young man sat behind a desk selling his books of wildlife photography to a long line of people. His wildlife photos seemed to be in great demand. I continued checking at the front desk, but no vacancy materialized. It seemed that we'd have to find a secluded, out-of-the-way place and lie down to sleep tucked off in a corner behind sofas somewhere. We'd just have to wait and outlast the tourists until things quieted down; then we'd hide and sleep. It was going to be a long night. We were beggars and thieves.

It was eight thirty at night when Team Locust reformed on the leather sofas in the living room of the second-in-size Old Faithful Lodge. We had our backpacks with us. The employee recreation center was in this building, and a couple of the young lodge workers had invited Porno to use it. We walked through an employee-only doorway at the end of a corridor and found a small employee gym that was dimly lit and had four basketball hoops, a Ping-Pong table and a stage. We played Ping-Pong and decided that we would sleep there, on the stage.

Porno somehow believed that he could take me in Ping-Pong, but he must've been on drugs. He'd beaten us all in foosball and pool—but this was a different matter. A ball and paddle game isn't as good for me as a ball and racquet game, but it's in the neighborhood. Porno was a good player, but outmatched. We had fun. It felt great to do what I did best. Then Brett disappeared to go do what he did best. He returned at nine thirty that night with extraordinary news—he'd secured us a room. He showed us the key. It was just like the car key that he'd scored from Aunt Martha back in Encampment. Brett was amazing. He was smooth like that. He'd gotten us a two hundred and forty dollar a night room with two queen beds and a cot, on the second floor of the main building, and he'd gotten it for free. We couldn't believe it. Only Brett could've worked that magic. He'd requested to meet with the manager, and in her back office he'd explained about the hike we were on, and how we had no place to sleep, and could she please find a way to help us. It was miraculous; that was all it took. I'd been requesting all day at the front desk to pay for a room and I'd gotten shot down every time.

We became giddy. We felt joyous. Our fortune had changed. We found a basketball and began shooting baskets. That quickly turned into a heated game of two-on-two. It was ten o'clock at night, and we were laughing wildly. I teamed with Porno. Todd with Brett. Gabe sat and watched. Our game in the dim gym began and remained violent and ugly. We hacked and pushed each other into oblivion, bodies flying everywhere. None of us were skyscrapers, so nobody had the advantage of height. Brett was a predictably decent ball handler, while Todd was far better than I ever would've expected. Porno, the strongest among us, was solid and I kept encouraging him to drive to the hoop. I kept calling him "Sir Charles!" for Charles Barkley, to egg on his aggressive play. That's what a coach does—finds a way to win. If calling your teammate Sir Charles helps you win, then you do it. We all crashed the board for rebounds, laughing and battling. Jason helped us eek out a ten-to-nine win. I had my Ping-Pong win, my basketball win, and we had our free room. So it'd turned into a positive day. Like Herman Hesse's Steppenwolf, I'd had several individual incidents during the day that I could call pleasurable occurrences—but lacking as always was that feeling of impossible-to-experience "happiness." Like how a thousand times a day I could identify views and moments that gave me what I could describe as pleasure—but that it doesn't add up to that overall feeling of contentment is the frustrating bane of my existence. I walked away from our basketball game with a jammed index finger on my left hand. It was a miracle that no one had gotten seriously injured. It was a crazy thing to have done. I couldn't imagine the feeling of defeat if one of us'd had to go home due to a broken ankle sustained during basketball in a dark employee gymnasium in a back room in Yellowstone National Park:

"You got hurt in Yellowstone? Was it an animal that got you?"

"No—late night basketball."

What were the chances of that?

200

Poison.

Gabe slept on the cot. Todd and I shared one queen bed while old fraternity roommates Jason and Brett shared the other. The others were accustomed to cramming into rooms, while I'd been sleeping mostly in singles and sometimes in doubles. It was fun being crammed together. More jokes. More shared stories. More ideas and joint planning. Worse mess. Worse smell. I could see the appeal. I was slowly coming around to their way of things. Our hiking junk filled the room to overflowing. Our room had a broken automatic fan which made a whirring noise. That was the secret to the free room. We didn't mind it at all, but the inn felt that they couldn't rent a room with a broken fan. When Brett had asked the manager if there was anything she could do for us, she'd thought of this solution. It worked very well for us.

Todd disappeared to play poker and drink and smoke with some young foreign workers he'd met. The staff in the park seemed to be mostly Eastern Europeans — young men and women from Bulgaria, Romania, Poland, and the Czech Republic. They lived all together in a mini-village dormitory. Todd stayed out most of the night, as he was prone to do, with his goofy way and his spiky hair. Porno and Gabe drank down in the basement bar. At three o'clock in the morning, I was awakened by the sound of violent retching. Surprisingly, it was Brett, who hadn't gone drinking. He was drenched in sweat and felt like he was going to die. A short while later, Gabe took his turn vomiting violently in the bathroom. Then Brett took round two; then Gabe took round two. None of the rest of us could sleep with all that going on. The two of them shared the same symptoms. In between bouts of vomiting, both claimed that they were freezing and needed more blankets. Both of them were sweating profusely to the point that their beds became swimming pools.

At sunrise, August 11, a Thursday, neither Brett nor Gabe was able to move a muscle. They couldn't rise from bed. They barely had energy enough to talk. They had fever, sweat, chills. They vomited some more. It was food poisoning. The day before, they'd both ordered Xanterra hamburgers at the Snow Lodge Café, while I'd eaten a veggie-burger and Todd and Porno'd had pizza. We felt certain that Xanterra was the cause. They were the food provider for all the national parks in America. None of their food tasted good. Now these two were violently ill. It necessitated a zero day. Otherwise, we would've up and skedaddled. Brett and Gabe slept through the afternoon with our window curtains drawn and every available blanket draped over them. They didn't leave the room all day. Their chills and fevers continued. Brett's only movement of the day came in calling and asking the manager to give us a second night. He asked if she'd please let us pay this time.

I helped Gabe hobble next door to the village's small medical center, called Medcor. They took his temperature, gave him pills, and charged him a hell of a lot of money for it. He had a 104 temperature. We asked about food poisoning, but they wouldn't comment. We pressed them, but they wouldn't say. We guessed it was something like how you're never supposed to admit fault at the scene of a car crash. They probably got food poisoning cases in there all the time.

Darwin.

Todd, Porno, and I watched an eruption of Old Faithful along with two thousand other people on the great wooden terrace and walkway. It felt quite communal. The geyser was something that I'd seen on TV, growing up. Now I was standing before it. It felt fine.

"I'm not hiking to Canada," I told Todd and Porno over dinner at the inn's banquet room.

Our two waitresses were from Russia and they sat down with us briefly. They'd met Todd at the employee poker game the night before. They treated us like one of their own, because we were scraping by, clawing, and surviving just like them instead of vacationing here with large families. They could relate to us—we were having an adventure, just trying to get by, just like them.

"What?"

"I'll never make it to Canada. I'm only going to hike to Helena, and then I'll fly home from there."

"Yeah, right."

"It's true."

It wasn't a big deal. I'd already known it for quite a while. I'd known it as far back as no-bathtub Salida in southern Colorado. The writing had been written on the wall that whole time. All that time I'd known how the summer was going to end. I was resigned to it by now. It was mid-August and I had to be back at work in two weeks. And we hadn't even reached Montana yet. It'd take more than two weeks to hike the state of Montana. Hence, I wouldn't reach Canada. I loved my job. I actually wanted to return to it. And I didn't feel like giving my boss the same phone call I'd given her six years earlier, back when I'd had to ask for extended time off so that I could complete the Pacific Crest Trail. Back then I showed up sixteen days into the school year, and I just couldn't in good conscience do that to them again. I wanted to stay and reach Canada, but it wouldn't be fair. Six years earlier I'd been willing to quit my job and even lose my marriage if need be, just to have my through-hike. I wasn't willing to quit my job this time. Strange what the years will do to a person.

We let it drop. They didn't believe that a person could do that—could hike all this way and then stop before finishing. It wasn't my job to convince them otherwise. I wasn't sharing to gain attention. I was just letting them know my situation. If they didn't believe me, that was okay. They'd find out soon enough. It'd been painful to take the long rest breaks throughout the days while hiking with this group—knowing all along what it'd mean—but I actually wouldn't have traded it for anything.

Todd went off to the employee dormitory to play poker with the waiters and waitresses again. It was our second night at the giant Old Faithful Inn. One year into the future, my mother and father would drive across the country from New York to Oregon, to visit my younger brother at his new job as a law school professor at the University of Oregon. On their return, my parents would drive through Yellowstone. They'd call me from the road the next day to share how amazed they'd been by the park. Mostly, they'd proclaim amazement that I'd walked through it. They'd say that they'd looked out their car windows and had tried to imagine me coming out of the woods and walking across the vast plains, wearing my backpack. My mother was thrilled to list the animals that they'd seen in Yellowstone:

"...bison, elk, a mule deer, a chipmunk..."

"Wait a minute!"—I would stop her—"Did you just say you saw a chipmunk?"

"Yes," she would say, "It ran across the road right in front of us. It was the first animal we saw."

I would get such a kick out of that.

"That's an amazing story," I'd say. "You drove through Yellowstone and you saw a chipmunk. It made the list! That is priceless."

Everybody always gets excited by seeing a chipmunk. I can identify. They really are cute little things, I admit.

On that trip through Yellowstone my father would pull to the side of the road upon sighting a single bison in a field. The bison would cross the field and approach their car. My mother would say, "Let's drive off now." My father would reply, "No, wait—let's see what it'll do!" There exists something called the Darwin Awards, which are annually designated posthumously to people who've died under self-inflicted circumstances that'd seem to the average person to be clearly not right. The idea is that the people who died actually are helping our species by no longer being able to pass on their genes. It's survival of the fittest and they've weeded themselves out. This was dialogue straight from the pages of the Darwin Awards: the last words that someone says of a large wild animal that's in close proximity are, "let's see what it'll do!" This, from the Rhodes Scholar. The bison would then walk around to my father's side of the car, at which point it'd change his perspective dramatically. My father would at that moment promptly drive off. No harm, no foul. No Darwin Award.

August 12, Brett and Gabe were again unable to hike. Their vomiting had abated because they'd nothing left to vomit, but they remained too weak to get out of bed. That left us to make a new plan. Todd, Porno, and I couldn't wait any longer. The three of us would hike westward to the next trail town, West Yellowstone, which lies in Montana. Brett and Gabe would rest one more day and then hitchhike over to meet us there. We needed to keep moving. We needed to keep pressing forward.

After breakfast, Todd sat in the bar for an hour, drinking and chatting with one of the Eastern European girls, a strikingly attractive woman from Romania. We were packed and ready to go, but Todd couldn't pull himself away. Porno and I had to grab hold of him and lift him from the table and pull him outside. We set out walking down the glorious wooden boardwalk nature trail which began outside the lodge and passed Old Faithful Geyser.

The boardwalk zigzagged us westward for two miles through bubbling blue geysers of all shapes and sizes. We ambled along slowly, reading the placards at each hot pool and mini-geyser to learn their names, history, and temperatures. It was leisurely strolling alongside children and families. But we were the only ones wearing backpacks. We took photographs. I walked for fifteen minutes with a man from Malaysia who was ethnically Chinese. He asked about the CDT and I shared a few stories.

At the end of the boardwalk, the tourists all looped back to the village; but Todd, Porno and I ducked under the railing and stepped off the far end of the boardwalk and set out southwestward along a sandy path, like in Jurassic Park, stepping off the car path and setting out into the pods. A few people watched us go, a little bewildered. I have to be perfectly honest here and say that we felt a bit like bad-asses, ducking under the railing and setting out across the land where the animals lived. That feeling alone kind of made the entire trip worthwhile. It made up for the pain of all the blisters, and all the dehydration and drought in the deserts. It made up for pornographic Haikus. It even made up for Giardia. It almost made up for the lightning scares.

We were carrying food for only two days. We walked a few miles and then climbed one thousand feet up a winding canyon, climbing back into the hills from up out of the Old Faithful basin. We had our pepper spray in our holsters at our hips. It was just the three of us. Instantly, our thoughts turned to grizzly bears again. We had just forty miles to go to reach the town of West Yellowstone. We hoped that Brett and Gabe would recover and meet us there.

16
Montana

A screaming comes across the sky.

—Thomas Pynchon, *Gravity's Rainbow*

IMAX.

The Bitterroot is Montana's state flower. It's purple, and the Native Americans made sauces, soups, and pudding from its bitter roots. Things like that can get lost on these hikes. The chance existed that perhaps Brett and Gabe wouldn't get better and wouldn't join us in West Yellowstone. And what would that mean for the hike? We kept our heads down and walked silently along. In Montana, the trail initially bumps westward on the Montana-Idaho border at around seven thousand feet elevation. It's an incredibly unspectacular stretch. The scenery finally improves halfway up the state as the trail straightens northward and gains elevation. The finale is two celebrated and grizzly-filled stretches: the Bob Marshall Wilderness and then Glacier National Park. I wished I could skip the tedium of southern Montana and end with the glorious glaciers, but that wasn't going to happen.

Todd, Porno, and I climbed eleven miles westward up out of the Old Faithful valley to a high plateau at eighty-five hundred feet. We set up our tents very close together, due to anxiety over grizzly bears. Our tents were actually touching, sandwiched under four tall trees in a thicket beside a lukewarm puddle called Summit Lake. It was the first trailside water past Old Faithful. It wasn't refreshing, but instead was like the Giardia-filled lake in Wyoming which'd crippled me. I used iodine pills this time. It was so that my Giardia wouldn't catch Giardia. Or so that I wouldn't catch Double-Giardia. For I still had an intruder in my system. A tapeworm can be nine feet long, or it can be fifty feet long. This was a parasite, but at least it wasn't a tapeworm.

The three of us occupied a subset in that we were the only Team Locust members who'd through-hiked the Pacific Crest Trail. That meant we'd experienced Big Miles, for big mileage days come easily on the PCT in northern California and Oregon. Every PCT through-hiker gets a taste of them. The reason that mattered was because we awoke on August 13 , twenty-nine miles shy of a spot called Mack's Inn, and we decided to hike it all the way in. We set out early and blazed away on flat, easy trail, making a westward beeline away from Summit Lake.

Midmorning, we stepped into Montana. Shortly afterward, we exited Yellowstone National Park, for the park boundary is beyond the state line. I felt melancholy from lack of Prozac. My hike was winding down. I needed to head home soon. I needed to get back to my job. The idea of trying to reach Helena before time ran out had gotten stuck in my mind. We took turns in the lead, and we stayed together. We saw a few deer. We walked dirt roads for a dozen miles. The route wasn't scenic or glamorous. This was the Mac's Inn Cutoff, another of Todd's Ley Alternate Routes.

Three final miles on a paved road brought us to the single-stop-sign town of Mack's Inn, Montana. It was the size of a grapefruit, yet it had a Montana feel. Like if you walked just a bit out of town, you'd get lost in the steep woods, and rain and snow would drop down on you. There was a river, a hotel, pizzeria, post office, and quite surprisingly a dinner-theatre. In the pizzeria I had the single worst-tasting pizza by far that I'd ever had in my forty-one years on the planet. It had a solid inch of cheese on top, which kind of tasted like underarm cheese. The pizzeria's teenage cook (just hired) admitted that he'd never made a pizza before. He was zero-for-one. We slept in the hotel.

We hitchhiked thirty miles off-trail to West Yellowstone, Montana, on the morning of August 14, to take a day off and hopefully meet up with Brett and Gabe. West Yellowstone was home to three thousand people and was a tourist trap with an IMAX movie theatre. Outside the theatre, in the middle of South Canyon Street at the south end of town, was a giant grizzly bear statue. The stone bear stood on its hind legs and reached up to a tremendous height. Town had cowboy hat stores, turquoise belt buckle stores, gem shops, antique shops, and Native American tourist trinket stores. The hotels had evocative names like One Horse Motel, Big Western Pine, Pony Express Motel, and the Stage Coach Inn. It was a bright, sunny day. Tourists ambled along the sidewalks. People stopped here just to pause and catch their breath before entering Yellowstone.

We took a room at the Ho-Hum Hotel on Canyon Street in the center of town. This was Highway 287, which we'd been paralleling beginning at the Great Divide Basin and leading diagonally all the way across Wyoming. It'd been the road which had led us into Yellowstone National Park's Grants

Village, and it was the road through Old Faithful Village. Here was the last that we'd see of it, for it headed northward up to Helena, while we'd head westward. We dumped our things and sat under an awning's shade outside the Book Peddler Café, which had an espresso bar. Todd bought Lolita, on my recommendation, and he sat reading it while Porno and I kept our eyes open for Brett and Gabe. Part of me wished that they'd be so weak that we'd all be forced to remain in West Yellowstone an extra day, because I just didn't feel like going anywhere. I was still sick myself, still weak and not eating much. But soon to our surprise here they came up the street saying that they were feeling better. Shit.

We ate a late lunch together in an otherwise empty Chinese restaurant. Warm tea tasted good to me. We then walked down to the IMAX theatre. An IMAX advertisement came on the screen and said: "We can take you places that you've only dreamed of." It felt very strange to hear that, as we weren't merely dreaming but were ourselves going to the places that they'd be show-ing us on screen. Granted, that wouldn't have been the case if the IMAX movie was a deep sea or space exploration—but the film we watched was The Lewis & Clark Journey, a reenactment of their westward exploration to the Pacific Ocean and back again, filmed with sweeping aerial views of the mountains and rivers. Included were grand scenes of the men, Sacajawea, and their dog Seaman boating westward, portaging, and mountain climbing. The film included tremendous aerial shots of the Great Falls in Montana, which had proven to be an enormous obstacle for them. Little could I have known it then, but in exactly six days I'd be standing alone at the base of the Great Falls as a tourist in street clothes.

Climate Change.

Lima, Montana, was the next trail town, about four days away. Early on August 15, the Fidel Castro hairy communists hitchhiked to Mack's Inn to collect their shared post office drop box. Star Trekkers Todd and I rose later. We took our time, did some grocery shopping. Finally, we walked to the end of town and stuck out our thumbs. It took us over an hour to get a ride. Again, cars passed filled with vacationing tourists who had no interest in picking us up. While waiting on the sidewalk, Todd called his girlfriend Cooper in Virginia on his cell phone and I sat listening to them argue for thirty minutes. Through-hikes take their toll on every couple.

A young female nurse picked us up. While driving us back to the trail at Mack's Inn where we'd left off, she explained that she was a Mormon. She let us out at a dirt road, one which Todd said led northward. We sat in the sun for an hour until finally Porno-Brett-Gabe stepped tan-clothed out of a truck. It never ceased to amaze me how we could keep meeting up like this. We never seemed to miss. It didn't matter if it was in town, or meeting at a lake, or meeting on a dirt road. On this crazy trail, with its limitless route options, we'd kept finding each other again and again.

Team Locust reunited, we climbed seven miles northwestward up the dirt road back into the mountains. We passed a few roadside homes, but as we climbed deeper inland from the highway, the homes tapered and ended. It was a long and gradual climb up 9,855-foot Taylor Mountain. We'd entered the Centennial Mountain Range. Two or three cars passed by, driving up to a scenic overlook on the mountaintop. I ran out of water. It's never enjoyable to run out of water. It's unbecoming to have to ask your fellow hikers for water, but sometimes it has to be done. We stopped to eat beside the road, just a half mile below the summit. A young park ranger pulled over in her truck and sat with us. She was friendly and pretty in a green government uniform. She saved me by giving me water.

We sat at the spot where we'd leave the mountain and veer ninety-degrees westward on the CDT, to head along the Montana-Idaho border. The park ranger said that she was up there studying the effect that mountain pine beetles were having on grizzly bears. It was all due to climate change, she told us. We'd heard about the pine beetles. She explained that the average temperature in the Rocky Mountains had risen two degrees in our lifetimes, and that the mountain pine beetle was living longer and causing more damage as a result. Before, cold winter temperatures at high elevation in the Rockies used to kill enough of the beetles to keep their population in check, but now the winters weren't cold enough to kill them, so beetles lived through the winters in greater numbers and infested and killed whole forests of white bark pine trees. White bark pines turn red when they die from beetle attack. We'd been seeing entire mountainsides of red, dead trees for weeks now. This was our first explanation for it. Millions of acres of trees had been killed by the beetles. In a negative feedback-loop, having fewer trees then further accelerates climate change. It was a downward spiral. Grizzly bears climbed to high elevation to eat the pine nuts on the trees in the late summer. Dead trees meant no pine nuts—meant starvation for the grizzlies. It's Koyaneskatsi, the web of life out of balance. Small differences in input can create vast differences in output.

She told us that climate change was affecting the ice up in Glacier National Park, too. She said that in 1968 there were sixty-eight glaciers in the park, but today there were just twenty-seven. Scientists have predicted that all the glaciers in the park will have melted by 2030. Soon, they'll have to rename Glacier National Park. Of course, the earth doesn't care about any of that. It doesn't have emotion. It'll go on without us long after humans are gone, and life of one kind or another will last here until the sun dies in five billion years, after the sun's elements swell and then swallow up earth in the final hour. It's a strange concept: one day that'll actually happen to our beloved planet. It's a fact. We'll be long gone by then. But maybe we'll last a thousand, or ten thousand more years in the meantime.

We followed the groove of the CDT for several miles along a westward trending ridge; then we set up our tents for the night on a rocky slope where level ground was in short supply. It was the best we could find. Early that next morning, August 16, we descended into a valley of dense underbrush. We lost the trail while pushing down through dew-wet killer weeds and bushes. We fanned out and fought our way descending westward into the valley. We picked our own way, following one of Todd's hunches. I felt perfectly uninspired.

Something inside me had changed. Something had turned. It was mid-August and I needed to be back at my job in two weeks. It'd be impossible for me to hike to Canada in time. By this point, I actually no longer felt bad about the thought of leaving. No, the bad feeling had come earlier. The awful, heart-wrenching feeling I'd had of the fated inevitability of all this—of this exact scenario had come many weeks before. By now, the pain had dulled. My only remaining plan was simply to get as far as I could before leaving. I'd considered Helena a target, but now I doubted that I'd make it even that far. Very soon, I'd have to jump on an airplane home. I'd need to figure out from which airport to depart. I'd have to abandon my motorcycle, too.

My uniform had changed through the years. Back on the Appalachian Trail, I'd hiked in sneakers and long socks and had worn gaiters up over my calves to keep from getting scratched. Now, I wore only ankle socks and no gaiters. I no longer cared if my legs got hacked. Usually, dense undergrowth wasn't an issue on the CDT, but in this spot a ridiculously large number of briars stuck to my sneakers and shoelaces so that it looked like I was wearing fuzzy slippers. Todd wore ankle socks, too, but the others all had traditional long socks and they instantly got briars all over them turning their lower legs into fluffy poodles. For hours, we pushed down lower into the valley.

We reached a winding stream lined with ten-foot-tall bushes. We slogged through the stream over sandbars and around river bends. It was the perfect home for grizzlies. It felt like the Grizzly Maze that Timothy Treadwell had found in Alaska, minus the very real threat that he'd faced (or rather, that he'd idiotically settled into). We made noise. We took turns hiking in front, teasing each other about it: "Your turn!" In the afternoon, we climbed westward out of the valley and found our unmarked dirt CDT. We came upon it just like that. The rest of the day took us up over tree line, traversing high around exposed mountainsides. We spread out, as we had no need to stick together. We could look out and see one another ahead and behind in the distance. It felt wonderful to have open views. We stopped for breaks and ate our snacks together. Todd was sure that we were on the CDT. I didn't have maps for this area. I was just going along.

The personality of our breaks had changed. Our multiple daily breaks were still the same duration, but now Team Locust had put all the jokes on hold and the others were reading books instead. As soon as we'd stop for a break, out'd come the books. Porno read Watership Down, which is an epic odyssey story; Brett read The Death of Ivan Illyich, just so that he could keep brooding some more; Todd read Lolita; and Gabe had finished Dharma Bums and now read The Tracker, based on Todd's recommendation—which was about the life of the Apache Scout Tom Brown. I didn't have a book. I just sat eating and watching the others, waiting for them to put their books down so that we could rise and continue.

Storm clouds blew toward us. The trail descended down into the trees. Gabe and I almost came to blows as we set up our tents. Something was coming to a head between us. Earlier, I'd called him out about his farting and about pornographic Haikus. This time he'd broken branches off a tree for his tent site, and when I asked what he was doing, he snapped at me. So I snapped at his snapping. I said something like, "Why do you always have to be an asshole? Always. *Why?*" Tempers can flare. I was at the end of my rope. I didn't mean to keep being so critical of Gabe. There were times when we had good talks and got along fine. It was just that he'd also get on my nerves. I was on edge and a little unstable. I instantly regretted confronting him yet again, but I was perfectly ready to fight. I was going to drop my gloves and go at it right there. I was ready to throw a punch. Me, the oldest one in the group. The others all just ignored us.

August 17, we awoke to drizzly, overcast, cold foggy grayness—the sky dark and threatening to storm. I kept my head down and hiked quietly, following in line. We walked westward and approached a mountain ridge that we'd need to scale. We reached its slopes midday just as light rain fell. We started a long steep climb. More storm clouds blew in. Our luck was about to run out. Instead of waiting down low where we'd risk possibly getting temporarily stuck on the southern side of this ridge, we took a chance by trying to get up and over it. We tried to hurry and scale the ridge before getting pinned down. We climbed for two hours. We almost made it. Thirty minutes more would've done it. We were up near the crest of the ridge when the lightning started.

Thunder and lightning cracked open the sky and forced us to huddle together on the ground. We were up so high that we had only miniature leafless trees around us, which offered no shelter. Cascading rain dumped down on us, and we draped our flimsy inadequate plastic tarps over our heads. The rain turned to hail and soon ice lay all around us, covering the ground in a blanket of white. I was freezing. I had no middle layer over my shirt and under my rain shell. Fall was approaching and I wasn't prepared for the cold. My only chance to stay warm was to keep moving, but violent lightning cracks kept striking all around. Scaling the ridge at that moment would've been suicidal. Yet again, it wasn't grizzlies but lightning that brought us near death (actually, hypothermia would've done nicely, too). Mark Twain had spent time out west and knew the reality: he'd said, "Thunder is good, thunder is impressive; but it is the lightning that does the work."

The lightning passed after thirty minutes, and the icy rain subsided. We

210

rose and shivered while climbing the final way over the ridge. We were exposed up high; the wind blew. The others paused to try to dry out their things, but I was so cold that I couldn't stop. The ground before us was rolling hills covered with ice. I was frozen to the bone. I felt miserable. I had to keep moving. Todd and I walked far out ahead of the others. After an hour, we stopped to wait. But they never came. We stood in a forest clearing shivering and stomping our feet beside an empty sheep corral and water trough, waiting for the Fidel Castro Trio to come down the plateau. Finally, they appeared from around a hillside, from a direction which didn't make sense and which we weren't expecting. They explained that they'd gotten lost. I was miserable. We pushed on. We spied a tent on a hillside and we guessed it belonged to a shepherd because beside it was a flock of sheep and also some sheep dogs who barked at us from a distance. We lost the trail at dusk. We crossed a creek and stopped to tent in a forest on complex terrain. I couldn't have known it at the time, but the next day would be my final day hiking on the Continental Divide Trail.

Done.

We awoke on Thursday, August 18, to fog and wet grass. We climbed up a wooded hillside. The trail had disappeared beneath our feet the night before and we had to search for it. Todd's map showed it snaking westward, then curving back eastward, so we gave up searching, and Todd picked a northward cross-country course and we set out climbing through trees and over rocks to cut the trail off at the hypotenuse. Soon, somebody screamed and we bumped smack into the trail. As usual, Todd's way worked. He was quite capable like that. As always. We came out of the forest and bumped up and down like a roller coaster climbing rocky hills and dirt hills for hours, until we came to at a landmark fence-line and followed it for one mile through tall wet grass in a slight drizzle to a dirt road that led six easy miles descending to Interstate 15 from where we'd exit to the town of Lima. The fog lifted as we walked the dirt road and sunshine poked through the clouds and warmed us. Everything was easy now. We took our time. Joked a little.

Up the road toward us came a young southbound solo through-hiker named Rick Harbison. We stood and chatted with him. He'd started at the Canadian border and was indeed planning to hike to Mexico. He was getting a late start. It was his first through-hike. It's difficult to learn the tricks of the trade by starting on the CDT. We told him that we'd seen a group of about six southbound through-hikers all bunched up together about a week earlier back in Dubois. I get nosy. I want to know what motivates other hikers. And I want to know whether we have any connection or commonality. The jackpot for me is to meet someone like Eddie-B, whom I'd actually met on a previous trail. I always want to see if I can meet AT hikers from 1993, or PCT hikers from 1999. Short of that, I always hope I'll meet Rochesterians. Or Mainers. Or students from the small Maine colleges of Bates, Bowdoin, and Colby. Incredibly, I was thrilled to learn that this young man was a recent Colby College graduate of 2003. Not only that, but astonishingly he'd played on the tennis team there. I looked at him and said,

"Who was your coach? Freddie?"

"Yeah, Freddie Brussell!"

"I know Freddie. He's a friend of mine. I was the men's tennis coach at Colby before Freddie. If I hadn't left Colby for Bates, then I would've been your coach."

The guy didn't care too much, but I was thrilled by it. It's a small world. These trails are amazing like that. Like how I'd ran into a Tennessee relative of mine named Frist while hiking the AT. Finally, we could see Interstate 15 down low in the distance. The southbound tennis player had given us the number for Jan's Cabins in Lima and Todd called there on his cell phone to arrange a ride. He explained that we were almost at I-15. Jan's husband promised to come pick us up on a gravel road beside the interstate and drive us twenty miles northward up I-15 to Lima. We walked down and waited on the gravel road. We sat for forty-five minutes, throwing pebbles at a small sign that gave information about a nearby goat sanctuary. Todd'd hit the sign and yell, "Bradley!" It was just like old times. The pickup truck came and whisked us away. My hike was over. I was done. I wouldn't take another step on the CDT.

Lima Beans.

From there, the trail arcs northwestward through the Bitteroot Mountains; then it leaves the Montana-Idaho border at a place called Chief Joseph Pass and arcs northeastward to Helena. From there, it climbs due-north up Montana's interior to the Canadian border. The remaining trail towns were Leadore (in Idaho), and then the Montana towns of Wisdom, Anaconda, Helena, Lincoln, Augusta, and East Glacier. Todd's planned town stops didn't correspond exactly to those of the others, but that'd be for them to work out. My part was over. I had twelve days left to get back to my job. I could've kept going for one or two more trail towns, but I didn't see the point. Those wouldn't even be northward-moving miles, anyway. No, my twelve-year project was complete.

I stood in the parking lot at Jan's Cabins in Lima, Montana, feeling just like Forest Gump when Tom Hanks as Forest has been running the country from end-to-end for a few years (just to "put the past behind") and has a following of people, when suddenly he just stops in the middle of the road way out west in the desert and stands still for a moment and then says: "I'm tired. I think I'll go home now." And just like that, he's done. Like so, with me: out there in Lima, with Giardia, with Team Locust, knowing that our pace hadn't allowed me to meet my deadline and reach Canada in time. I was missing my squash teams and my players, missing my job. I knew I was done.

212

Lima's population was 242 people. Jan's Cabins was adjacent to a diner and large parking lot. The area was seemingly the extent of town and was located practically underneath a raised overpass span of Interstate 15 at the western end of the diner's parking lot. We looked up at it. It felt like looking up at the Brooklyn Bridge or the Golden Gate Bridge. We could see only the tops of the cars and trucks in the far-right northbound lane racing along. The diner's parking lot served as a bus stop for Greyhound. Interstate 15 stretched northward to Butte, Helena, and Great Falls on its way to Canada where it changed names and led to Calgary. I'd ride a Greyhound to Butte. Make my way home from there.

"I'm done," I said.

They could see that I was serious, and that it was real. My agenda was now different from theirs. The others busied themselves with the things a through-hiker does: eat, clean, restock, organize. It wasn't like I was expecting them to stop and cry or anything. I busied myself with departure. I'd mailed my blue jeans and a thin sweatshirt ahead to myself, but I couldn't remember to which town I'd mailed them. When I stopped in at the Lima PO, here quite fortuitously was the box waiting for me with my new, clean clothes. Sometimes you get lucky like that. I must've known that I'd last only this long. Back at Jan's Cabins I showered, shaved, and dressed as a civilian. I borrowed a saw from Jan's husband and sawed off the top third of my hiking stick, to never use it again, but instead to save it as a memento to commemorate my CDT hike—to remember Team Locust. I returned to the PO and mailed home my backpack, hiking gear, and the saved top third of my hiking stick. I kept only a few papers, a road map of Montana, and a toothbrush. I felt wonderful.

Two decaled vans in the parking lot were alongside some cyclists from Austria. Their van said: Pan-American AIDS Awareness Expedition 2005. We spoke with them for a little while, but we lacked the energy and desire to fully engage and hear all about their endurance trip, which apparently was twenty-three thousand kilometers through North, Central, and South America in thirty-five days.

We ate together in the diner. It was large and spacious. Had comfortable, padded chairs and easy décor. The food was delicious and the owners were friendly. In came a young man from Ireland who was through-hiking the three triple crown trails all in this one single summer. It's something of which only a few human beings could be capable. This guy was incredible, otherworldly. He was absolutely not massive. He stood only five foot nine and weighed one hundred fifty-five pounds. He sat with us and we asked about his summer. He'd started five months earlier and had already through-hiked the Appalachian Trail southbound, and then the Pacific Crest Trail northbound. Two weeks ago, he'd stepped off the northern end of the PCT at the Canadian border and it'd taken him only a few hours to hitchhike westward to Glacier National Park where he'd immediately started hiking southward down the CDT—on the same day.

213

He was holding up fine. It was easy, he told us. His routine involved rising early each morning and hiking positively mammoth, nonstop hiking days. Long hours, no breaks, light pack. Nothing under thirty-five miles a day; routine forty-plus mileage days, with not infrequent fifty-mile days thrown in, too. He never slept over in towns, he said. Washing laundry meant lying down for a few moments in a stream. No tent, just a tarp. No post office drop boxes, as they're restrictive.

Sitting at our table, he ate the largest meal I'd ever seen. He ate two mushroom cheeseburgers, a large milkshake, and two tall plates of steak fries, pouring ranch salad dressing all over his two flowing plates and dipping his cheeseburgers and french fries in the dressing with every bite, to add calories. It wasn't just the size of the meal that was extraordinary, but it was the pace and the rhythm with which he ate. He didn't rush. But he never let up and he never slowed down until the final bite was gone and there was no evidence whatsoever that any food had ever been on either plate at all. He answered our questions as he ate. When he'd finished, he rose and excused himself. And set back out for the trail.

Mere mortals by comparison, we were spending the night at Jan's Cabins. I'd a single, while the others shared a bunk-bed quad, all sandwiched in just the way that they liked it. We walked down and ate dinner in a nonvegetarian-friendly steakhouse in an old warehouse where they hand you raw meat and you stand and cook your own steak. I ate a salad and two baked potatoes. We all drank beer. The restaurant was empty except for us. It had a bar, pool tables, and juke box. It was mostly country music on the juke box, but I put in my quarters and quite amazingly found The Cars' "It's All I Can Do." It made me feel like I was floating in outer space. That song has always made me think of a girl that I knew back in high school. I could close my eyes and see her standing in front of me.

Four teenagers entered and shot pool. Then in came a young, married, attractive couple who exuded athleticism. They sat with us at our long table and asked what'd brought us there. We told them about the trail. They were out here from New York City. The husband was six foot four and muscular. His name was Chris Anthony and he was a professional football player in the Arena Football League. He was number eighty-six, and a wide receiver for the New York Dragons. His team was based in western Long Island and he got time off in the summer. They were out here because he'd just completed a one-month wilderness first aide course. I told them that I was a college squash coach. They asked where. I answered Bates College, in Maine, and Chris' wife Anne perked up and said that she was a dancer and had just the other day finished taking three weeks of classes at the Bates Dance Festival. Dancers from New York City take classes and train at Bates every summer. They sit outside the gym smoking cigarettes and eating yogurt and bananas. Tour groups of prospective students walk by during summer vacation and see spandex-clad

214

skinny women sitting on the Bates gym steps, smoking. Banana peels lying about. Earlier in the day, I'd met a graduate of Maine's Colby College, and now on my last day of the summer, I'd finally met a person with some affiliation to Bates. The couple was very nice. Wife Anne was down-to-earth and terrifically pretty, but we mostly ignored her and spent all our time asking Chris about arena football. He answered our questions. Team Locust knows all about Arena Football now. Gabe turned to the rest of us and plaintively whined,

"How come we can't play Arena Football?"

Porno, the frankest one of all, put the matter to rest by answering: "Because we're not big, we're not strong, we're not fast, and we're not athletic."

A weird thing occurred between Gabe and me over the motorcycle. Team Locust had known all along that I'd motorcycled from Maine to Mexico, and that my bike was down in New Mexico with Jessie Gibbins. I'd told them that I didn't know if I'd ever get it back. That'd prompted Gabe to ask if he could buy it from me. It wasn't worth much, so on my final few days of hiking into Lima, I'd told Gabe that he could just have it. I'd give it to him. Maybe I'd been trying to create peace and make up for the constant internecine battles in which he and I'd kept finding ourselves engaged with in Team Locust. But now he told me that he didn't have his motorcycle license and that he'd never ridden one before — so I changed my mind and said that I wouldn't give it to him after all. Gabe was irked that I'd rescinded the offer, but I'd never have been able to live with myself if I gave him the bike and then he crashed and killed himself or someone else in trying to ride it back to California without a license. He hadn't known that it takes awhile to learn to ride a bike and to gain a feel for it.

I ate breakfast with the others that next morning, August 19. Then they packed and made final departure preparations. I couldn't express how glad I felt not to be going with them. A little before noon, they piled on the back of Jan's husband's pickup truck. I stood wearing my blue jeans and pullover and I waved them off. It was a warm, sunny day. It was nearly fall, and it could snow on them up in the mountains at any time from here to Canada. At their pace, they had one month to go. They waved out the back of the pickup truck, and then they were gone. I'd never see any of them again.

2:00 AM.

A northbound Greyhound Bus was scheduled to pull into the Lima Diner parking lot at a quarter to four in the afternoon, but it passed by on the interstate without stopping. My heart sank because I'd stood looking up helplessly while watching it drive right by. It was an awful feeling. It might've been better if I'd had my Prozac. I entered the diner and asked the owners:

"Was that the bus that was supposed to stop?"

"Did the bus go by?" the wife asked.

"Goddam it!" the husband said. "Sometimes they do that."

The owners were angry. It wasn't some scam that they'd all worked out to keep me in town longer to spend more money. The husband called the bus company and expressed his feelings forcefully. He hung up and apologized to me. It wasn't their fault. I was bored and had nothing to do. I'd already checked out of my room. The next bus was scheduled for one thirty in the morning. The diner owners called the bus company back and asked them to please be sure that the middle-of-the-night bus stopped in Lima, as I was going to be on it. I paid for another night in the hotel; then I napped through the afternoon. I closed my eyes and felt very restful. I could hardly believe that my hike was over. I was perfectly happy about it. Even relieved. No more sun, wind, hail, rain, meals out of a little stove, nights on the ground in a sleeping bag. No more burs on my sneakers.

At one o'clock in the morning, I walked out in the darkness and stood in the parking lot outside the diner. The diner was closed. The lights were off. I went early to be sure not to miss the bus. It was bitterly cold. The wind blew, adding wind chill. I wore my blue jeans and long-sleeved pullover. I paced back and forth to stay warm. I could imagine Team Locust out in their tents somewhere fast asleep. On their way to the next town. Continuing. Hiking onward. At two o'clock in the morning, the Interstate 15 northbound Greyhound pulled up. It was thirty minutes late. It'd had me worried, but at least this time it stopped. Riding to Butte in the early hours of the morning, I couldn't sleep but just leaned my head against the window with my eyes closed. It always takes awhile to get home.

216

17
Rent-a-Car

Whenever the moon and stars are set,
Whenever the wind is high
All night long in the dark and wet,
A man goes riding by.
Late in the night where the fires are out.
Why does he gallop and gallop about?

— Robert Louis Stevenson, "Windy Nights"

Tourist.

Returning to life after the CDT was much the same as it'd been after finishing my other hikes. On all three occasions, I'd no choice but to resume work and daily functioning immediately. That's not recommended, but there's usually no way to avoid it. It took about a year's time before I felt truly normal again. Overeating occurs. Through-hikes teach the brain to crave calories, and once home you eat every day all day long. You're rail thin and famished when you finish a through-hike, so you eat every morsel of food that's anywhere nearby. You eat like you think you might never have food again. It's practically impossible not to gain weight as the pendulum swings the other way. Thus, this startling conclusion: through-hiking makes you fat! To avoid it, you have to be careful and stay disciplined, that's all. That's easier said than done, though, especially for all those addictive-personality types who get drawn into through-hiking for reasons of insatiability in the first place. You have to take what your brain is telling you is the correct portion size, and then cut it in half. Meta-Knowledge: the ability to assess the quality of your own knowledge. Otherwise, you bulge.

I lingered in Montana before returning home, to treat myself to exploring the state. I debarked the night bus in Butte and slept from four in the morning until nine in the morning in a cheap hotel; and then I took a taxi to the airport and rented a car for three days. My plan was to drive up north on the eastern side of the Rockies, and then cross over to the western side through Glacier National Park and drive down to Missoula and fly home from there. Jessie had promised to hang on to my broken motorcycle for me.

I drove my rental car northward on August 21, stopping to buy running shoes and a red winter jacket at the Capital Hill Mall in Helena. It felt nice to move by the push of my foot and to feel the wind rush in my open window. I continued northward to the small city of Great Falls, and then across the plains north of town to the side road that leads eastward to the waterfall. The landscape was rolling, yellow grassland. From a distance it looked inviting, but up close each seemingly innocuous rise, gentle hill, and valley revealed unexpected and unforgiving elevation changes. I drove the seven-mile dirt side road and felt disoriented dropping down between the mounds. At the Great Falls was a power station, a public park, and a lodge. The parking lot was filled with cars from a wedding reception. I walked down and gazed at the waterfall. It was no Niagara Falls, but impressive nonetheless. This was the waterfall that'd given Lewis and Clarke the roughest portage of their three-and-a-half-year western exploration.

Continuing up I-15 northbound, by car, I gazed at the mountains beside me, parallel to my west. They rose like a wall. They looked fake, like a movie backdrop. I stopped at the tiny roadside Old Trail Museum (optional donations appreciated!). A large part of the reason why I'd stopped at that small shack was because it was next to an ice cream store, and I figured that I could kill two birds with one stone. Or, being a vegetarian, not kill any birds, but just check out the museum and then have a frozen ice slushie. Inside the mini-museum, quite incredibly, were one-hundred-million-year-old fossils. No lie. It was amazing. Jack Horner, the renowned paleontologist from Montana State University in Bozeman, who's portrayed in the Jurassic Park movies, frequently came and dug in the dusty foothills nearby, just west off I-15. He'd found great numbers of dinosaur bones there. Ten miles away was Egg Mountain, the most concentrated egg and nesting dinosaur site in the world. They told me that in the museum offhandedly, like it was no big deal. Everyday stuff. Just go out and find some hundred-million-year-old dinosaur eggs!

Continuing northward, I stopped at two fossil stands and looked at rocks. I passed by a few more dinosaur museums. I pulled into the parking lot of the Museum of the Plains Indians at dinnertime. I walked to the door and found to my great disappointment that they'd just closed for the day. I pressed my hands and face against the glass and through the windows saw the elaborate and colorful headdresses of the Native American Plains Indians on statues. I would've loved to have seen that museum. I would've loved to have been a Plains Indian. I reached Glacier National Park by evening. The snow-covered

218

mountains seemed so high that I'd difficultly imagining anyone could hike through them. But I knew better. I grabbed a quick bite to eat in the town of East Glacier; then I took "Going to the Sun Highway" through the mountains and over to the western side of the Rockies. I drove southward and spent the night in a hotel in the small city with the lovely sounding name of Kalispell— the mouth performing gentle calisthenics to pronounce that word. I felt calm and eager to fly home.

Monday morning, August 22, I drove farther southward to Missoula. I took a room at a Ramada and lay in bed for hours. I rose from bed only to buy junk food next door at a gas station. My flight out was for noon the next day. It was all over now. I hadn't the slightest regret. I wanted to get back to Maine. My August 23 plane ride home was routine. At a layover in Chicago, I sat beside an old man who wore medals around his neck. He said that he'd won them in an age group national track event. It sounded cool. But I pretty much knew in my heart that I really didn't want to go that way. Age group tennis and squash tournaments loomed on my horizon. Age group marathon racing, too—things of that sort. Those old competitors are good and they take it seriously, out there duking it out like nothing has changed. But by then I want something to have changed. I hope that something will change for me. I'd like to gracefully welcome a change. I hope I can work it out. I have to find a way to grow into that. It just seems weird to conceive of competing from the cradle all the way to the grave. There's supposed to be something more to life. A chance to smell the roses. A time to give. A time for peace.

Five weeks after returning home, a light suddenly went off in my brain that things still weren't right, that my stomach was still burbling, and that I quite obviously still had Giardia. I don't know why it'd taken me so long for that fact to sink in. It may have been the stress of returning to life off the trail and getting my things in order. So finally I got myself to a doctor. They diagnosed me quite easily and gave me a prescription for pills with the perfectly awful sounding name of Flagyl (metronidazole), an antiprotozoal and antibacterial antibiotic. The pills were gigantic. I took two a day for three days, and that was it. The Giardia was cured. It couldn't have been any simpler. I should've taken care of that on the trail. Then I would've been able to eat. And maybe in those last couple weeks I would've been able to think just that little bit clearer.

Team Locust Finishes.

On September 24, 2005, Team Locust touched the stone obelisk at the Canadian border on the western shore of Waterton Lake in Glacier National Park. I learned that from Porno, who wrote to tell me that he was starting graduate school in engineering. He told me the names of some of the spots that I'd missed: Ippity Bop, Leepers Motel, Lumberjack Inn, Blondies, Whistle Stop Restaurant. I'd missed hiking underneath a spot I'd seen in photographs,

219

called The Chinese Wall. Porno said that Gabe had given Todd a Mohawk haircut with a razor in their final trail town of Darby, Montana. He called it a compact town, a restaurant offering the best food on the trail, and a hotel café that served huckleberry milkshakes. It was the final trail town for northbounders. I imagined how glorious it'd feel to enter it on foot knowing that it was the final stop: Raise high the roof beams, Carpenter! It'd feel like it had walking northbound into Monson, Maine, on the Appalachian Trail; and like it had walking northward into Stehekin, Washington, on the Pacific Crest Trail.

They hadn't seen any grizzly bears, but on their second-to-last day they'd seen fresh grizzly tracks in the trail. The tracks went in the opposite direction—descending the same trail that they were ascending—so they hadn't been in danger of bumping into the bear. They hadn't had too much problem with snow. It'd snowed on them overnight on the twenty-second and the twenty-third. Before that, they'd had a stretch of remarkable weather where they hadn't had to set up their tents for over a week.

They'd reached the Canadian customs station a few miles before the actual border. The border cut across Waterton Lake, with tourists taking boat rides from one end of the lake to the other. A load of tourists had arrived by boat while Team Locust had sat at the dock on the Canadian side, swimming and sunbathing. Brett's parents drove in and met them there and gave them beer and champagne at the lake to celebrate. It was fortunate that nobody drowned. I asked Porno if they'd gotten accused of being Amateur Assholes while in Glacier. He said that he might've "beaten the shit" out of anyone who said that to them. I told him that I was writing a story about the hike. He said: "Please don't portray me as Lenny in Of Mice and Men." I was glad to know that they'd made it.

Full Circle.

I'd once dated a crazy woman who loved to travel and see new places. She'd been to thirty-six countries and was hungry for more. She never went back to the same place twice. It always had to be someplace new. When I mentioned my desire to return to Germany to see my old village and the old tennis club where I'd once played, she'd looked at me as if I'd had two heads; or at least as if my face was running, like maybe my nose was melting hot wax sending it dripping down to my chin. But I always like to go back and see things, like where I used to live, where I used to attend school, where I used to play tennis. I'd love to return to the Pagosa Springs Resort in Colorado someday. I know that one day I will. I've climbed Maine's Mt. Katahdin twelve times now, and it never gets old. I always love returning to the Adirondack Mountains, where I'd hiked as a kid. It's more than simply geographical, too, for I like to go back and remember the old times in my life—the people I used to know. I guess I'm entirely nostalgic like that.

I can honestly say that I'd love to go back and repeat the Appalachian Trail one day. I don't need that to be anytime soon. Maybe I'll wait and do it on the twentieth anniversary of my 1993 hike in 2013. That'd be fun. I'd revisit the towns and the places I'd been. I'd see all the mountains again and see if I could recognize paths and hillsides and cliffs and landmarks and sections of trail. It'd be a welcome and fantastic feeling to walk toward a town, knowing all the while exactly what I could expect to find there. Yet I can't say for sure that will happen. For I've stepped over into the second half of my life now. On some days my paternal instincts are raging. It's time to shift gears and start the second half of my life with a family and with children of my own. We never know what the future will bring.

Jessie Gibbins asked me to visit Silver City in the summer of 2006, but I couldn't. In the summer of 2007, I spent a week in Oregon; then I flew down to El Paso and rode an airport shuttle van three hours up into the hills to Silver City. I got to see Jessie and her friends again—drink wine at the Vine. My motorcycle was a mess. It'd sat idle for two years with some gas in the tank and the motorcycle shop couldn't fix it. So I sold it to them and flew home to Maine. My older brother sold me his Mazda Miata. So I have a convertible now instead of a motorcycle. I love the car. I put the top down and it's just like the motorcycle. Except this time if I have an itch, I can scratch it.

At the end of that 2007 summer, I took my dream job, leaving Bates and Maine to become the squash coach at Middlebury College in Vermont. I'd liked it in Maine and would've stayed there coaching for another twenty years, except that Middlebury offered something that Bates didn't: mountains. Maine certainly had mountains, but from flat Lewiston I'd had to drive about three hours just to reach them. It's quite different in Middlebury, with the Adirondack Mountains just a few miles to the west, across Lake Champlain, and the Green Mountains of Vermont just a dozen miles to the east. Middlebury's campus is on rolling hills and has mountains surrounding it. It has the most beautiful campus that I've ever seen. It's beautiful. Stunning.

So off I went in the fall of 2007 after seventeen years in Maine, leaving my teams and my friends behind to start a new life. The Chimney Point Bridge over Lake Champlain into New York State is just twelve miles west of my office. In that regard, I have brought my life around full circle. I can't get over that fact. I have to pinch myself constantly. The Adirondacks of Northern New York were where it had all started for me. It's where I'd spent a few summers at a boys' camp and had learned to love the mountains. Now, I'm there in a finger snap.

Lake Placid, in the heart of the Adirondacks, was where I'd had my first apartment twenty years earlier. It'd been immediately after college. Back then, I'd taught tennis down on Long Island in the summers and had lived in Lake Placid for two winters while trying to figure out just what in the hell I should to do with my life. I'd read a lot. Took warm baths. Had become vegetarian

221

and found my way. Every night I'd walked three miles around Mirror Lake. If I'd been able to find a way to remain in Lake Placid back then, I would've stayed there all this time. Instead of coaching and distance-hiking. It was a roundabout course that has only just now led me back just in time. Man In the Middle. In the middle of my life. Now in Middlebury.

I've a room three miles from the gym, in a neighboring town that was incorporated before the birth of our nation and in late summer is filled with corn. I look out my window and see the Adirondacks' silhouette in the west. I live in Vermont, but look over at land that lies in the state where I was born. From my driveway out front I see Vermont's Green Mountains in the east, up where Robert Frost had lived for many years. There's nothing to do here but exercise. But that's okay, I'm embracing it. I run the roads outside town and smell manure on spring days, which takes me back to the smell of Bavaria with the cows in southern Germany. There's an amazing food cooperative in Middlebury. There're lots of vegetarians here. There're also pickup trucks with bumper stickers that say: "GUT DEER?" When I'm bored, I drive to Burlington. Montreal and New York City are easy to reach. And I can return to my family in Rochester easier now than I could from Maine. That's important.

The fierce Vermont winter of 2007–2008 had weekly snowstorms. I slid all over the road in my little Miata. It's quiet at night. I hear crickets. See stars in the sky. I've somehow incorporated mountains into my life of racquet sports. They're the two great loves of my life. I have both now. I sometimes wonder how it all worked out—was it luck or skill? Maybe that's just what happens when you work for seventeen years with single-minded purpose toward a goal. My career's been a through-hike all its own. But I've missed things along the way. I've missed having a family. Perhaps it isn't too late. I'll have to see how that goes. See where life takes me. Cristina, Steve, and their little boy Francis have come and visited me, and a few times I drove back to visit them in Maine. Now they're getting ready to move to Spain. Cristina will always be dear to me. Her little boy is my favorite. I'm crazy for that little peanut. One day when he's much older he'll learn that Uncle Johnny was once married to his mother. His jaw will drop. He'll say, "Huh?" We'll explain it to him.

I have a whole new family of squash players. I used to take my Bates' players on a preseason climb up Mt. Katahdin in Maine every fall, but now at Middlebury I take my players over to Keene Valley in the Adirondacks, and we hike three miles into the woods to spend the night at the Johns Brook Lodge lean-tos, and then the following morning, we rise early and climb four mountains in one day: Haystack, Basin, Saddleback, and Gothics. I love to share that with them.

Eyes and Ears Open.

I have no regrets. If I had to do it again, I'd make the exact same decisions.

I keep my eyes and ears open. I'll occasionally hear things about the trail. My Continental Divide through-hike was more than just a hike in itself. It was the end of a three-trail odyssey that oftentimes left me feeling on the CDT like I'd the kind of momentum generated by a large boulder that'd already rolled more than halfway down a steep hill. My Appalachian Trail and Pacific Crest Trail through-hikers had generated such long-distance hiking momentum for me that going to hike the CDT was inevitable.

One of the strangest things happened when I read an April 18, 2008, very large New York Times sports page piece about a guy named Chris Anthony, who was a wide receiver for the New York Dragons in the Arena Football League. It was the same guy that I'd met at the slaughter-house steak-bar with Team Locust back in Lima, Montana, on my final day on the CDT. He'd been there with his wife Anne who'd just taken the Bates College summer dance session. The article said that he was in his sixth season with Dragons and was premed at Hunter College. It said that he was twenty-nine years old, and that he'd earned his emergency medical training certification in the summer of 2005. It fit perfectly, for we'd met him in 2005 when he'd just finished a monthlong wilderness emergency training course that would help him transition into a medical career. It felt amazing and strange to have met that guy in Lima, Montana, and then to read about him in the New York Times three years later. It was kind of like spending fifteen minutes with a guy named Eddie-B on my fourth day of my Appalachian Trail hike and then bumping into the guy twelve years later in the desert of Wyoming.

I don't have any sources to provide me with updates about the trail, and I'm not much in touch with any past hiker-friends. No one to tell me things like how Reserve's Elk Country Café was sold and now called Frisco Lodging Company. Things like that, for the landscape keeps constantly changing. But of course my hiking friends and the town people live on in my memory. I've said it before: they're perfect there. On my final day in Maine, before moving to Middlebury, my telephone rang in an otherwise empty apartment that I'd just spent lots of time vacating. It was my final hour of moving out, and at the time of the phone call there wasn't a single possession of mine left in the apartment except for the telephone on the floor. It was Todd, of Team Locust fame. It seemed like a fitting circumstance in which to receive a call from crazy spiky-haired barfly Todd. He said that everything was going great and that he was, as always, "fon-tostic."

Listening to Todd's voice, alone in that empty apartment, suddenly I was back on the trail. I could see things, smell things, feel things. It's like how Marcel Proust wrote in his life's work In Search of Lost Time, how smells can trigger memories and actually transport you back in time. Like that, little things happen to trigger my memories, like watching the Daniel Day Lewis movie There Will Be Blood, one of the characters introduces himself and explains how he'd traveled to California after having just come from New Mexico, "from Silver City," he says. I hear that and my ears prick up. Suddenly I'm sitting in the Javalina Café drinking coffee with Jessie Gibbins. I'm sitting there and she's telling me all about the Vietnam Vet who dives under the tables in restaurants when cars backfire, and about the old artist who creates paintings of women's vaginas. I'm sitting there with her, and I haven't yet met the Hermit. I haven't yet crawled on my belly like a snake off-trail in the Gila Wilderness searching for my route to the river. I haven't even yet risen from the coffee shop and walked down the street with her to come face-to-face with the guy with the cockatiel on his shoulder. How I felt then at that moment is an emotion far different than how I rationally look back on it as an event on the continuum of my life. To actually go back to that rush of emotion is a gift. I feel it and sit a little straighter. I think of the trail towns.

Through-hikes give you the chance to live simply and pare things down. It's changed me. I'm not scared when it's quiet. I can survive when I'm cold, wet, tired, lost. I appreciate the little things. I've met so many people. I'd wanted to see that stuff. I'd wanted to get out there. I'd needed to get out there. It's how homo sapiens populated the globe, by setting out. And I got myself out there. I feel glad about that. I needed to see the things that I saw. It's a lousy thing to feel so restless that it pulls on you like that. If there's a person who doesn't have that tug, then I consider them lucky and I envy them. Maybe that's what it's all about. Maybe that's part of what it's done for me—let me know who I am.

Discovering ourselves is a lifelong process. Wisdom comes from age, to be certain. But I had a blast, walking out there in the mountains. All three trails had been different. The Appalachian Trail was the celebrity and the popular one of the Triple Crown, but one day the CDT will gather itself up and get itself together and get off the roads, and then it will be fabulous and wildly popular. I feel no need to return to hike my missing piece in Montana. I'm okay with the way it went. My hikes can live on in my memory now. People ask me about the trails. I feel I could go on a lecture tour. Through-hikes aren't for everyone, but some people just can't help themselves. They've helped me and for a time they've fulfilled me. Still, the restlessness inside never seems to go completely away. It still echoes. Still rattles around in my brain.

Printed in the United States
213082BV00002B/1/P